Roundell Palmer Selborne

The Book of Praise

From the Best English Hymn Writers

Roundell Palmer Selborne

The Book of Praise
From the Best English Hymn Writers

ISBN/EAN: 9783744692373

Printed in Europe, USA, Canada, Australia, Japan

Cover: Foto ©Lupo / pixelio.de

More available books at **www.hansebooks.com**

THE
BOOK OF PRAISE

FROM THE BEST ENGLISH HYMN WRITERS

SELECTED AND ARRANGED BY

ROUNDELL PALMER

MACMILLAN AND CO.
London and Cambridge.
1863.

PREFACE.

THE present is an attempt, not to add to the great and constantly increasing multitude of hymn-books intended for congregational use; but to present, under a convenient arrangement, a collection of such examples of a copious and interesting branch of popular literature, as, after a study of the subject which for several years has occupied part of his leisure hours, have seemed to the Editor most worthy of being separated from the mass to which they belong.

A good hymn should have simplicity, freshness, and reality of feeling; a consistent elevation of tone, and a rhythm easy and harmonious, but not jingling or trivial. Its language may be homely; but should not be slovenly or mean. Affectation or visible artifice is worse than excess of homeliness: a hymn is easily spoiled by a single falsetto note. Nor will the most exemplary soundness of doctrine atone for doggrel, or redeem from failure a prosaic didactic style.

There are many hymns in the English language, which will bear the test of these rules, as well, perhaps, as those of Germany, or of the ancient Latin Church. But they are apt to be presented in such company, or in such a manner, as to detract much from their effect. From the operation of causes connected with the nature of such compositions, it happens, that writers, who do not in general rise above mediocrity, sometimes produce beautiful hymns; while, on the other hand, there is far more dross than gold in the works of all voluminous hymn-writers. Nor are the principles, on which popular collections of hymns for congregational use are formed, favourable to that kind of selection, which is here attempted. In such collections, as a general rule, the taste of the compilers is regulated by their theology: they seem to be very easily satisfied with all that they think orthodox and edifying, or liturgically appropriate; they do not submit hymns, derived from sources which they respect, to any free or independent criticism; and, on the other hand, they reject, with morbid fastidiousness, every sentiment and expression in which they think they detect the traces of opinions which they dislike. It is also their frequent habit to cut down the compositions which they approve, with little discrimination or judgment, to such arbitrary dimensions, as suit their ideas of the time which ought to be occupied, during Divine service, by congregational singing.

The same regard to motives of (real, or supposed,) convenience and edification has introduced a system of tampering with the text of hymns, which has now grown into so great an abuse, that to meet with any author's genuine text, in a book of this kind, is quite the exception. Censurable as this practice is, in a literary point of view, it must be confessed that those who adopt it may plead, in their excuse, the examples of many of the writers, whose compositions they alter. The Wesleys altered the compositions of George Herbert, Sandys, Austin, and Watts. Toplady, Madan, and others, altered some of Charles Wesley's hymns, much to his brother John's discontent, as he testifies in the preface to his *Hymn-Book for Methodists*. Toplady's own hymns, even the "Rock of Ages," have not escaped similar treatment. James Montgomery complains much, in the preface to the edition of his collected hymns published in 1853, of his share in this peculiar cross of hymn-writers, as he calls it. But he had himself, about thirty years before, altered the works of other men, in his *Christian Psalmist.* Bishop Heber, scholar as he was, and editor of Jeremy Taylor's works, silently altered Taylor's Advent Hymn in his own hymn-book; and the hymns of Heber himself, and of writers still living, such as Keble, Milman, Alford, and Neale, are met with every day in a variety of forms, which their authors would hardly recognize. Perhaps, when the masters of the art have taken such liberties, it may be explained on the same principle as that on which musicians, and particularly the composers of anthems, produce variations from, and improvements upon, the works of their predecessors: and, indeed, some such variations of hymns are sufficiently good to take rank as new compositions; better than those by which they were suggested. But this is a rare felicity; and the result is widely different, when the work of alteration is undertaken by incompetent hands.

In the present volume, while the Editor has not thought it necessary to give the whole of every composition, from which a selection of parts might, in his judgment, more advantageously be made, it has been his desire and aim to adhere strictly, in all cases in which it could be ascertained, to the genuine uncorrupted text of the authors themselves. Great pains have been taken to trace out and ascertain the true authorship of such hymns, as were either without names of authors, or attributed to authors by whom they were not really written, in the books from which the Editor in the first instance took them. This was a task, which he could himself scarcely have undertaken, and in which he certainly could not have hoped to succeed, but for the assistance of Mr. Sedgwick, of No. 81, Sun Street, Bishopsgate; who has bestowed much time and attention on this branch of literature, and has attained to a knowledge of it, probably not possessed by any other Englishman. By his valuable help, the authorship of about thirteen-fourteenths of the compositions here collected has been traced, and the text collated with the original works of the authors. Thus aided, the Editor has been enabled, before finally completing his selection, to go through all, or almost all, the original publications containing hymns or sacred poetry of (amongst others), George Herbert, Sandys, Wither, Quarles, Crashaw, John Austin, Baxter, Bishop Taylor, Bishop Patrick, Bishop Ken, John Mason, Thomas Shepherd, Samuel Crossman, and Lancelot Addison (of the seventeenth century); Joseph Addison, Watts, Simon Browne,

Ralph Erskine, Doddridge, Hammond, John and Charles Wesley, Cennick, Seagrave, Grigg, Berridge, Olivers, William Williams, Toplady, Cowper, John Newton, Anne Steele, Hart, Gibbons, Michael Bruce, Logan, Byrom, Skelton, Swain, Daniel Turner, Ryland, Stennett, Needham, Beddome, Medley, Henry Moore, and Mrs. Barbauld (of the eighteenth century); Gisborne, Kirke White, Anne Flowerdew, Drennan, Bowdler, Kelly, James Montgomery, Sir Robert Grant, Bishop Heber, Bishop Mant, Bathurst, Lyte, Edmeston, Bernard Barton, Grinfield, and Chandler (of the present century); besides other writers, still living, whom it is unnecessary to name; and many miscellaneous collections, old and modern. Of the names thus enumerated, several are not represented at all in this collection; as the Editor did not find anything in their works which appeared to him to be suitable for his purpose, and equal to the general standard of merit, which he desired to maintain. But of the great majority, as well as of some other writers whose works are not accessible in a collected form, specimens more or less numerous will be found. A few examples of successful variations or centoes (in all instances but two, by known authors) from earlier compositions, have also been included; together with three original hymns, out of several which have been communicated to the Editor, by the kindness of the authors, in manuscript. Upon the works of living authors generally, the Editor has not thought it expedient to draw with the same freedom, as upon those of earlier generations; although he has not deemed it necessary to forego altogether the advantage of including in his book specimens of those works, especially of such of them as have obtained general currency in popular hymn-books.

The arrangement which has been adopted in this volume (and upon which some care has been bestowed), may be explained in a few words. The Catholic Creeds, and the Lord's Prayer, presenting in their simplest forms, and in their natural order, all the fundamental points of Christianity, both objective and subjective, appeared to the Editor to be the best basis for a classification of those hymns of faith and devotion, which express feelings at all times appropriate to a Christian profession. These two groups of hymns constitute Parts I. and II. of the Collection. The Third Part consists of hymns distinguished chiefly from those of the two former classes, by having a special reference to particular times and occasions. In the Fourth Part will be found distributed, under suitable heads, compositions of a kind intermediate between hymns for general use and private meditations; which (although the distinction is better marked in some cases than in others) seem to breathe, upon the whole, the accents of particular, rather than general, consciousness and experience. On this account, they are, for the most part, out of place in ordinary hymn-books, and unfit to be sung by public congregations; but their tone is not the less spiritual and real; and those who know anything of their own wants, and of the power of religion, can scarcely fail to be impressed with their beauty and truth.

The Editor is not sure, whether it may not appear to some to be an objection to this classification, that, by bringing closely together a number of hymns on one subject, a sense of repetition and monotony is created, which might have been avoided by a different method. The repetition, however, which will undoubtedly be met with in the works, not only of different, but even of the same hymn-writers, is of a kind appropriate to such compositions; and, therefore, it ought not to be withdrawn from observation. All lovers of Art are familiar with the habitual repetition of Holy Families, and other sacred subjects, by the early painters, down to and including Raffaelle. The constant enthusiastic contemplation of a few subjects, dear to the universal heart of Christendom, and embodying the highest conceptions of Divine purity and beauty, produced a simplicity, refinement, and spirituality of style, which never tires, notwithstanding its limited range. These are the hymns of painters, addressed to the sense of sight. A similar law has always governed, and to this day governs Christian Hymnody; binding together by the force of a central attraction, more powerful than all causes of difference, times ancient and modern, nations of various race and language, Churchmen and Nonconformists, Churches reformed and unreformed. It is refreshing to turn aside from the divisions of the Christian world, and to rest for a little time in the sense of that inward unity, which, after all, subsists among all good Christians, and which (is it too much to hope?) may perhaps receive some illustration, even from a volume like this.

Throughout the volume, the names of the authors, when known, are affixed to their hymns. When more authors than one have been concerned in the composition of a hymn, or when it is a cento or variation by one person from the work of another, the names of all the writers concerned (so far as known) are given. The dates added to the names signify, when without brackets, the time at which each hymn is believed to have been first composed or published: when within brackets, the date of the edition or copy, from which the text of a hymn (known or believed to have been published at an earlier date, not correctly ascertained), has been taken by the Editor. The text has been verified by collation with the original work of the author, or an authentic copy, in every case, except those specified in the notes at the end of the volume. The notes also show in what cases the text consists of any selected parts or part, less than the whole, of an original work. When a double date is appended to a single name, it signifies that the work, published at the earlier date, was afterwards altered by the author himself, the text of the later date being that adopted.

The Editor cannot conclude without returning his thanks to many friends, and to some not personally known to him, for the kind assistance, and offers of assistance, which he has received from them, while this work was in progress. His obligations to some of them will be found specially acknowledged in the notes. He has also to thank the owners of copyrights in many of the more modern hymns, which are included in the volume, for the consent which they have, in all cases when applied to, kindly given to the use of their works. And if, in any instances, he has, either through ignorance of the existence of a copyright, or for want of means of communication, made use of any work, in respect of which a similar permission ought to have been obtained, without actually obtaining it, he ventures to hope that the oversight may be excused, and the same liberality extended to him, as if a request for permission had been previously made.

CONTENTS.

PART THE FIRST.

HYMNS ARRANGED ACCORDING TO THE SUBJECTS OF THE CREED.

		HYMN	PAGE
I.	The Holy Trinity	I. to VII.	1
II.	God the Creator	VIII. to XXIX.	7
III.	Christ Incarnate	XXX. to XLVII.	32
IV.	Christ Crucified	XLVIII. to LVII.	53
V.	Christ Risen	LVIII. to LXIV.	61
VI.	Christ Ascended	LXV. to LXXIII.	69
VII.	Christ's Kingdom and Judgment	LXXIV. to XCII.	83
VIII.	God the Holy Ghost	XCIII. to CVII.	104
IX.	The Holy Catholic Church	CVIII. to CXXIX.	120
X.	The Communion of Saints	CXXX. to CXLI.	144
XI.	The Forgiveness of Sins	CXLII. to CXLVIII.	155
XII.	Resurrection and Eternal Life	CXLIX. to CLXVIII.	162

PART THE SECOND.

HYMNS ARRANGED ACCORDING TO THE SUBJECTS OF THE LORD'S PRAYER.

	"Lord, teach us to pray"	CLXIX.	185
I.	"Our Father, which art in heaven, hallowed be Thy Name"	CLXX. to CLXXIII.	186
II.	"Thy kingdom come"	CLXXIV. to CLXXX.	191
III.	"Thy will be done in earth, as it is in heaven"	CLXXXI. to CCIV.	198
IV.	"Give us this day our daily bread"	CCV. to CCXVIII.	222
V.	"And forgive us our trespasses, as we forgive them that trespass against us"	CCXIX. to CCXXVI.	234
VI.	"And lead us not into temptation; but deliver us from evil"	CCXXVII. to CCXLII.	240
VII.	"For Thine is the kingdom, the power, and the glory, for ever and ever. Amen"	CCXLIII. to CCXLV.	253

PART THE THIRD.

HYMNS FOR NATURAL AND SACRED SEASONS.

	HYMN	PAGE
I. Day and Night	CCXLVI. to CCLXVI.	257
II. Seed Time and Harvest	CCLXVII. to CCLXXIV.	286
III. The Old and New Year	CCLXXV. to CCLXXX.	294
IV. Baptism and Childhood	CCLXXXI. to CCXCI.	299
V. Holy Communion	CCXCII. to CCXCVIII.	310
VI. Holy Matrimony	CCXCIX.	317
VII. The Burial of the Dead	CCC. to CCCVI.	318
VIII. Church Dedication	CCCVII. to CCCIX.	323
IX. The Lord's Day	CCCX. to CCCXXI.	326

PART THE FOURTH.

SONGS OF THE HEART.

	HYMN	PAGE
I. The Call.—"Rise; He calleth thee." (Mark x. 49)	CCCXXII. to CCCXXXIV.	341
II. The Answer.—"I will arise, and go to my Father." (Luke xv. 18)	CCCXXXV. to CCCXLIV.	355
III. Faith.—"Looking unto Jesus, the Author and Finisher of our Faith." (Heb. xii. 2)	CCCXLV. to CCCLI.	365
IV. Love.—"If ye love Me, keep my commandments." (John xiv. 15)	CCCLII. to CCCLX.	375
V. Hope.—"Set your affections on things above; not on things on the earth." (Col. iii. 2)	CCCLXI. to CCCLXXVI.	387
VI. Joy.—"In whom, though now ye see Him not, yet believing, ye rejoice with joy unspeakable, and full of glory." (1 Pet. i. 8)	CCCLXXVII. to CCCLXXXVI.	404
VII. Discipline.—"Whom the Lord loveth, He chasteneth." (Heb. xii. 6)	CCCLXXXVII. to CCCXCIX.	414
VIII. Patience.—"Be patient, therefore, brethren, unto the coming of the Lord." (James v. 7)	CCCC. to CCCCXII.	426

NOTES	449
LIST OF AUTHORS	461
INDEX OF FIRST LINES	465

PART I.

HYMNS ARRANGED ACCORDING TO THE SUBJECTS OF THE CREED.

The Book of Praise.

PART THE FIRST.

I.

THE HOLY TRINITY.

"The Catholic Faith is this: that we worship one God in Trinity, and Trinity in Unity."

I.

Holy, holy, holy, Lord God Almighty!
    Early in the morning our song shall rise to Thee;
Holy, holy, holy! Merciful and Mighty!
    God in Three Persons, blessed Trinity!

Holy, holy, holy! all the saints adore Thee,
    Casting down their golden crowns around the glassy sea,
Cherubim and seraphim falling down before Thee,
    Which wert, and art, and evermore shalt be.

Holy, holy, holy! though the darkness hide Thee,
    Though the eye of sinful man Thy glory may not see,
Only Thou art holy, there is none beside Thee,
    Perfect in power, in love and purity.

Holy, holy, holy, Lord God Almighty!
    All Thy works shall praise Thy Name in earth and sky and sea;
Holy, holy, holy! Merciful and Mighty!
    God in Three Persons, blessed Trinity!

Bishop Reginald Heber. 1827.

II.

Round the Lord in glory seated
    Cherubim and seraphim
Fill'd His temple, and repeated
    Each to each th' alternate hymn.

"Lord, Thy glory fills the heaven,
    "Earth is with its fulness stor'd;
"Unto Thee be glory given,
    "Holy, holy, holy Lord!"

Heaven is still with glory ringing,
    Earth takes up the angels' cry,
"Holy, holy, holy," singing,
    "Lord of hosts, the Lord most High!"

With His seraph train before Him,
    With His holy Church below,
Thus conspire we to adore Him,
    Bid we thus our anthem flow:

"Lord, Thy glory fills the heaven,
    "Earth is with its fulness stor'd;
"Unto Thee be glory given,
    "Holy, holy, holy Lord!"
        Bishop Richard Mant. 1837.

III.

Holy, holy, holy, Lord,
    God of hosts! When heaven and earth
Out of darkness, at Thy word,
    Issued into glorious birth,
All Thy works before Thee stood,
And Thine eye beheld them good,
While they sang, with one accord,
Holy, holy, holy, Lord!

Holy, holy, holy! Thee,
  One Jehovah evermore,
Father, Son, and Spirit, we,
  Dust and ashes, would adore:
Lightly by the world esteemed,
From that world by Thee redeemed,
Sing we here, with glad accord,
Holy, holy, holy Lord!

Holy, holy, holy! All
  Heaven's triumphant choir shall sing,
When the ransomed nations fall
  At the footstool of their King:
Then shall saints and seraphim,
Hearts and voices, swell one hymn,
Round the Throne with full accord,
Holy, holy, holy, Lord!

James Montgomery. 1853.

IV.

Te Deum Laudamus.

God eternal, Lord of all,
Lowly at Thy feet we fall,
All the earth doth worship Thee;
We amidst the throng would be.

All the holy angels cry,
Hail, thrice holy, God most High!
Lord of all the heavenly powers,
Be the same loud anthem ours.

Glorified apostles raise
  Night and day continual praise;
Has Thou not a mission too
  For thy children here to do?

With Thy prophets' goodly line
We in mystic bond combine;
For Thou hast to babes revealed
Things that to the wise were sealed.

Martyrs, in a noble host,
Of Thy cross are heard to boast;
Since so bright the crown they wear,
Early we Thy cross would bear.

All Thy Church in heaven and earth,
Jesus! hail Thy spotless birth;
Own the God, who all has made;
And the Spirit's soothing aid.

Offspring of a Virgin's womb;
Slain, and Victor o'er the tomb;
Seated on the Judgment-throne,
Number us among Thine own!

Day by day we magnify Thee,
And would evermore be nigh Thee:
Keep us from the Tempter's snare;
Spare Thy people, Jesu, spare!

James Elwin Millard. 1848.

V.

Te Deum Laudamus.

Thee we adore, eternal Lord!
We praise Thy Name with one accord;
Thy saints, who here Thy goodness see,
Through all the world do worship Thee.

To Thee aloud all angels cry,
And ceaseless raise their songs on high,

Both cherubin and seraphin,
The heavens and all the powers therein.

The Apostles join the glorious throng;
The Prophets swell the immortal song;
The Martyrs' noble army raise
Eternal anthems to Thy praise.

Thee, Holy, holy, holy King!
Thee, O Lord God of hosts, they sing:
Thus earth below, and heaven above,
Resound Thy glory and Thy love.
Anon. [1842.]

VI.

I give immortal praise
    To God the Father's love,
For all my comforts here
    And better hopes above;
He sent His own eternal Son
To die for sins that man had done.

To God the Son belongs
    Immortal glory too,
Who bought us with His blood
    From everlasting woe;
And now He lives, and now He reigns,
And sees the fruit of all His pains.

To God the Spirit's name
    Immortal worship give,
Whose new-creating power
    Makes the dead sinner live;
His work completes the great design,
And fills the soul with joy divine.

Almighty God, to Thee
  Be endless honours done ;
The undivided Three,
  And the mysterious One !
Where reason fails with all her powers,
There faith prevails, and love adores.
Isaac Watts. 1709.

VII.

O King of kings, before whose throne
  The angels bow, no gift can we
Present that is indeed our own,
  Since heaven and earth belong to Thee :
Yet this our souls through grace impart,
The offering of a thankful heart.

O Jesu, set at God's right hand,
  With Thine eternal Father plead
For all Thy loyal-hearted band,
  Who still on earth Thy succour need ;
For them in weakness strength provide,
And through the world their footsteps guide.

O Holy Spirit, Fount of breath,
  Whose comforts never fail nor fade,
Vouchsafe the life that knows no death,
  Vouchsafe the light that knows no shade ;
And grant, that we through all our days
May share Thy gifts, and sing Thy praise.
Anon. [1857.]

II.

GOD THE CREATOR.

"I believe in one God, the Father Almighty, Maker of heaven and earth, and of all things visible and invisible."

VIII.

Psalm C.

Before Jehovah's awful throne,
  Ye nations, bow with sacred joy;
Know that the Lord is God alone,
  He can create, and He destroy.

His sov'reign power, without our aid,
  Made us of clay, and formed us men;
And when like wandering sheep we stray'd,
  He brought us to His fold again.

We'll crowd Thy gates with thankful songs,
  High as the heavens our voices raise;
And earth, with her ten thousand tongues,
  Shall fill Thy courts with sounding praise.

Wide as the world is Thy command,
  Vast as eternity Thy love;
Firm as a rock Thy truth must stand,
  When rolling years shall cease to move.

Isaac Watts. 1719.
Varied by Charles Wesley. 1741.

IX.

Psalm XCIII.

The Lord Jehovah reigns
  And royal state maintains,
His head with awful glories crown'd;
  Arrayed in robes of light,
  Begirt with sovereign might,
And rays of majesty around.

  Upheld by Thy commands,
  The world securely stands,
And skies and stars obey Thy word:
  Thy throne was fixed on high
  Before the starry sky:
Eternal is Thy kingdom, Lord.

  In vain the noisy crowd,
  Like billows fierce and loud,
Against Thine empire rage and roar:
  In vain, with angry spite,
  The surly nations fight,
And dash like waves against the shore.

  Let floods and nations rage,
  And all their powers engage;
Let swelling tides assault the sky:
  The terrors of Thy frown
  Shall beat their madness down:
Thy throne for ever stands on high.

  Thy promises are true,
  Thy grace is ever new;
There fixed, Thy Church shall ne'er remove:
  Thy saints with holy fear
  Shall in Thy courts appear,
And sing Thine everlasting love.

Isaac Watts. 1719.

God the Creator.

X.

Let all the world rejoice,
　The great Jehovah reigns;
The thunders are His awful voice;
　Our life His will ordains;
　The glories of His Name
The lightnings, floods, and hail proclaim.

He rules by sea and land,
　O'er boundless realms He sways;
He holds the oceans in His hand,
　And mighty mountains weighs:
　Unequalled and alone
In majesty He fills His throne.

The universe He made
　By His prevailing might;
The earth's foundations He hath laid,
　And scattered ancient night;
　When heaven, and earth, and sea,
Proclaimed His awful majesty.

When the bright orb of day
　First gleamed with ruddy light,
And yonder moon, with silver ray,
　Marched up the vault of night;
　And stars bedecked the skies,
That seemed creation's thousand eyes;

And earth's fair form was seen,
　With flowers and blossoms drest;
And trees, and fields, and meadows green,
　Adorned her youthful breast,
　Hung out in boundless space,
Amid the ocean's cool embrace;

Glad was the angel throng
  To see His might prevail;
And loud they sung a joyful song
  This universe to hail,
  While yet in youth it stood;
The Maker, too, pronounced it good.

But this fair world shall die,
  The creature of a day;
In ashes and in ruins lie,
  Its glory passed away:
  As when before her birth,
Again shall be this mighty earth.

Soon shall the day be o'er
  Of yonder brilliant sun;
And he shall set to rise no more,
  His race of glory run;
  And soon, alas! all soon
Shall fade the stars, and yon pale moon.

But ever fix'd, the throne
  Of the Eternal One
Shall stand, when all creation's gone,
  Unequalled and alone;
  New worlds to make at will,
And His own wise designs fulfil.

John Hunt. 1853.

XI.

PSALM CXV.

Not unto us, Almighty Lord,
  But to Thyself the glory be!
Created by Thy awful word,
  We only live to honour Thee.

Where is their God? the heathen cry,
  And bow to senseless wood and stone;
Our God, we tell them, fills the sky,
  And calls ten thousand worlds his own.

Vain gods! vain men! the Lord alone
  Is Israel's worship, Israel's friend;
O fear His power, His goodness own,
  And love Him, trust Him, to the end.

Who lean on Him, from strength to strength,
  From light to light, shall onward move,
Till through the grave they pass at length,
  To sing on high His saving love.
                    Henry Francis Lyte. 1834.

XII.

Psalm CXLVI.

Happy the man, whose hopes rely
On Israel's God; He made the sky,
  And earth and seas with all their train;
His truth for ever stands secure,
He saves the opprest, He feeds the poor;
  And none shall find his promise vain.

The Lord hath eyes to give the blind;
The Lord supports the sinking mind;
  He sends the labouring conscience peace;
He helps the stranger in distress,
The widow and the fatherless,
  And grants the prisoner sweet release.

I'll praise Him while He lends me breath,
And when my voice is lost in death

Praise shall employ my nobler powers:
My days of praise shall ne'er be past,
While life and thought and being last,
Or immortality endures.

Isaac Watts. 1719.

XIII.

Psalm XIX.

The spacious firmament on high,
With all the blue ethereal sky,
And spangled heavens, a shining frame,
Their great Original proclaim.
The unwearied sun, from day to day,
Does his Creator's power display,
And publishes to every land
The work of an Almighty hand.

Soon as the evening shades prevail,
The moon takes up the wondrous tale,
And nightly to the listening earth
Repeats the story of her birth;
Whilst all the stars that round her burn,
And all the planets in their turn,
Confirm the tidings, as they roll,
And spread the truth from pole to pole.

What, though in solemn silence all
Move round the dark terrestrial ball;
What, though no real voice or sound
Amidst their radiant orbs be found;
In reason's ear they all rejoice,
And utter forth a glorious voice,
For ever singing, as they shine,
"The hand that made us is Divine."

Joseph Addison. 1728.

God the Creator.

XIV.

There is a book, who runs may read,
  Which heavenly truth imparts,
And all the lore its scholars need,
  Pure eyes and Christian hearts.

The works of God, above, below,
  Within us and around,
Are pages in that book, to show
  How God Himself is found.

The glorious sky, embracing all,
  Is like the Maker's love,
Wherewith encompass'd, great and small
  In peace and order move.

The moon above, the Church below,
  A wondrous race they run;
But all their radiance, all their glow,
  Each borrows of its sun.

The Saviour lends the light and heat
  That crowns His holy hill;
The saints, like stars, around His seat
  Perform their courses still.

The saints above are stars in Heaven;
  What are the saints on earth?
Like trees they stand, whom God has given,
  Our Eden's happy birth.

Faith is their fix'd unswerving root,
  Hope their unfading flower;
Fair deeds of charity their fruit,
  The glory of their bower.

The dew of heaven is like Thy grace;
   It steals in silence down;
But, where it lights, the favoured place
   By richest fruits is known.

One name, above all glorious names,
   With its ten thousand tongues
The everlasting sea proclaims,
   Echoing angelic songs.

The raging fire, the roaring wind,
   Thy boundless power display:
But in the gentler breeze we find
   Thy Spirit's viewless way.

Two worlds are ours: 'tis only sin
   Forbids us to descry,
The mystic heaven and earth within,
   Plain as the sea and sky.

Thou who hast given us eyes to see
   And love this sight so fair,
Give us a heart to find out Thee,
   And read Thee everywhere.

John Keble. 1827.

XV.

PSALM LXV.

On God the race of man depends,
Far as the earth's remotest ends,
Where the Creator's name is known
By nature's feeble light alone.

He bids the noisy tempests cease;
He calms the raging crowd to peace,

God the Creator.

When a tumultuous nation raves
Wild as the winds, and loud as waves.

Whole kingdoms, shaken by the storm,
He settles in a peaceful form;
Mountains, establish'd by His hand,
Firm on their old foundations stand.

Behold His ensigns sweep the sky;
New comets blaze, and lightnings fly!
The heathen lands, with swift surprise,
From the bright horrors turn their eyes.

At His command the morning ray
Smiles in the east, and leads the day;
He guides the sun's declining wheels
Over the tops of western hills.

Seasons and times obey His voice;
The evening and the morn rejoice
To see the earth made soft with showers,
Laden with fruit, and drest in flowers.

'Tis from His watery stores on high
He gives the thirsty ground supply;
He walks upon the clouds, and thence
Doth His enriching drops dispense.

The desert grows a fruitful field,
Abundant food the valleys yield;
The valleys shout with cheerful voice,
And neighbouring hills repeat their joys.

Thy works pronounce Thy power divine;
O'er every field Thy glories shine;
Through every month thy gifts appear;
Great God! Thy goodness crowns the year!

Isaac Watts. 1719.

XVI.

Thy goodness, Lord, our souls confess,
   Thy goodness we adore;
A spring, whose blessings never fail,
   A sea without a shore.

Sun, moon, and stars, Thy love attest
   In every cheerful ray;
Love draws the curtains of the night,
   And love restores the day.

Thy bounty every season crowns
   With all the bliss it yields,
With joyful clusters bend the vines,
   With harvests wave the fields.

But chiefly Thy compassions, Lord,
   Are in the Gospel seen;
There, like the Sun, Thy mercy shines
   Without a cloud between.

Thomas Gibbons. 1784.

XVII.

I sing th' almighty power of God,
   That made the mountains rise,
That spread the flowing seas abroad,
   And built the lofty skies.

I sing the wisdom that ordain'd
   The sun to rule the day:
The moon shines full at His command,
   And all the stars obey.

God the Creator.

I sing the goodness of the Lord
   That filled the earth with food ;
He formed the creatures with His word,
   And then pronounced them good.

Lord, how Thy wonders are display'd,
   Where'er I turn my eye ;
If I survey the ground I tread,
   Or gaze upon the sky !

There's not a plant or flower below,
   But makes Thy glories known ;
And clouds arise, and tempests blow,
   By order from Thy throne.

Creatures, as numerous as they be,
   Are subject to Thy care ;
There's not a place where we can flee
   But God is present there.

In Heaven He shines with beams of love,
   With wrath in hell beneath ;
'Tis on His earth I stand or move,
   And 'tis His air I breathe.

His hand is my perpetual guard ;
   He keeps me with His eye :
Why should I then forget the Lord,
   Who is for ever nigh ?

Isaac Watts. 1720.

XVIII.

Yes, God is good ; in earth and sky,
  From ocean-depths and spreading wood,
Ten thousand voices seem to cry,
  " God made us all, and God is good."

The sun that keeps his trackless way,
  And downward pours his golden flood,
Night's sparkling hosts, all seem to say
  In accents clear, that God is good.

The merry birds prolong the strain,
  Their song with every spring renewed ;
And balmy air, and falling rain,
  Each softly whisper, " God is good."

I hear it in the rushing breeze ;
  The hills that have for ages stood,
The echoing sky and roaring seas,
  All swell the chorus, " God is good."

Yes, God is good, all Nature says,
  By God's own hand with speech endued ;
And man, in louder notes of praise,
  Should sing for joy that God is good.

For all Thy gifts we bless Thee, Lord ;
  But chiefly for our heavenly food,
Thy pardoning grace, Thy quick'ning word ;
  These prompt our song, that God is good.

John Hampden Gurney. 1851.

XIX.

Nil laudibus nostris eges.

Our praise Thou need'st not ; but Thy love,
    Our Father and our Friend,
Would have our prayers thus soar above,
    In blessings to descend.

Thy secret judgments' depths profound
    Still sings the silent night ;
The day upon his golden round
    Thy pity infinite.

The soul lost in astonishment
    Would speechless wonder fill ;
But, in the ravish'd bosom pent,
    Love cannot all be still.

Feeble and faint, she fain would tell
    Of our great Father's love,
Tempering the ills that with us dwell,
    And pledging good above.

Thither would our best thoughts aspire,
    But chains on us abide ;
O quicken Thou our faint desire,
    And to Thy presence guide !
              Isaac Williams. 1839.

XX.

Let all the world in every corner sing
    My God and King !
  The heavens are not too high ;
  His praise may thither fly :

The earth is not too low;
His praises there may grow.

Let all the world in every corner sing
    My God and King!
The Church with psalms must shout;
No door can keep them out:
But, above all, the heart
Must bear the longest part.

Let all the world in every corner sing
    My God and King!

George Herbert. 1632.

XXI.

Psalm CIV.

O worship the King,
  All glorious above;
O gratefully sing
  His power and His love;
Our Shield and Defender,
  The Ancient of days,
Pavilioned in splendour,
  And girded with praise.

O tell of His might,
  O sing of His grace,
Whose robe is the light,
  Whose canopy space;
His chariots of wrath
  Deep thunder-clouds form,
And dark is His path
  On the wings of the storm.

God the Creator.

The earth, with its store
   Of wonders untold,
Almighty, Thy power
   Hath founded of old,
Hath stablish'd it fast
   By a changeless decree,
And round it hath cast,
   Like a mantle, the sea.

Thy bountiful care
   What tongue can recite?
It breathes in the air,
   It shines in the light;
It streams from the hills,
   It descends to the plain,
And sweetly distils
   In the dew and the rain.

Frail children of dust,
   And feeble as frail,
In Thee do we trust,
   Nor find Thee to fail:
Thy mercies how tender!
   How firm to the end!
Our Maker, Defender,
   Redeemer, and Friend!

O measureless Might!
   Ineffable Love!
While angels delight
   To hymn Thee above,
The humbler creation,
   Tho' feeble their lays,
With true adoration
   Shall lisp to Thy praise.

Sir Robert Grant. [1839.]

XXII.

Sing to the Lord with cheerful voice,
    From realm to realm the notes shall sound;
And Heaven's exulting sons rejoice
    To bear the full Hosanna round.

When, starting from the shades of night,
    At dread Jehovah's high behest,
The Sun arrayed his limbs in light,
    And Earth her virgin beauty drest;

Thy praise transported Nature sung
    In pealing chorus loud and far;
The echoing vault with rapture rung,
    And shouted every morning star.

When, bending from His native sky,
    The Lord of Life in mercy came,
And laid His bright effulgence by,
    To bear on earth a human name;

The song, by cherub voices raised,
    Roll'd through the dark blue depths above;
And Israel's shepherds heard amazed
    The seraph notes of peace and love.

And shall not man the concert join,
    For whom this bright creation rose;
For whom the fires of morning shine,
    And eve's still lamps, that woo repose?

And shall not he the chorus swell,
    Whose form the Incarnate Godhead wore;
Whose guilt, whose fears, whose triumph tell
    How deep the wounds his Saviour bore?

Long as yon glittering arch shall bend,
   Long as yon orbs in glory roll,
Long as the streams of life descend
   To cheer with hope the fainting soul,

Thy praise shall fill each grateful voice,
   Shall bid the song of rapture sound :
And heaven's exulting sons rejoice
   To bear the full Hosanna round.
                       John Bowdler. 1814.

XXIII.

Psalm CIII.

Praise, my soul, the King of heaven ;
   To His feet thy tribute bring ;
Ransomed, healed, restored, forgiven,
   Who like me His praise should sing?
      Praise Him! praise Him!
      Praise the everlasting King!

Praise Him for His grace and favour,
   To our fathers in distress ;
Praise Him, still the same for ever,
   Slow to chide, and swift to bless ;
      Praise Him ! praise him !
      Glorious in His faithfulness!

Father-like He tends and spares us ;
   Well our feeble frame he knows ;
In His hands He gently bears us,
   Rescues us from all our foes :
      Praise Him ! praise him !
      Widely as His mercy flows!

Angels, help us to adore Him,
  Ye behold Him face to face ;
Sun and moon, bow down before Him,
  Dwellers all in time and space,
    Praise Him! praise Him!
  Praise with us the God of grace!
        Henry Francis Lyte. 1834.

XXIV.

Psalm CL.

Praise the Lord, His glories show,
Saints within His courts below,
Angels round His throne above,
All that see and share His love.
Earth to heaven, and heaven to earth,
Tell his wonders, sing his worth ;
Age to age, and shore to shore,
Praise Him, praise Him, evermore!

Praise the Lord, His mercies trace ;
Praise His providence and grace,
All that He for man hath done,
All He sends us through His Son :
Strings and voices, hands and hearts,
In the concert bear your parts ;
All that breathe, your Lord adore,
Praise Him, praise Him, evermore!
        Henry Francis Lyte. 1834.

XXV.

Psalm CXLVIII.

Praise the Lord of Heaven, praise Him in the height,
Praise Him, all ye angels, praise Him, stars and light;
Praise Him, skies, and waters, which above the skies,
When His word commanded, 'stablished did arise.

Praise the Lord, ye fountains of the deeps and seas,
Rocks and hills and mountains, cedars and all trees;
Praise Him, clouds and vapours, snow, and hail, and fire,
Stormy wind, fulfilling only His desire.

Praise Him, fowls and cattle, princes and all kings,
Praise Him, men and maidens, all created things;
For the Name of God is excellent alone;
Over earth His footstool, over heaven His throne.

T. B. Browne. 1844.

XXVI.

Hark, my soul, how every thing
Strives to serve our bounteous King;
Each a double tribute pays,
Sings its part, and then obeys.

Nature's chief and sweetest quire
Him with cheerful notes admire;
Chanting every day their lauds,
While the grove their song applauds.

Though their voices lower be,
Streams have too their melody;
Night and day they warbling run,
Never pause, but still sing on.

All the flowers that gild the spring
Hither their still music bring;
If Heaven bless them, thankful they
Smell more sweet, and look more gay.

Only we can scarce afford
This short office to our Lord;
We, on whom His bounty flows,
All things gives, and nothing owes.

Wake, for shame, my sluggish heart,
Wake, and gladly sing thy part;
Learn of birds, and springs, and flowers,
How to use thy nobler powers.

Call whole nature to thy aid,
Since 'twas He whole nature made;
Join in one eternal song,
Who to one God all belong.

Live for ever, glorious Lord!
Live, by all Thy works ador'd!
One in Three, and Three in One,
Thrice we bow to Thee alone!

John Austin. 1668.

XXVII.

Come, O come! in pious lays
Sound we God Almighty's praise;
Hither bring, in one consent,
Heart, and voice, and instrument:
Music add of every kind,
Sound the trump, the cornet wind,
Strike the viol, touch the lute,
Let not tongue nor string be mute;
Nor a creature dumb be found
That hath either voice or sound.

Let those things which do not live
In still music praises give;
Lowly pipe, ye worms that creep
On the earth or in the deep:
Loud aloft your voices strain,
Beasts and monsters of the main;
Birds, your warbling treble sing;
Clouds, your peals of thunder ring;
Sun and moon, exalted higher,
And bright stars, augment the choir.

Come, ye sons of human race,
In this chorus take your place,
And amid the mortal throng
Be you masters of the song:
Angels and supernal powers,
Be the noblest tenor yours:
Let, in praise of God, the sound
Run a never-ending round,
That our song of praise may be
Everlasting, as is He.

From earth's vast and hollow womb,
Music's deepest base may come;
Seas and floods, from shore to shore,
Shall their counter-tenors roar:
To this concert, when we sing,
Whistling winds your descants bring;
That our song may over-climb
All the bounds of place and time,
And ascend, from sphere to sphere,
To the great Almighty's ear.

So from Heaven on earth He shall
Let His gracious blessings fall;
And this huge wide orb we see
Shall one choir, one temple be;
Where in such a praiseful tone
We will sing what He hath done,
That the cursed fiends below
Shall thereat impatient grow:
Then, O come, in pious lays
Sound we God Almighty's praise!

George Wither. 1641.

XXVIII.

To God, ye choir above, begin
   A hymn so loud and strong,
That all the universe may hear
   And join the grateful song.

Praise Him, thou sun, Who dwells unseen
   Amidst transcendent light,
Where thy refulgent orb would seem
   A spot, as dark as night.

Thou silver moon, ye host of stars,
    The universal song
Through the serene and silent night
    To listening worlds prolong.

Sing Him, ye distant worlds and suns,
    From whence no travelling ray
Hath yet to us, through ages past,
    Had time to make its way.

Assist, ye raging storms, and bear
    On rapid wings His praise,
From north to south, from east to west,
    Through heaven, and earth, and seas.

Exert your voice, ye furious fires
    That rend the watery cloud,
And thunder to this nether world
    Your Maker's words aloud.

Ye works of God, that dwell unknown
    Beneath the rolling main;
Ye birds, that sing among the groves,
    And sweep the azure plain;

Ye stately hills, that rear your heads,
    And towering pierce the sky;
Ye clouds, that with an awful pace
    Majestic roll on high;

Ye insects small, to which one leaf
    Within its narrow sides
A vast extended world displays,
    And spacious realms provides;

Ye race, still less than these, with which
    The stagnant water teems,
To which one drop, however small,
    A boundless ocean seems;

Whate'er ye are, where'er ye dwell,
    Ye creatures great or small,
Adore the wisdom, praise the power,
    That made and governs all.

And if ye want or sense or sounds,
    To swell the grateful noise,
Prompt mankind with that sense, and they
    Shall find for you a voice.

From all the boundless realms of space
    Let loud Hosannas sound;
Loud send, ye wondrous works of God,
    The grateful concert round.

Philip Skelton. 1784.

XXIX.

The strain upraise of joy and praise,
        Alleluia!
 To the glory of their King
 Shall the ransomed people sing,
        Alleluia!
 And the choirs that dwell on high
 Shall re-echo through the sky,
        Alleluia!
They through the fields of Paradise who roam,
The blessed ones, repeat through that bright home,
        Alleluia!

The planets glittering on their heavenly way,
The shining constellations, join and say,
Alleluia!

    Ye clouds that onward sweep,
    Ye winds on pinions light,
  Ye thunders, echoing loud and deep,
    Ye lightnings, wildly bright,
In sweet consent unite your Alleluia!
    Ye floods and ocean billows,
    Ye storms and winter snow,
    Ye days of cloudless beauty,
    Hoar frost and summer glow;
    Ye groves that wave in spring,
    And glorious forests, sing
Alleluia!

First let the birds, with painted plumage gay,
Exalt their great Creator's praise, and say
Alleluia!

Then let the beasts of earth, with varying strain,
Join in creation's hymn, and cry again,
Alleluia!

Here let the mountains thunder forth sonorous,
Alleluia!

There let the valleys sing in gentler chorus,
Alleluia!

Thou jubilant abyss of ocean, cry
Alleluia!

Ye tracts of earth and continents, reply
Alleluia!

    To God, Who all creation made,
    The frequent hymn be duly paid;
Alleluia!

This is the strain, the eternal strain, the Lord
    Almighty loves;
Alleluia!

This is the song, the heavenly song, that Christ
  Himself approves ;
            Alleluia !
Wherefore we sing, both heart and voice awaking,
            Alleluia !
And children's voices echo, answer making,
            Alleluia !
  Now from all men be outpoured
  Alleluia to the Lord ;
  With Alleluia evermore
  The Son and Spirit we adore.
Praise be done to the Three in One,
Alleluia ! Alleluia ! Alleluia ! Alleluia !
        John Mason Neale. 1851.

CHRIST INCARNATE.

III.

"*And in one Lord Jesus Christ, the only-begotten Son of God, begotten of His Father before all worlds, God of God, Light of Light, Very God of Very God, Begotten, not made, being of one Substance with the Father, by Whom all things were made:*
"*Who for us men, and for our salvation, came down from Heaven, and was Incarnate by the Holy Ghost of the Virgin Mary, and was made man.*"

XXX.

"*Jam desinant suspiria.*"

  Away with sorrow's sigh,
  Our prayers are heard on high ;
  And through Heaven's crystal door
  On this our earthly floor
Comes meek-eyed Peace to walk with poor mortality.

Christ Incarnate.

In dead of night profound,
There breaks a seraph sound
Of never-ending morn;
The Lord of glory born
Within a holy grot on this our sullen ground.

Now with that shepherd crowd
If it might be allowed,
We fain would enter there
With awful hastening fear,
And kiss that cradle chaste in reverend worship bowed.

O sight of strange surprise
That fills our gazing eyes:
A manger coldly strew'd,
And swaddling bands so rude,
A leaning mother poor, and child that helpless lies.

Art Thou, O wondrous sight,
Of lights the very Light;
Who holdest in Thy hand
The sky and sea and land;
Who than the glorious heavens art more exceeding bright?

'Tis so; faith darts before,
And, through the cloud drawn o'er,
She sees the God of all,
Where angels prostrate fall,
Adoring tremble still, and trembling still adore.

No thunders round Thee break;
Yet doth Thy silence speak
From that, Thy Teacher's seat,
To us around Thy feet,
To shun what flesh desires, what flesh abhors to seek.

D

Within us, Babe divine,
Be born, and make us Thine;
Within our souls reveal
Thy love and power to heal;
Be born, and make our hearts Thy cradle and Thy shrine.

Isaac Williams. 1839.

XXXI.

What sudden blaze of song
    Spreads o'er the expanse of Heaven?
In waves of light it thrills along,
    Th' angelic signal given:
Glory to God! from yonder central fire
Flows out the echoing lay beyond the starry quire.

Like circles widening round
    Upon a clear blue river,
Orb after orb, the wondrous sound
    Is echoed on for ever:
"Glory to God on high, on earth be peace,
And love towards men of love, salvation and release!"

Yet stay, before thou dare
    To join that festal throng;
Listen, and mark what gentle air
    First stirred the tide of song:
'Tis not, "the Saviour born in David's home,
To whom for power and health obedient worlds should come."

'Tis not, "the Christ the Lord:"
    With fixed adoring look

The quire of angels caught the word,
    Nor yet their silence broke :
But when they heard the sign, where Christ
    should be,
In sudden light they shone, and heavenly harmony.

Wrapped in His swaddling bands,
    And in His manger laid,
The Hope and Glory of all lands
    Is come to the world's aid :
No peaceful home upon His cradle smil'd ;
Guests rudely went and came, where slept the royal
    Child.

But where Thou dwellest, Lord,
    No other thought should be,
Once duly welcomed and ador'd.
    How should I part with Thee ?
Bethlehem must lose Thee soon ; but Thou wilt
    grace
The single heart to be Thy sure abiding place.

Thee, on the bosom laid
    Of a pure virgin mind,
In quiet ever and in shade
    Shepherd and sage may find ;
They, who have bowed untaught to Nature's
    sway,
And they, who follow Truth along her star-paved
    way.

The pastoral spirits first
    Approach Thee, Babe divine ;
For they in lowly thoughts are nurst,
    Meet for Thy lowly shrine :

Sooner than they should miss where Thou dost dwell,
Angels from Heaven will stoop to guide them to Thy cell.

Still, as the day comes round
   For Thee to be reveal'd,
By wakeful shepherds Thou art found
   Abiding in the field :
All though the wintry heaven and chill night air
In music and in light Thou dawnest on their prayer.

O faint not ye for fear !
   What though your wandering sheep,
Reckless of what they see and hear
   Lie lost in wilful sleep ?
High Heaven, in mercy to your sad annoy,
Still greets you with glad tidings of immortal joy.

Think on the eternal home
   The Saviour left for you ;
Think on the Lord most Holy, come
   To dwell with hearts untrue :
So shall ye tread untired His pastoral ways,
And in the darkness sing your carol of high praise.
                  John Keble. 1827.

XXXII.

'Tis come, the time so oft foretold,
   The time eternal love forecast ;
Four thousand years of hope have rolled,
   And God hath sent His Son at last ;
Let heaven, let earth, adore the plan ;
Glory to God, and grace to man !

To swains that watch'd their nightly fold,
   Of lowly lot, of lowly mind,
To these the tidings first were told,
   That told of hope for lost mankind ;
God gives His Son ; no more He can ;
Glory to God, and grace to man !

And well to shepherds first 'tis known,
   The Lord of angels comes from high,
In humblest aspect like their own,
   Good Shepherd, for His sheep to die :
O height and depth, which who shall span ?
Glory to God, and grace to man !

Fain with those meek, those happy swains,
   Lord, I would hear that angel quire ;
Till, ravished by celestial strains,
   My heart responds with holy fire ;
(That holy fire Thy breath must fan ;)
Glory to God, and grace to man !
Thomas Grinfield. 1836.

XXXIII.

While shepherds watched their flocks by night
   All seated on the ground,
The angel of the Lord came down,
   And glory shone around.

" Fear not," said he ; (for mighty dread
   Had seized their troubled mind ;)
" Glad tidings of great joy I bring
   " To you and all mankind.

" To you, in David's town, this day
  " Is born of David's line
" The Saviour, who is Christ the Lord;
  " And this shall be the sign.

" The heavenly Babe you there shall find
  " To human view displayed,
" All meanly wrapt in swathing bands,
  " And in a manger laid."

Thus spake the Seraph; and forthwith
  Appeared a shining throng
Of angels, praising God, and thus
  Address'd their joyful song.

" All glory be to God on high,
  " And to the earth be peace;
" Good will henceforth from Heaven to men
  " Begin, and never cease!"

Nahum Tate. 1703.

XXXIV.

Hark! how all the welkin rings
Glory to the King of kings!
Peace on earth, and mercy mild,
God and sinners reconciled!
Joyful, all ye nations, rise,
Join the triumph of the skies;
Universal nature say,
Christ the Lord is born to-day!

Christ, by highest Heaven adored;
Christ, the Everlasting Lord;
Late in time behold Him come,
Offspring of a Virgin's womb:

Christ Incarnate.

Veiled in flesh the Godhead see;
Hail, th' Incarnate Deity,
Pleased as man with men to appear,
Jesus, our Immanuel here!

Hail! the heavenly Prince of Peace!
Hail! the Sun of Righteousness!
Light and life to all He brings,
Risen with healing in His wings.
Mild He lays His glory by,
Born that man no more may die,
Born to raise the sons of earth,
Born to give them second birth.

Come, Desire of nations, come,
Fix in us Thy humble home!
Rise, the Woman's conquering Seed,
Bruise in us the Serpent's head!
Now display Thy saving power,
Ruined nature now restore,
Now in mystic union join
Thine to ours, and ours to Thine!

Adam's likeness, Lord, efface;
Stamp Thy image in its place;
Second Adam from above,
Reinstate us in Thy love!
Let us Thee, though lost, regain,
Thee, the Life, the Heavenly Man:
O! to all Thyself impart,
Formed in each believing heart!

Charles Wesley. 1743.

XXXV.

We'll sing, in spite of scorn:
   Our theme is come from Heaven:
To us a Child is born,
   To us a Son is given;
The sweetest news that ever came
We'll sing, though all the world should blame.

The long-expected morn
   Has dawn'd upon the earth;
The Saviour Christ is born,
   And angels sing His birth:
We'll join the bright seraphic throng,
We'll share their joys, and swell their song.

O! 'tis a lofty theme,
   Supplied by angels' tongues!
All other objects seem
   Unworthy of our songs.
This sacred theme has boundless charms,
It fills, it captivates, it warms.

Now sing of peace divine,
   Of grace to guilty man;
No wisdom, Lord, but Thine
   Could form the wondrous plan;
Where peace and righteousness embrace,
And justice goes along with grace.

Give praise to God on high,
   With angels round His throne;
Give praise to God with joy,
   Give praise to God alone!
'Tis meet His saints their songs should raise,
And give the Saviour endless praise.
                  Thomas Kelly. 1806—1836.

XXXVI.

The scene around me disappears,
   And, borne to ancient regions,
While time recalls the flight of years,
   I see angelic legions
Descending in an orb of light:
Amidst the dark and silent night
   I hear celestial voices.

Tidings, glad tidings from above
   To every age and nation!
Tidings, glad tidings! God is Love,
   To man He sends salvation!
His Son beloved, His only Son,
The work of mercy hath begun;
   Give to His Name the glory!

Through David's city I am led;
   Here all around are sleeping;
A Light directs to yon poor shed;
   There lonely watch is keeping:
I enter; ah! what glories shine!
Is this Immanuel's earthly shrine,
   Messiah's infant Temple?

It is, it is; and I adore
   This Stranger meek and lowly,
As saints and angels bow before
   The throne of God thrice Holy!
Faith through the veil of flesh can see
The Face of Thy Divinity,
   My Lord, my God, my Saviour!

James Montgomery. 1825.

XXXVII.

Though rude winds usher thee, sweet day,
   Though clouds thy face deform,
Though nature's grace is swept away
   Before thy sleety storm;
Ev'n in thy sombrest wintry vest,
Of blessed days thou art most blest.

Nor frigid air nor gloomy morn
   Shall check our jubilee;
Bright is the day when Christ was born,
   No sun need shine but He;
Let roughest storms their coldest blow,
With love of Him our hearts shall glow.

Inspired with high and holy thought,
   Fancy is on the wing;
It seems as to mine ear it brought
   Those voices carolling,
Voices through heaven and earth that ran,
Glory to God, good will to man.

I see the shepherds gazing wild
   At those fair spirits of light;
I see them bending o'er the Child
   With that untold delight
Which marks the face of those who view
Things but too happy to be true.

There, in the lowly manger laid,
   Incarnate God they see;
He stoops to take, through spotless maid,
   Our frail humanity:
Son of high God, creation's Heir,
He leaves His Heaven to raise us there.

Through Him, Lord, we are born anew,
   Thy children once again;
Oh! day by day our hearts renew,
   That Thine we may remain,
And, angel-like, may all agree,
One sweet and holy family.

Oft, as this joyous morn doth come
   To speak our Saviour's love,
Oh, may it bear our spirits home,
   Where He now reigns above;
That day which brought Him from the skies,
And man restores to Paradise!

Then let winds usher thee, sweet day,
   Let clouds thy face deform;
Though nature's grace is swept away
   Before thy sleety storm;
Ev'n in thy sombrest wintry vest
Of blessed days thou art most blest.
              Samuel Rickards. 1825.

XXXVIII.

It came upon the midnight clear,
   That glorious song of old,
From angels bending near the earth
   To touch their harps of gold:
" Peace to the earth, goodwill to men
   From Heaven's all-gracious King:"
The world in solemn stillness lay
   To hear the angels sing.

Still through the cloven skies they come
   With peaceful wings unfurl'd;

And still their heavenly music floats
  O'er all the weary world :
Above its sad and lowly plains
  They bend on heavenly wing,
And ever o'er its Babel sounds
  The blessed angels sing.

Yet with the woes of sin and strife
  The world has suffered long ;
Beneath the angel-strain have rolled
  Two thousand years of wrong ;
And men, at war with men, hear not
  The love-song which they bring :
Oh ! hush the noise, ye men of strife,
  And hear the angels sing !

And ye, beneath life's crushing load
  Whose forms are bending low,
Who toil along the climbing way
  With painful steps and slow ;
Look now ! for glad and golden hours
  Come swiftly on the wing :
Oh ! rest beside the weary road,
  And hear the angels sing !

For lo ! the days are hastening on,
  By prophet-bards foretold,
When with the ever-circling years
  Comes round the age of gold ;
When Peace shall over all the earth
  Its ancient splendours fling,
And the whole world send back the song
  Which now the angels sing.

Edmund H. Sears. [1860.]

XXXIX.

The race that long in darkness pined
    Have seen a glorious Light;
The people dwell in Day, who dwelt
    In Death's surrounding night.

To hail Thy rise, Thou better Sun,
    The gathering nations come,
Joyous as when the reapers bear
    The harvest-treasures home.

For Thou our burden hast removed,
    And quell'd th' oppressor's sway,
Quick as the slaughtered squadrons fell
    In Midian's evil day.

To us a Child of Hope is born,
    To us a Son is given;
Him shall the tribes of earth obey,
    Him all the hosts of heaven.

His Name shall be the Prince of Peace,
    For evermore adored,
The Wonderful, the Counsellor,
    The great and mighty Lord.

His power increasing still shall spread,
    His reign no end shall know:
Justice shall guard His throne above,
    And Peace abound below.

John Morrison. 1770.

XL.

Bright was the guiding star that led
   With mild benignant ray
The Gentiles to the lowly shed,
   Where the Redeemer lay.

But lo! a brighter, clearer light
   Now points to His abode;
It shines through sin and sorrow's night,
   To guide us to our God.

O haste to follow where it leads;
   The gracious call obey;
Be rugged wilds, or flowery meads,
   The Christian's destined way.

O gladly tread the narrow path
   While light and grace are given!
Who meekly follow Christ on earth,
   Shall reign with Him in heaven.
        Anon. " Spirit of the Psalms." 1829.

XLI.

As with gladness men of old
Did the guiding star behold;
As with joy they hailed its light,
Leading onward, beaming bright;
So, most gracious God, may we
Evermore be led by Thee.

As with joyful steps they sped
To that lowly manger-bed;
There to bend the knee before
Him whom heaven and earth adore;

So may we with willing feet
Ever seek Thy mercy-seat.

As they offered gifts most rare
At that manger rude and bare;
So may we with holy joy,
Pure, and free from sin's alloy,
All our costliest treasures bring,
Christ, to Thee, our heavenly King.

Holy Jesus! every day
Keep us in the narrow way;
And, when earthly things are past,
Bring our ransomed souls at last
Where they need no star to guide,
Where no clouds Thy glory hide.

In the heavenly country bright
Need they no created light;
Thou its Light, its Joy, its Crown,
Thou its Sun, which goes not down:
There for ever may we sing
Hallelujahs to our King.
William Chatterton Dix. 1860.

XLII.

Hark, the glad sound! the Saviour comes,
   The Saviour promised long;
Let every heart prepare a throne,
   And every voice a song!

He comes, the prisoners to release
   In Satan's bondage held;
The gates of brass before Him burst,
   The iron fetters yield.

He comes, from thickest films of vice
    To clear the mental ray,
And on the eye-balls of the blind
    To pour celestial day.

He comes, the broken heart to bind,
    The bleeding soul to cure,
And with the treasures of His grace
    To enrich the humble poor.

Our glad Hosannas, Prince of Peace,
    Thy welcome shall proclaim,
And heaven's eternal arches ring
    With thy belovèd name.
              Philip Doddridge. 1755.

XLIII.

Lo! He comes! let all adore Him!
    'Tis the God of grace and truth!
Go! prepare the way before Him,
    Make the rugged places smooth!
Lo! He comes, the mighty Lord!
Great His work, and His reward.

Let the valleys all be raisèd;
    Go, and make the crooked straight;
Let the mountains be abasèd;
    Let all nature change its state;
Through the desert mark a road,
Make a highway for our God.

Through the desert God is going,
    Through the desert waste and wild,
Where no goodly plant is growing,
    Where no verdure ever smiled;

But the desert shall be glad,
And with verdure soon be clad.

Where the thorn and briar flourish'd,
    Trees shall there be seen to grow,
Planted by the Lord and nourish'd,
    Stately, fair, and fruitful too;
They shall rise on every side,
They shall spread their branches wide.

From the hills and lofty mountains
    Rivers shall be seen to flow,
There the Lord will open fountains,
    Thence supply the plains below;
As He passes, every land
Shall confess His powerful hand.
Thomas Kelly. 1809.

XLIV.

Psalm XCVIII.

Joy to the world, the Lord is come:
    Let earth receive her King;
Let every heart prepare Him room,
    And heaven and nature sing.

Joy to the earth! the Saviour reigns;
    Let men their songs employ;
While fields and floods, rocks, hills, and plains
    Repeat the sounding joy.

No more let sins and sorrows grow,
    Nor thorns infest the ground:
He comes to make His blessings flow
  ·Far as the curse is found.

He rules the world with truth and grace,
  And makes the nations prove
The glories of His righteousness,
  And wonders of His love.
Isaac Watts. 1709.

XLV.

Thus saith God of His Anointed;
  He shall let My people go;
'Tis the work for Him appointed,
  'Tis the work that He shall do;
    And My city
He shall found, and build it too.

He whom man with scorn refuses,
  Whom the favoured nation hates,
He it is Jehovah chooses,
  Him the highest place awaits;
    Kings and princes
Shall do homage at His gates.

He shall humble all the scorners,
  He shall fill His foes with shame;
He shall raise and comfort mourners
  By the sweetness of His Name;
    To the captives
He shall liberty proclaim.

He shall gather those that wander'd;
  When they hear the trumpet's sound,
They shall join the sacred standard,
  They shall come and flock around;
    He shall save them,
They shall be with glory crown'd.
Thomas Kelly. 1809.

XLVI.

O for a thousand tongues to sing
   My dear Redeemer's praise,
The glories of my God and King,
   The triumphs of His grace!

My gracious Master and my God,
   Assist me to proclaim,
To spread, through all the earth abroad,
   The honours of Thy Name.

Jesus, the Name that charms our fears,
   That bids our sorrows cease;
'Tis music in the sinner's ears,
   'Tis life, and health, and peace!

He speaks, and, listening to His voice,
   New life the dead receive;
The mournful, broken hearts rejoice,
   The humble poor believe.

Hear Him, ye deaf; His praise, ye dumb,
   Your loosened tongues employ;
Ye blind, behold your Saviour come,
   And leap, ye lame, for joy!
               Charles Wesley. 1743.

XLVII.

How sweet the Name of Jesus sounds
   In a believer's ear!
It soothes his sorrows, heals his wounds,
   And drives away his fear!

It makes the wounded spirit whole,
    And calms the troubled breast;
'Tis manna to the hungry soul,
    And to the weary rest.

Dear Name! the rock on which I build,
    My shield and hiding-place,
My never-failing treasury, fill'd
    With boundless stores of grace,

By Thee my prayers acceptance gain,
    Although with sin defiled;
Satan accuses me in vain,
    And I am owned a child.

Jesus, my Shepherd, Husband, Friend,
    My Prophet, Priest, and King,
My Lord, my Life, my Way, my End,
    Accept the praise I bring.

Weak is the effort of my heart,
    And cold my warmest thought;
But, when I see Thee as Thou art,
    I'll praise Thee as I ought.

Till then, I would Thy love proclaim
    With every fleeting breath;
And may the music of Thy Name
    Refresh my soul in death!

John Newton. 1779.

IV.

"And was Crucified for us under Pontius Pilate; He suffered, and was buried."

XLVIII.

When I survey the wondrous cross
   On which the Prince of glory died,
My richest gain I count but loss,
   And pour contempt on all my pride.

Forbid it, Lord, that I should boast
   Save in the death of Christ, my God;
All the vain things that charm me most
   I sacrifice them to His blood.

See from His head, His hands, His feet,
   Sorrow and love flow mingled down!
Did e'er such love and sorrow meet,
   Or thorns compose so rich a crown?

Were the whole realm of nature mine,
   That were a present far too small;
Love so amazing, so divine,
   Demands my soul, my life, my all.
              Isaac Watts. 1709.

XLIX.

We sing the praise of Him Who died,
   Of Him Who died upon the cross;
The sinner's hope let men deride.
   For this we count the world but loss.

Inscribed upon the cross we see
   In shining letters, God is Love;
He bears our sins upon the tree,
   He brings us mercy from above.

The Cross! it takes our guilt away;
   It holds the fainting spirit up;
It cheers with hope the gloomy day,
   And sweetens every bitter cup;

It makes the coward spirit brave,
   And nerves the feeble arm for fight;
It takes its terror from the grave,
   And gilds the bed of death with light;

The balm of life, the cure of woe,
   The measure and the pledge of love,
The sinner's refuge here below,
   The angels' theme in heaven above.
Thomas Kelly. 1820.

L.

Lord Jesu, when we stand afar
   And gaze upon Thy Holy Cross,
In love of Thee and scorn of self,
   Oh! may we count the world as loss.

When we behold Thy bleeding wounds,
   And the rough way that Thou hast trod,
Make us to hate the load of sin
   That lay so heavy on our God.

Oh holy Lord! uplifted high
   With outstretched arms, in mortal woe,
Embracing in Thy wondrous love
   The sinful world that lies below.

Give us an ever living faith
   To gaze beyond the things we see;
And in the mystery of Thy Death
   Draw us and all men unto Thee!
          William Walsham How. [1860.]

LI.

Beneath Thy cross I lay me down,
And mourn to see Thy bloody crown;
Love drops in blood from every vein;
Love is the spring of all His pain.

Here, Jesus, I shall ever stay,
And spend my longing hours away,
Think on Thy bleeding wounds and pain,
And contemplate Thy woes again.

The rage of Satan and of sin,
Of foes without, and fears within,
Shall ne'er my conquering soul remove
Or from Thy cross, or from Thy love.

Secured from harms beneath Thy shade,
Here death and hell shall ne'er invade;
Nor Sinai, with its thundering noise,
Shall e'er disturb my happier joys.

O unmolested happy rest!
Where inward fears are all supprest;
Here I shall love, and live secure,
And patiently my cross endure.
          William Williams. 1772.

LII.

Plunged in a gulf of dark despair
   We wretched sinners lay,
Without one cheerful beam of hope,
   Or spark of glimmering day.

With pitying eyes the Prince of Grace
   Beheld our helpless grief:
He saw, and oh! amazing love!
   He ran to our relief.

Down from the shining seats above
   With joyful haste He fled;
Entered the grave in mortal flesh,
   And dwelt among the dead.

Oh! for this love, let rocks and hills
   Their lasting silence break,
And all harmonious human tongues
   The Saviour's praises speak!

Angels, assist our mighty joys;
   Strike all your harps of gold!
But, when you raise your highest notes,
   His love can ne'er be told.
                      Isaac Watts. 1709.

LIII.

PSALM VIII.

O Lord, how good, how great art Thou,
   In heaven and earth the same!
There angels at Thy footstool bow,
   Here babes Thy grace proclaim.

When glorious in the nightly sky
    Thy moon and stars I see,
O, what is man! I wondering cry,
    To be so loved by Thee!

To him Thou hourly deign'st to give
    New mercies from on high;
Didst quit Thy Throne with him to live,
    For him in pain to die.

Close to Thine own bright seraphim
    His favoured path is trod;
And all beside are serving him,
    That he may serve his God.

O Lord, how good, how great art Thou,
    In heaven and earth the same!
There angels at Thy footstool bow,
    Here babes Thy grace proclaim.
               Henry Francis Lyte. 1834.

LIV.

    Blow ye the trumpet, blow,
        The gladly solemn sound;
    Let all the nations know,
        To earth's remotest bound;
The year of Jubilee is come;
Return, ye ransomed sinners, home.

    Jesus, our great High Priest,
        Hath full atonement made;
    Ye weary spirits, rest;
        Ye mournful souls, be glad:
The year of Jubilee is come;
Return, ye ransomed sinners, home.

Extol the Lamb of God,
  The all-atoning Lamb;
Redemption in His blood
  Throughout the world proclaim:
The year of Jubilee is come;
Return, ye ransomed sinners, home.

Ye slaves of sin and hell,
  Your liberty receive;
And safe in Jesus dwell,
  And blest in Jesus live:
The year of Jubilee is come;
Return, ye ransomed sinners, home.

Ye, who have sold for nought
  Your heritage above,
Shall have it back unbought,
  The gift of Jesus' love;
The year of Jubilee is come;
Return, ye ransomed sinners, home.

The Gospel Trumpet hear,
  The news of heavenly grace;
And, saved from earth, appear
  Before your Saviour's face:
The year of Jubilee is come;
Return, ye ransomed sinners, home.
Charles Wesley. 1751.

LV.

Now let us join with hearts and tongues,
And emulate the angels' songs;
Yea, sinners may address their King
In songs that angels cannot sing.

They praise the Lamb who once was slain;
But we can add a higher strain;
Not only say, He suffered thus,
But that He suffered all for us.

Jesus, who pass'd the angels by,
Assumed our flesh to bleed and die;
And still He makes it His abode;
As man He fills the throne of God.

Our next of kin, our Brother now,
Is He to whom the angels bow;
They join with us to praise His Name,
But we the nearest interest claim.

But ah! how faint our praises rise!
Sure 'tis the wonder of the skies,
That we, who share His richest love,
So cold and unconcern'd should prove.

O glorious hour! it comes with speed,
When we, from sin and darkness freed,
Shall see the God who died for man,
And praise Him more than angels can.
John Newton. 1779.

LVI.

O Saviour, may we never rest
   Till Thou art form'd within;
Till Thou hast calm'd our troubled breast,
   And crush'd the power of sin.

O may we gaze upon Thy cross,
   Until the wondrous sight
Makes earthly treasures seem but dross,
   And earthly sorrows light.

Until, releas'd from carnal ties,
   Our spirit upward springs,
And sees true peace above the skies,
   True joy in heavenly things.

There as we gaze, may we become
   United, Lord, to Thee;
And in a fairer, happier home,
   Thy perfect beauty see.

William Hiley Bathurst. 1831.

LVII.

Saviour, I lift my trembling eyes
   To that bright seat, where, placed on high,
The great, the atoning Sacrifice,
   For me, for all, is ever nigh.

Be Thou my guard on peril's brink;
   Be Thou my guide through weal or woe;
And teach me of Thy cup to drink,
   And make me in Thy path to go.

For what is earthly change or loss?
   Thy promises are still my own:
The feeblest frame may bear Thy cross,
   The lowliest spirit share Thy Throne.

Anon. "*M. G. T.*" 1831.

V.

CHRIST RISEN.

"*And the third day He rose again, according to the Scriptures.*"

LVIII.

Again the Lord of Life and Light
    Awakes the kindling ray,
Unseals the eyelids of the morn,
    And pours increasing day.

O what a night was that which wrapt
    The heathen world in gloom!
O what a sun, which broke this day
    Triumphant from the tomb!

This day be grateful homage paid,
    And loud hosannas sung;
Let gladness dwell in every heart,
    And praise on every tongue.

Ten thousand differing lips shall join
    To hail this welcome morn,
Which scatters blessings from its wings
    To nations yet unborn.

The powers of darkness leagued in vain
    To bind His Soul in death;
He shook their kingdom, when He fell,
    With His expiring breath.

And now His conquering chariot wheels
   Ascend the lofty skies ;
While broke beneath His powerful cross
   Death's iron sceptre lies.

Exalted high at God's right hand,
   The Lord of all below,
Through Him is pardoning love dispens'd,
   And boundless blessings flow.

And still for erring guilty man
   A Brother's pity flows ;
And still His bleeding heart is touch'd
   With memory of our woes.

To Thee, my Saviour and my King,
   Glad homage let me give ;
And stand prepared like Thee to die,
   With Thee that I may live !
          Anna Lætitia Barbauld. 1825.

LIX.

Christ the Lord is risen to-day,
Sons of men and angels say :
Raise your joys and triumphs high,
Sing, ye heavens, and earth reply.

Love's redeeming work is done,
Fought the fight, the battle won :
Lo ! our Sun's eclipse is o'er ;
Lo ! He sets in blood no more.

Vain the stone, the watch, the seal ;
Christ hath burst the gates of hell !

Christ Risen.

Death in vain forbids His rise;
Christ hath open'd Paradise!

Lives again our glorious King:
Where, O Death, is now thy sting?
Once He died, our souls to save:
Where thy victory, O Grave?

Soar we now where Christ has led,
Following our exalted Head;
Made like Him, like Him we rise;
Ours the cross, the grave, the skies.

What though once we perish'd all,
Partners in our parents' fall?
Second life we all receive,
In our Heavenly Adam live.

Risen with Him, we upward move;
Still we seek the things above;
Still pursue, and kiss the Son
Seated on His Father's Throne.

Scarce on earth a thought bestow,
Dead to all we leave below;
Heav'n our aim, and loved abode,
Hid our life with Christ in God:

Hid, till Christ our Life appear
Glorious in His members here;
Join'd to Him, we then shall shine,
All immortal, all divine.

Hail the Lord of Earth and Heaven!
Praise to Thee by both be given!
Thee we greet triumphant now!
Hail, the Resurrection Thou!

King of glory, Soul of bliss!
Everlasting life is this,
Thee to know, Thy power to prove,
Thus to sing, and thus to love!

Charles Wesley. 1743.

LX.

Jesus Christ is risen to-day,	Hallelujah!
Our triumphant holy day,	Hallelujah!
Who did once upon the cross	Hallelujah!
Suffer to redeem our loss;	Hallelujah!
Hymns of praise then let us sing	Hallelujah!
Unto Christ our heavenly King,	Hallelujah!
Who endured the cross and grave,	Hallelujah!
Sinners to redeem and save;	Hallelujah!
But the pain which He endured,	Hallelujah!
Our salvation has procured:	Hallelujah!
Now above the sky He's king,	Hallelujah!
Where the angels ever sing	Hallelujah!
Sing we to our God above	Hallelujah!
Praise eternal as His love;	Hallelujah!
Praise Him, all ye heavenly host,	Hallelujah!
Father, Son, and Holy Ghost;	Hallelujah!

Anon. [1762.]
(*Last stanza by Charles Wesley.*)

LXI.

Ad templa nos rursus vocat.

Now morning lifts her dewy veil
  With new-born blessings crown'd:
Oh! haste we then her light to hail
  In courts of holy ground!

Christ Risen.

But Christ, triumphant o'er the grave,
   Shines more divinely bright:
Oh! sing we then His power to save,
   And walk we in His light!

When from the swaddling bands of shade,
   Sprang forth the world so fair,
In robes of brilliancy arrayed,
   Oh, what a Power was there!

When He, who gave His guiltless Son
   A guilty world to spare,
Restored to life the Holy One,
   Oh, what a Love was there!

When forth from its Creator's hand
   The earth in beauty stood,
All decked with light at His command,
   He saw, and called it good.

But still more lovely in His sight,
   The earth still fairer stood,
When the Holy Lamb had wash'd it white
   In His atoning blood.

Still, as the morning rays return,
   To the pious soul 'tis given
In fancy's mirror to discern
   The radiant domes of Heaven.

But now that our eternal Sun
   Hath shed His beams abroad,
In Him we see the Holy One,
   And mount at once to God.

Oh, holy, blessed Three in One!
    May Thy pure light be given,
That we the paths of death may shun,
    And keep the road to Heaven!

John Chandler. 1837.

LXII.

The Son of God! the Lord of Life!
    How wondrous are His ways!
O for a harp of thousand strings,
    To sound abroad his praise!
How passing strange, to leave the seat
    Of Heaven's eternal throne,
And hosts of glittering Seraphim,
    For guilty man alone!

And did He bow His sacred head,
    And die a death of shame?
Let men and angels magnify
    And bless His holy name!
O let us live in peace and love,
    And cast away our pride,
And crucify our sins afresh.
    As He was crucified!

He rose again; then let us rise
    From sin, and Christ adore,
And dwell in peace with all mankind,
    And tempt the Lord no more:
The Son of God! the Lord of Life!
    How wondrous are His ways!
O for a harp of thousand strings
    To sound abroad His praise!

A. Gray. [1851.]

LXIII.

Salvation ! oh ! the joyful sound !
   'Tis pleasure to our ears !
A sovereign balm for every wound,
   A cordial for our fears !

Buried in sorrow and in sin,
   At hell's dark door we lay ;
But we arise, by grace Divine,
   To see a heavenly day.

Salvation ! let the echo fly
   The spacious earth around,
While all the armies of the sky
   Conspire to raise the sound !

Isaac Watts. 1709.

LXIV.

The foe behind, the deep before,
   Our hosts have dared and past the sea :
And Pharaoh's warriors strew the shore,
   And Israel's ransom'd tribes are free.
Lift up, lift up your voices now !
The whole wide world rejoices now !
The Lord hath triumph'd gloriously !
The Lord shall reign victoriously !
      Happy morrow,
      Turning sorrow
         Into peace and mirth !
      Bondage ending,
      Love descending
         O'er the earth !

Seals assuring,
Guards securing,
   Watch His earthly prison:
Seals are shattered,
Guards are scattered,
   Christ hath risen!

No longer must the mourners weep,
  Nor call departed Christians dead;
For death is hallowed into sleep
  And every grave becomes a bed.
    Now once more,
    Eden's door
Open stands to mortal eyes:
For Christ hath risen, and men shall rise:
    Now at last,
    Old things past,
Hope and joy and peace begin:
For Christ hath won, and man shall win.

It is not exile, rest on high:
  It is not sadness, peace from strife:
To fall asleep is not to die;
  To dwell with Christ is better life.
    Where our banner leads us,
      We may safely go:
    Where our Chief precedes us,
      We may face the foe.
    His right arm is o'er us,
      He will guide us through;
    Christ hath gone before us;
      Christians! follow you!

John Mason Neale. 1851

VI.

CHRIST ASCENDED.

"And ascended into Heaven; and sitteth on the right hand of the Father."

LXV.

Thou art gone up on high
  To mansions in the skies,
And round Thy throne unceasingly
  The songs of praise arise.
But we are lingering here
  With sin and care oppress'd;
Lord! send Thy promised Comforter,
  And lead us to Thy rest!

Thou art gone up on high:
  But Thou didst first come down,
Through earth's most bitter misery
  To pass unto Thy crown:
And girt with griefs and fears
  Our onward course must be;
But only let that path of tears
  Lead us, at last, to Thee!

Thou art gone up on high:
  But Thou shalt come again
With all the bright ones of the sky
  Attendant in Thy train.
Oh! by Thy saving power
  So make us live and die,
That we may stand, in that dread hour,
  At Thy right hand on high!

Anon. [1853.]

LXVI.

Thou, who didst stoop below
  To drain the cup of woe
And wear the form of frail mortality,
  Thy blessed labours done,
  Thy crown of victory won,
Hast pass'd from earth, pass'd to Thy home on
    high.

It was no path of flowers
  Through this dark world of ours,
Beloved of the Father, Thou didst tread:
  And shall we in dismay
  Shrink from the narrow way,
When clouds and darkness are around it spread?

O Thou, who art our life,
  Be with us through the strife!
Thy own meek head by rudest storms was bowed;
  Raise Thou our eyes above,
  To see a Father's love
Beam, like a bow of promise, through the cloud.

E'en through the awful gloom
  Which hovers o'er the tomb,
That light of love our guiding star shall be:
  Our spirits shall not dread
  The shadowy way to tread,
Friend, Guardian, Saviour! which doth lead to
    Thee.

Sibella Elizabeth Miles. [1840.]

LXVII.

To Him, who for our sins was slain,
To Him, for all His dying pain,
   Sing we Hallelujah!
To Him, the Lamb our sacrifice,
Who gave His soul our ransom-price,
   Sing we Hallelujah!

To Him, who died that we might die
To sin, and live with Him on high,
   Sing we Hallelujah!
To Him, who rose that we might rise
And reign with Him beyond the skies,
   Sing we Hallelujah!

To Him, who now for us doth plead
And helpeth us in all our need,
   Sing we Hallelujah!
To Him, who doth prepare on high
Our home in immortality,
   Sing we Hallelujah!

To Him be glory evermore;
Ye heavenly hosts, your Lord adore;
   Sing we Hallelujah!
To Father, Son, and Holy Ghost,
One God most great, our joy and boast,
   Sing we Hallelujah!

    Arthur Tozer Russell. 1851.

LXVIII.

Saviour, when in dust to Thee
Low we bend the adoring knee;
When repentant to the skies
Scarce we lift our weeping eyes;

Oh! by all the pains and woe
Suffer'd once for man below,
Bending from Thy throne on high,
Hear our solemn Litany!

By Thy helpless infant years,
By Thy life of want and tears,
By Thy days of sore distress
In the savage wilderness;
By the dread mysterious hour
Of the insulting tempter's power;
Turn, oh! turn a favouring eye,
Hear our solemn Litany!

By the sacred griefs that wept
O'er the grave where Lazarus slept;
By the boding tears that flowed
Over Salem's lov'd abode;
By the anguish'd sigh that told
Treachery lurk'd within Thy fold;
From Thy seat above the sky,
Hear our solemn Litany!

By Thine hour of dire despair;
By Thine agony of prayer;
By the cross, the nail, the thorn,
Piercing spear, and torturing scorn;
By the gloom that veil'd the skies
O'er the dreadful sacrifice;
Listen to our humble cry,
Hear our solemn Litany!

By Thy deep expiring groan;
By the sad sepulchral stone;
By the vault, whose dark abode
Held in vain the rising God;

Oh! from earth to heaven restored,
Mighty re-ascended Lord,
Listen, listen to the cry
Of our solemn Litany!
Sir Robert Grant. [1839.]

LXIX.

Saviour, who, exalted high
In Thy Father's majesty,
Yet vouchsaf'st Thyself to show
To Thy faithful flock below;
Foretaste of that blissful sight,
When, arrayed in glorious light,
Beaming with paternal grace,
They shall see Thee face to face:
Saviour, though this earthly shroud
Now my mortal vision cloud,
Still Thy presence let me see,
Manifest Thyself to me!

Son of God, to Thee I cry:
By the holy mystery
Of Thy dwelling here on earth,
By thy pure and holy birth,
Offspring of the Virgin's womb;
By the light, through midnight gloom
Bursting on the shepherds' gaze;
By the angels' song of praise:
By the leading of the star,
The Eastern sages' guide from far;
By their gifts, with worship meet
Offer'd at thy infant feet:
Lord, Thy presence let me see,
Manifest Thyself to me!

Man of sorrows, hear me cry!
By Thy great humility;

By Thy meckly-bowed head;
By Thy gentle spirit, fled
To the mansions of the dead;
By the wound, whence issuing flow'd
Water mingled with Thy blood;
By Thy breathless body, laid
In the rock's sepulchral shade,
Where man ne'er before reposed,
Straightly watch'd, securely closed;
Lord, Thy presence let me see,
Manifest Thyself to me!

Lord of Glory, God most high,
Man exalted to the sky,
God and man, to Thee I cry!
With Thy love my bosom fill,
Prompt me to perform Thy will;
Grant me, what Thou bidd'st, to do;
What Thou proffer'st to pursue:
So may He, the Sire above,
Guard me with a Parent's love!
So may He, the Spirit blest,
Whisper comfort, hope, and rest!
So mayst Thou, my Saviour, come,
Make this froward heart Thy home,
And manifest Thyself to me
In the Triune Deity!
Bishop Richard Mant. 1831.

LXX.

Jesu! behold, the Wise from far,
Led to Thy cradle by a star,
   Bring gifts to Thee, their God and King!
O guide us by Thy light, that we
The way may find, and still to Thee
   Our hearts, our all, for tribute bring!

Christ Ascended.

Jesu! the pure, the spotless Lamb,
Who to the Temple humbly came,
   Duteous, the legal rites to pay!
O make our proud, our stubborn will
All Thy wise, gracious laws fulfil,
   Whate'er rebellious nature say!

Jesu! who on the fatal wood
Pour'dst out Thy life's last drop of blood,
   Nailed to the accursed shameful cross!
O may we bless Thy love, and be
Ready, dear Lord, to bear for thee
   All shame, all grief, all pain, and loss!

Jesu! who, by Thine own love slain,
By Thine own Power took'st life again,
   And Conqueror from the grave didst rise!
O may Thy death our souls revive,
And ev'n on earth a new life give,
   A glorious life, that never dies!

Jesu! who to Thy heaven again
Return'dst in triumph, there to reign,
   Of men and angels sovereign king!
O may our parting souls take flight
Up to that land of joy and light,
   And there for ever grateful sing!

All glory to the sacred Three,
One undivided Deity!
   All honour, power, and love, and praise!
Still may Thy blessed Name shine bright
In beams of uncreated light,
   Crown'd with its own eternal rays!

Variation from John Austin. 1668.
By John Wesley, 1739.

LXXI.

Hail, Thou once despised Jesus,
    Hail, thou Galilean king!
Thou didst suffer to release us,
    Thou didst free salvation bring:
Hail, Thou agonizing Saviour,
    Bearer of our sin and shame;
By Thy merits we find favour;
    Life is given through Thy Name!

Paschal Lamb, by God appointed,
    All our sins were on Thee laid;
By Almighty Love anointed,
    Thou hast full atonement made:
All Thy people are forgiven
    Through the virtue of Thy Blood;
Opened is the gate of Heaven;
    Peace is made 'twixt man and God.

Jesus, hail! enthroned in glory,
    There for ever to abide;
All the heavenly hosts adore Thee,
    Seated at Thy Father's side.
There for sinners Thou art pleading;
    There Thou dost our place prepare;
Ever for us interceding
    Till in glory we appear.

Worship, honour, power, and blessing,
    Thou art worthy to receive;
Loudest praises, without ceasing,
    Meet it is for us to give!
Help, ye bright angelic spirits,
    Bring your sweetest, noblest lays;
Help to sing our Saviour's merits,
    Help to chant Immanuel's praise!

Soon we shall, with those in glory,
  His transcendent grace relate;
Gladly sing th' amazing story
  Of His dying love so great:
In that blessed contemplation
  We for evermore shall dwell,
Crown'd with bliss and consolation,
  Such as none below can tell.
John Bakewell. 1760.

LXXII.

  Join all the glorious names
  Of wisdom, love, and power,
  That ever mortals knew,
  That angels ever bore;
All are too mean to speak His worth,
Too mean to set my Saviour forth.

  But oh! what gentle terms,
  What condescending ways,
  Doth our Redeemer use
  To teach His heavenly grace!
Mine eyes with joy and wonder see
What forms of love He bears for me.

  Array'd in mortal flesh
  He like an Angel stands,
  And holds the promises
  And pardons in His hands;
Commission'd from His Father's throne
To make His grace to mortals known.

  Great Prophet of my God,
  My tongue would bless Thy Name;
  By Thee the joyful news
  Of our salvation came;

The joyful news of sins forgiven,
Of hell subdued, and peace with Heaven.

 Be Thou my Counsellor,
 My Pattern, and my Guide;
 And through this desert land
 Still keep me near Thy side:
Oh, let my feet ne'er run astray,
Nor rove, nor seek the crooked way!

 I love my Shepherd's voice;
 His watchful eyes shall keep
 My wandering soul among
 The thousands of His sheep:
He feeds His flock, He calls their names,
His bosom bears the tender lambs.

 To this dear Surety's hand
 Will I commit my cause;
 He answers and fulfils
 His Father's broken laws:
Behold my soul at freedom set;
My Surety paid the dreadful debt.

 Jesus, my great High Priest,
 Offer'd His Blood and died;
 My guilty conscience seeks
 No sacrifice beside:
His powerful Blood did once atone,
And now it pleads before the Throne.

 My advocate appears
 For my defence on high;
 The Father bows His ears
 And lays His thunder by:
Not all that hell or sin can say
Shall turn His heart, His love away.

Christ Ascended.

My dear Almighty Lord,
My Conqueror and my King,
Thy sceptre and Thy sword,
Thy reigning grace, I sing:
Thine is the power: behold I sit
In willing bonds before Thy feet!

Now let my soul arise,
And tread the Tempter down;
My Captain leads me forth
To conquest and a crown;
A feeble saint shall win the day,
Though death and hell obstruct the way.

Should all the hosts of death
And powers of hell unknown
Put their most dreadful forms
Of rage and mischief on,
I shall be safe; for Christ displays
Superior power, and guardian grace.

Isaac Watts. 1709.

LXXIII.

Beyond the glittering starry globe
  Far as th' eternal hills,
There, in the boundless worlds of light,
  Our great Redeemer dwells.

Immortal angels, bright and fair,
  In countless armies shine,
At His right hand, with golden harps,
  To offer songs divine.

"Hail! Prince," they cry, "for ever hail!
  Whose unexampled love
Moved Thee to quit these glorious realms
  And royalties above!"

While Thou didst condescend on earth
    To suffer rude disdain,
They cast their honours at Thy feet,
    And waited on Thy train.

Blest Angels, who adoring wait
    Around the Saviour's Throne,
Oh! tell us, for your eyes have seen,
    The wonders He has done.

Ye saw Him, when the heavens and earth
    A chaos first, He made,
And night involved the formless deep
    In her tremendous shade.

And when, amidst the darksome void,
    He bade the light arise,
And kindled up those shining orbs
    That now adorn the skies,

Ye saw;—and in melodious song
    Your powerful voices raise,
While all the new-born worlds resound
    Their great Creator's praise.

And, when on earth He deign'd to dwell,
    In mortal flesh array'd,
Ye wondering saw the Holy Child
    In Bethlehem's stable laid.

While in the lowly crib reposed,
    His Mother's tender care,
Ye stood around His homely bed,
    And watch'd His slumbers there.

Christ Ascended.

When fasting in the desert long
   His spotless soul was tried,
Ye saw Him there the Tempter foil,
   And soon His wants supplied.

Ye heard what gracious words He spoke,
   The hearts of men to win;
And saw, well pleased, the listening crowd
   Drink the sweet doctrine in;

Beheld diseases, tempests, death,
   His sovereign word obey,
And how, on dark benighted minds,
   He poured eternal day.

Saw Him, from busy scenes retired
   To spend the midnight hours,
While pure devotion fill'd His soul
   With all her rapturous powers.

When on the sacred mount He shone,
   In His own light array'd,
Ye saw, and own'd your Sovereign there,
   And your just homage paid;

Saw, when o'er Salem's fearful doom
   He shed the tender tear;
And how, to all His gracious calls,
   She turned the deafened ear.

In all his toils, and dangers too,
   Ye did His steps attend;
Oft paused, and wondered, how at last
   This scene of love would end.

And when the Powers of Hell combined
  To fill His cup of woe,
Your pitying eyes beheld His tears
  In bloody anguish flow.

As on the torturing Cross He hung,
  And darkness veil'd the sky,
Ye saw, aghast, that awful sight,
  The Lord of Glory die!

Astonish'd, here ye search and learn
  High Heaven's mysterious ways,
That thus to guilty dying man
  Immortal life conveys.

Anon He bursts the gates of death,
  Subdues the tyrant's power:
Ye saw th' illustrious Conqueror rise,
  And hailed the blissful hour,

Tended His chariot up the sky,
  And bore Him to His Throne;
Then swept your golden harps, and cried
  "The glorious work is done!"

My soul the joyful triumph feels,
  And thinks the moments long,
Ere she her Saviour's glory sees,
  And joins your rapturous song.

James Fanch and Daniel Turner. [1791.]

VII.

CHRIST'S KINGDOM AND JUDGMENT.

"*And He shall come again with Glory, to judge both the quick and the dead: whose Kingdom shall have no end.*"

LXXIV.

Now is the hour of darkness past;
  Christ has assumed His reigning power;
Behold the great accuser cast
  Down from the skies to rise no more.

'Twas by Thy Blood, immortal Lamb,
  Thine armies trod the Tempter down;
'Twas by Thy word and powerful Name
  They gained the battle and renown.

Rejoice, ye heavens! let every star
  Shine with new glories round the sky!
Saints, while ye sing the heavenly war,
  Raise your Deliverer's Name on high!

Isaac Watts. 1709.

LXXV.

Rejoice, the Lord is King,
  Your Lord and King adore;
Mortals, give thanks and sing,
  And triumph evermore:
Lift up your heart, lift up your voice;
Rejoice, again I say, rejoice.

Jesus the Saviour reigns,
    The God of truth and love;
When he had purged our stains,
    He took His seat above:
Lift up your heart, lift up your voice;
Rejoice, again I say, rejoice.

His kingdom cannot fail;
    He rules o'er earth and Heaven;
The keys of death and hell
    Are to our Jesus given:
Lift up your heart, lift up your voice;
Rejoice, again I say, rejoice.

He sits at God's right hand,
    Till all His foes submit,
And bow to His command,
    And fall beneath His feet:
Lift up your heart, lift up your voice;
Rejoice, again I say, rejoice.

He all His foes shall quell,
    Shall all our sins destroy,
And every bosom swell
    With pure seraphick joy:
Lift up your heart, lift up your voice,
Rejoice, again I say, Rejoice.

Rejoice in glorious hope;
    Jesus the Judge shall come,
And take His servants up
    To their eternal home:
We soon shall hear th' archangel's voice,
The Trump of God shall sound, rejoice.

                    Charles Wesley. 1745.

LXXVI.

The Lord is King! lift up thy voice,
O earth, and all ye heavens, rejoice!
From world to world the joy shall ring,
The Lord Omnipotent is King.

The Lord is King! who then shall dare
Resist His will, distrust His care,
Or murmur at His wise decrees,
Or doubt His royal promises?

The Lord is King! Child of the dust,
The Judge of all the earth is just:
Holy and true are all His ways:
Let every creature speak His praise.

He reigns! ye saints, exalt your strains;
Your God is King, your Father reigns;
And He is at the Father's side,
The Man of Love, the crucified.

Come, make your wants, your burdens known,
He will present them at the Throne;
And angel bands are waiting there
His messages of love to bear.

O, when His wisdom can mistake,
His might decay, His love forsake,
Then may His children cease to sing,
The Lord Omnipotent is King.

Alike pervaded by His eye,
All parts of His dominion lie;
This world of ours, and worlds unseen;
And thin the boundary between.

One Lord, one empire, all secures;
He reigns, and life and death are yours:
Through earth and heaven one song shall ring,
The Lord Omnipotent is King.

Josiah Conder. 1856.

LXXVII.

He, Who on earth as man was known,
    And bore our sins and pains,
Now, seated on th' eternal Throne,
    The God of Glory reigns.

His hands the wheels of Nature guide
    With an unerring skill,
And countless worlds, extended wide,
    Obey His sovereign will.

While harps unnumbered sound His praise
    In yonder world above,
His saints on earth admire His ways
    And glory in His love.

His Righteousness, to faith reveal'd,
    Wrought out for guilty worms,
Affords a hiding-place and shield
    From enemies and storms.

This land, through which His pilgrims go,
    Is desolate and dry;
But streams of grace from Him o'erflow,
    Their thirst to satisfy.

When troubles, like a burning sun,
    Beat heavy on their head,
To this Almighty Rock they run,
    And find a pleasing shade.

How glorious He! how happy they
    In such a glorious Friend!
Whose love secures them all the way,
    And crowns them at the end.
John Newton. 1779.

LXXVIII.

The Head that once was crown'd with thorns,
    Is crown'd with glory now;
A royal diadem adorns
    The mighty Victor's brow.

The highest place that Heaven affords
    Is His, is His by right,
The King of kings, and Lord of lords,
    And Heaven's eternal Light.

The joy of all who dwell above,
    The joy of all below,
To whom He manifests His love,
    And grants His Name to know.

To them the Cross, with all its shame,
    With all its grace, is given;
Their name an everlasting name,
    Their joy the joy of Heaven.

They suffer with their Lord below,
    They reign with Him above,
Their profit and their joy to know
    The mystery of His love.

The cross He bore is life and health,
    Though shame and death to Him
His people's hope, His people's wealth,
    Their everlasting theme.
Thomas Kelly. 1820.

LXXIX.

Hosanna! raise the pealing hymn
    To David's Son and Lord;
With Cherubim and Seraphim
    Exalt the Incarnate Word.

Hosanna! Lord, our feeble tongue
    No lofty strains can raise:
But Thou wilt not despise the young,
    Who meekly chant Thy praise.

Hosanna! Sovereign, Prophet, Priest,
    How vast Thy gifts, how free!
Thy Blood, our life; Thy word, our feast;
    Thy Name, our only plea.

Hosanna! Master, lo! we bring
    Our offerings to Thy Throne;
Not gold, nor myrrh, nor mortal thing,
    But hearts to be Thine own.

Hosanna! once Thy gracious ear
    Approved a lisping throng;
Be gracious still, and deign to hear
    Our poor but grateful song.

O Saviour, if, redeem'd by Thee,
    Thy temple we behold,
Hosannas through eternity
    We'll sing to harps of gold.
                Anon. [1842.]

LXXX.

Psalm LXXII.

Hail to the Lord's Anointed,
  Great David's greater Son!
Hail, in the time appointed,
  His reign on earth begun!
He comes to break oppression,
  To let the captive free,
To take away transgression,
  And rule in equity.

He comes with succour speedy,
  To those who suffer wrong;
To help the poor and needy,
  And bid the weak be strong:
To give them songs for sighing,
  Their darkness turn to light,
Whose souls, condemn'd and dying,
  Were precious in His sight.

He shall come down like showers
  Upon the fruitful earth,
And love, joy, hope, like flowers,
  Spring in His path to birth;
Before Him, on the mountains,
  Shall peace, the herald, go,
And righteousness, in fountains,
  From hill to valley flow.

Arabia's desert-ranger
  To Him shall bow the knee;
The Ethiopian stranger
  His glory come to see:

With offerings of devotion
  Ships from the Isles shall meet,
To pour the wealth of ocean
  In tribute at His feet.

Kings shall fall down before Him,
  And gold and incense bring;
All nations shall adore Him,
  His praise all people sing;
For He shall have dominion
  O'er river, sea, and shore;
Far as the eagle's pinion,
  Or dove's light wing, can soar.

For Him shall prayer unceasing,
  And daily vows ascend,
His kingdom still increasing,
  A kingdom without end:
The mountain-dews shall nourish
  A seed, in weakness sown,
Whose fruit shall spread and flourish,
  And shake like Lebanon.

O'er every foe victorious
  He on His throne shall rest,
From age to age more glorious,
  All blessing and all-blest:
The tide of time shall never
  His covenant remove;
His Name shall stand for ever,
  That Name to us is Love.
James Montgomery. 1822.

LXXXI.

Behold! the Mountain of the Lord
   In latter days shall rise
On mountain tops, above the hills,
   And draw the wondering eyes.

To this the joyful nations round,
   All tribes and tongues shall flow;
Up to the hill of God, they'll say,
   And to His house we'll go.

The beam that shines from Zion hill
   Shall lighten every land;
The King who reigns in Salem's towers
   Shall all the world command.

No strife shall vex Messiah's reign,
   Or mar the peaceful years;
To ploughshares men shall beat their swords,
   To pruning-hooks their spears.

No longer hosts encountering hosts
   Their millions slain deplore;
They hang the trumpet in the hall,
   And study war no more.

Come, then! O, come, from every land,
   To worship at His shrine;
And, walking in the Light of God,
   With holy beauties shine.

Michael Bruce. 1768.

LXXXII.

Psalm LXXII.

Jesus shall reign where'er the sun
Does his successive journeys run ;
His kingdom stretch from shore to shore,
Till moons shall wax and wane no more.

For Him shall endless prayer be made,
And praises throng to crown His Head ;
His Name, like sweet perfume, shall rise
With every morning sacrifice.

People and realms of every tongue
Dwell on His love with sweetest song,
And infant voices shall proclaim
Their early blessings on His Name.

Blessings abound where'er He reigns ;
The prisoner leaps to lose his chains ;
The weary find eternal rest,
And all the sons of want are blest.

Where He displays His healing power,
Death and the curse are known no more ;
In Him the tribes of Adam boast
More blessings than their father lost.

Let every creature rise, and bring
Peculiar honours to our King ;
Angels descend with songs again,
And earth repeat the long Amen !

Isaac Watts. 1719.

LXXXIII.

Psalm LXXII.

Great God, Whose universal sway
The known and unknown worlds obey,
Now give the kingdom to Thy Son,
Extend His power, exalt His throne.

As rain on meadows newly mown,
So shall He send His influence down;
His grace on fainting souls distils
Like heavenly dew on thirsty hills.

The heathen lands, that lie beneath
The shade of overspreading death,
Revive at His first dawning light,
And deserts blossom at the sight.

The saints shall flourish in His days,
Dress'd in the robes of joy and praise;
Peace, like a river, from His Throne
Shall flow to nations yet unknown.
Isaac Watts. 1719.

LXXXIV.

From Greenland's icy mountains,
   From India's coral strand,
Where Afric's sunny fountains
   Roll down their golden sand,
From many an ancient river,
   From many a palmy plain,
They call us to deliver
   Their land from error's chain.

What though the spicy breezes
    Blow soft o'er Ceylon's isle;
Though every prospect pleases,
    And only man is vile;
In vain with lavish kindness
    The gifts of God are strown;
The heathen in his blindness
    Bows down to wood and stone.

Can we, whose souls are lighted
    With wisdom from on high,
Can we to men benighted
    The lamp of life deny?
Salvation! O salvation!
    The joyful sound proclaim,
Till each remotest nation
    Has learnt Messiah's Name.

Waft, waft, ye winds, His story,
    And you, ye waters, roll,
Till like a sea of glory
    It spreads from pole to pole;
Till o'er our ransomed nature
    The Lamb for sinners slain,
Redeemer, King, Creator,
    In bliss returns to reign.
              Bishop Reginald Heber. 1827.

LXXXV.

On the mountain's top appearing,
    Lo! the sacred herald stands,
Welcome news to Zion bearing,
    Zion long in hostile lands;
        Mourning captive!
God Himself will loose thy bands.

Has thy night been long and mournful?
  Have thy friends unfaithful proved?
Have thy foes been proud and scornful,
  By thy sighs and tears unmoved?
    Cease thy mourning!
Zion still is well beloved!

God, thy God, will now restore thee;
  He Himself appears thy friend;
All thy foes shall flee before thee;
  Here their boasts and triumphs end:
    Great deliverance
Zion's King vouchsafes to send!

Enemies no more shall trouble;
  All thy wrongs shall be redress'd;
For thy shame thou shalt have double,
  In thy Maker's favour bless'd;
    All thy conflicts
End in everlasting rest!

Thomas Kelly. 1804.

LXXXVI.

O house of Jacob, come,
  And walk with us in light:
No more bewildered roam
  Like wanderers in the night;
The Hope of Israel calls you near,
And Abraham's shield, and Isaac's fear.

  O thou by tempests toss'd,
    Reviled, distress'd, trod down,
  In every region cross'd,
    With grief familiar grown,
Scattered and abject, peel'd, forlorn,
Thy name a taunt, thyself a scorn;

Though thou art fill'd, alas!
And drunk with misery,
That cup begins to pass
To them that hated thee:
But know, we honour Israel's name,
Our God and Abraham's is the same.

Rise, Jacob, from thy woes,
And thy Messiah see;
He, Who thy fathers chose,
Has not forgotten thee:
At His command, we bid you come;
Her Israel Zion welcomes home.
William Hurn. 1813.

LXXXVII.

The Lord of Might from Sinai's brow
  Gave forth His voice of thunder;
And Israel lay on earth below,
  Outstretch'd in fear and wonder:
Beneath His feet was pitchy night,
And at His left hand and His right
  The rocks were rent asunder.

The Lord of Love on Calvary,
  A meek and suffering stranger,
Upraised to heaven His languid eye
  In nature's hour of danger;
For us He bore the weight of woe,
For us He gave His blood to flow,
  And met His Father's anger.

The Lord of Love, the Lord of Might,
    The King of all created,
Shall back return to claim His right
    On clouds of glory seated;
With trumpet-sound, and angel-song,
And hallelujahs loud and long,
    O'er death and hell defeated.
Bishop Reginald Heber. 1827.

LXXXVIII.

See, the ransomed millions stand,
Palms of conquest in their hand;
This before the Throne their strain;
" Hell is vanquish'd; death is slain;
" Blessing, honour, glory, might,
" Are the Conqueror's native right;
" Thrones and powers before Him fall;
" Lamb of God, and Lord of all!"

Hasten, Lord! the promised hour;
Come in glory and in power;
Still Thy foes are unsubdued;
Nature sighs to be renewed:
Time has nearly reach'd its sum,
All things with Thy Bride say, Come;
Jesus, whom all worlds adore,
Come, and reign for evermore!
Josiah Conder. 1856.

LXXXIX.

Thou Judge of quick and dead,
    Before whose bar severe
With holy joy, or guilty dread,
    We all shall soon appear;

Our cautioned souls prepare
  For that tremendous Day,
And fill us now with watchful care,
  And stir us up to pray.

To pray, and wait the hour,
  The awful hour unknown,
When, robed in majesty and power,
  Thou shalt from Heaven come down,
  The immortal Son of Man,
  To judge the human race,
With all Thy Father's dazzling train,
  With all Thy glorious grace.

To damp our earthly joys,
  To increase our duteous fears,
For ever let the Archangel's voice
  Be sounding in our ears ;
  The solemn midnight cry,
  " Ye Dead, the Judge is come !
" Arise, and meet Him in the sky,
  " And meet your instant doom !"

O may we thus be found,
  Obedient to His word,
Attentive to the trumpet's sound,
  And looking for our Lord :
  O may we thus insure
  Our lot among the blest,
And watch a moment, to secure
  An everlasting rest !

Charles Wesley. 1749.

XC.

Lo! He comes, with clouds descending,
  Once for favoured sinners slain:
Thousand thousand saints attending
  Swell the triumph of His train:
    Hallelujah!
  God appears, on earth to reign!

Every eye shall now behold Him,
  Robed in dreadful majesty;
Those who set at nought and sold Him,
  Pierced, and nailed Him to the Tree,
    Deeply wailing,
  Shall the true Messiah see.

Every island, sea, and mountain,
  Heaven and earth shall flee away;
All who hate Him must, confounded,
  Hear the trump proclaim the day;
    Come to judgment!
  Come to judgment, come away!

Now Redemption, long expected,
  See in solemn pomp appear!
All His saints, by man rejected,
  Now shall meet Him in the air:
    Hallelujah!
  See the day of God appear!

Answer Thine own Bride and Spirit;
  Hasten, Lord, the general doom;
The new Heaven and earth t' inherit
  Take Thy pining exiles home:
    All creation
  Travails, groans, and bids Thee come!

Yea, Amen ! let all adore Thee,
   High on Thine eternal throne :
Saviour, take the power and glory ;
   Claim the kingdom for Thine own :
      O, come quickly,
Everlasting God, come down !
     Variation by Martin Madan. 1760.
  From Charles Wesley and John Cennick

XCI.

Lo ! He comes with clouds descending !
   Hark ! the trump of God is blown,
And th' Archangel's voice attending
   Makes the high procession known :
      Sons of Adam !
Rise, and stand before your God !

Crowns and sceptres fall before Him,
   Kings and conquerors own His sway ;
Haughtiest monarchs now adore Him,
   While they see His lightnings play :
      How triumphant
Is the world's Redeemer now !

Hear His voice, as mighty thunder
   Sounding in eternal roar,
While its echo rends in sunder
   Rocks and mountains, sea and shore :
      Hark ! His accents
Through th' unfathomed deep resound !

"Come, Lord Jesus ! O come quickly !"
   Oft has prayed the mourning Bride :
"Lo !" He answers, "I come quickly !"

Who Thy coming may abide?
　　All who loved Him,
All who long'd to see His day.

"Come," He saith, "ye heirs of glory;
　"Come, ye purchase of my blood;
"Claim the Kingdom now before you,
　"Rise, and fill the mount of God,
　　"Fix'd for ever
"Where the Lamb on Sion stands."

See! ten thousand burning seraphs
　From their thrones as lightnings fly;
"Take," they cry, "your seats above us,
　"Nearest Him that rules the sky!"
　　Patient sufferers,
How rewarded are ye now!

Now their trials all are ended:
　Now the dubious warfare's o'er;
Joy no more with sorrow blended,
　They shall sigh and weep no more;
　　God for ever
Wipes the tear from every eye.

Through His passion all victorious
　Now they drink immortal wine;
In Emmanuel's likeness glorious
　As the firmament they shine;
　　Shine for ever,
With the bright and morning Star.

Shout aloud, ye ethereal choirs!
　Triumph in Jehovah's praise!
Kindle all your heavenly fires,
　All your palms of victory raise!
　　Shout His conquests,
Shout salvation to the Lamb!

In full triumph see them marching
   Through the gates of massy light,
While the City walls are sparkling
   With meridian glory bright;
     O how lovely
Are the dwellings of the Lamb!

Hosts angelic all adore Him
   Circling round His orient seat;
Elders cast their crowns before Him,
   Fall and worship at His feet;
     O how holy
And how reverend is Thy Name!

Hail, Thou Alpha and Omega!
   First and Last, of all alone!
He that is, and was, and shall be,
   And beside whom there is none!
     Take the Glory,
Great Eternal Three in One!
Thomas Olivers. [1757.]

XCII.

Dies iræ, dies illa.

Day of anger, that dread Day
Shall the Sign in Heaven display,
And the Earth in ashes lay.

O what trembling shall appear,
When His coming shall be near,
Who shall all things strictly clear!

When the Trumpet shall command
Through the tombs of every land
All before the Throne to stand.

Death shall shrink and Nature quake,
When all creatures shall awake,
Answer to their God to make.

See the Book divinely penn'd,
In which all is found contain'd,
Whence the world shall be arraign'd!

When the Judge is on His Throne,
All that's hidden shall be shown,
Nought unpunish'd or unknown!

What shall I before Him say?
How shall I be safe that day,
When the righteous scarcely may?

King of awful majesty,
Saving sinners graciously,
Fount of mercy, save Thou me!

Leave me not, my Saviour, one
For whose soul Thy course was run,
Lest I be that day undone.

Thou didst toil my soul to gain;
Didst redeem me with Thy pain;
Be such labour not in vain!

Thou just Judge of wrath severe,
Grant my sins remission here,
Ere Thy reckoning day appear.

My transgressions grievous are;
Scarce look up for shame I dare;
Lord, Thy guilty suppliant spare!

Thou didst heal the sinner's grief,
And didst hear the dying thief:
Even I may hope relief.

All unworthy is my prayer;
Make my soul Thy mercy's care,
And from fire eternal spare!

Place me with Thy sheep, that band
Who shall separated stand
From the goats, at Thy right hand!

When Thy voice in wrath shall say,
Cursèd ones, depart away!
Call me with the blest, I pray!

Lord, Thine ear in mercy bow!
Broken is my heart and low:
Guard of my last end be Thou!

In that day, that mournful day,
When to judgment wakes our clay,
Show me mercy, Lord, I pray!

Henry Alford. 1845.

VIII.

"*And I believe in the Holy Ghost, the Lord and Giver of Life; who proceedeth from the Father and the Son; who with the Father and the Son together is worshipped and glorified; who spake by the Prophets.*"

XCIII.

When God of old came down from Heaven,
 In power and wrath He came;
Before His feet the clouds were riven,
 Half darkness and half flame.

Around the trembling mountain's base
  The prostrate people lay;
A day of wrath, and not of grace;
  A dim and dreadful day.

But, when He came the second time,
  He came in power and love;
Softer than gale at morning prime,
  Hover'd His holy Dove.

The fires, that rush'd on Sinai down
  In sudden torrents dread,
Now gently light, a glorious crown,
  On every sainted head.

Like arrows went those lightnings forth,
  Wing'd with the sinner's doom:
But these, like tongues, o'er all the earth,
  Proclaiming life to come.

And, as on Israel's awe-struck ear
  The voice exceeding loud,
The trump, that angels quake to hear,
  Thrill'd from the deep dark cloud;

So, when the Spirit of our God
  Came down, His flock to find,
A voice from heaven was heard abroad,
  A rushing mighty wind.

Nor doth the outward ear alone
  At that high warning start;
Conscience gives back th' appalling tone;
  'Tis echoed in the heart.

It fills the Church of God, it fills
    The sinful world around ;
Only in stubborn hearts and wills
    No place for it is found.

To other strains our souls are set ;
    A giddy whirl of sin
Fills ear and brain, and will not let
    Heav'n's harmonies come in.

Come, Lord ! come Wisdom, Love, and Power ;
    Open our ears to hear !
Let us not miss the accepted hour ;
    Save, Lord, by love or fear !

John Keble. 1827.

XCIV.

Veni Creator Spiritus.

Come, Holy Ghost, our souls inspire,
And lighten with celestial fire ;
Thou the Anointing Spirit art,
Who dost Thy sevenfold gifts impart.
Thy blessed unction from above
Is comfort, life, and fire of love :
Enable with perpetual light
The dulness of our blinded sight ;
Anoint and cheer our soilèd face
With the abundance of Thy grace ; .
Keep far our foes ; give peace at home ;
Where Thou art guide, no ill can come ;
Teach us to know the Father, Son,
And Thee of Both, to be but One :

That, through the ages all along,
This may be our endless song,
"Praise to Thy Eternal merit,
"Father, Son, and Holy Spirit!"
     Amen!
  Anon. (Ordination Service). 1662.

XCV.

Veni Creator Spiritus.

Holy Spirit, gently come,
Raise us from our fallen state,
Fix Thy everlasting home
In the hearts Thou didst create!
 Gift of God most High!
Visit every troubled breast :
Light and Life and Love supply ;
Give our spirits perfect rest !

Heavenly Unction from above,
Comforter of weary saints,
Fountain, Life, and Fire of Love,
Hear, and answer our complaints !
 Thee we humbly pray,
Finger of the Living God,
Now Thy sevenfold grace display,
Shed our Saviour's love abroad !

Now Thy quickening influence bring,
On our spirits sweetly move ;
Open every mouth to sing
Jesus' everlasting love !
 Lighten every heart ;
Drive our enemies away ;
Joy and peace to us impart ;
Lead us in the heavenly way !

Take the things of Christ and show
What our Lord for us hath done;
May we God the Father know
Only in and through the Son:
   Nothing will we fear,
Though to wilds and deserts driven,
While we feel Thy Presence near,
Witnessing our sins forgiven.

Glory be to God alone,
God, whose hand created all!
Glory be to God the Son,
Who redeem'd us from our fall!
   To the Holy Ghost
Equal praise and glory be,
When the course of time is lost,
Lost in wide eternity!

William Hammond. 1745.

XCVI.

Come, Holy Spirit, heavenly Dove,
My sinful maladies remove;
Be Thou my Light, be Thou my Guide,
O'er every thought and step preside.

The light of truth to me display,
That I may know and choose my way;
Plant holy fear within mine heart,
That I from God may ne'er depart.

Conduct me safe, conduct me far
From every sin and hurtful snare;
Lead me to God, my final Rest,
In His enjoyment to be blest.

Lead me to Christ, the Living Way,
Nor let me from His pastures stray:
Lead me to Heaven, the seat of bliss,
Where pleasure in perfection is.

Lead me to holiness, the road
That I must take to dwell with God;
Lead to Thy Word, that rules must give,
And sure directions how to live.

Lead me to means of grace, where I
May own my wants, and seek supply:
Lead to Thyself, the Spring from whence
To fetch all quickening influence.

Thus I, conducted still by Thee,
Of God a child beloved shall be,
Here to His family pertain,
Hereafter with Him ever reign.
Simon Browne. 1720.

XCVII.

Come, Holy Spirit, heavenly Dove,
   With all Thy quickening powers,
Kindle a flame of sacred love
   In these cold hearts of ours.

Look how we grovel here below,
   Fond of these trifling toys;
Our souls can neither fly nor go
   To reach eternal joys!

In vain we tune our formal songs,
   In vain we strive to rise;
Hosannas languish on our tongues,
   And our devotion dies.

Dear Lord, and shall we ever lie
    At this poor dying rate?
Our love so faint, so cold to Thee,
    And Thine to us so great!

Come, Holy Spirit, heavenly Dove,
    With all Thy quickening powers!
Come, shed abroad a Saviour's love,
    And that shall kindle ours.
Isaac Watts. 1709.

XCVIII.

Come, Holy Spirit, come
    Let Thy bright beams arise,
Dispel the darkness from our minds,
    And open all our eyes.

Cheer our desponding hearts,
    Thou heavenly Paraclete;
Give us to lie, with humble hope
    At our Redeemer's feet.

Revive our drooping faith,
    Our doubts and fears remove,
And kindle in our breasts the flame
    Of never-dying love.

Convince us of our sin,
    Then lead to Jesus' blood,
And to our wondering view reveal
    The secret love of God.

Show us that loving Man
    That rules the courts of bliss,
The Lord of hosts, the Mighty God,
    The Eternal Prince of Peace.

'Tis Thine to cleanse the heart,
  To sanctify the soul,
To pour fresh life in every part,
  And new-create the whole.

Dwell therefore in our hearts,
  Our minds from bondage free;
Then we shall know, and praise, and love
  The Father, Son, and Thee!
                    Joseph Hart. 1759.

XCIX.

Lord God the Holy Ghost,
  In this accepted hour,
As on the day of Pentecost,
  Descend in all Thy power!
  We meet with one accord
  In our appointed place,
And wait the promise of our Lord,
  The Spirit of all grace.

Like mighty rushing wind
  Upon the waves beneath,
Move with one impulse every mind
  One soul, one feeling breathe:
  The young, the old, inspire
  With wisdom from above,
And give us hearts and tongues of fire
  To pray, and praise, and love.

Spirit of Light, explore
  And chase our gloom away,
With lustre shining more and more
  Unto the perfect day!

Spirit of Truth, be Thou
In life and death our Guide!
O Spirit of adoption, now
May we be sanctified!

James Montgomery. 1819.

C.

O du allersüste Freude. (Paul Gerhardt.)

Holy Ghost, dispel our sadness,
  Pierce the clouds of sinful night;
Come, Thou source of sweetest gladness,
  Breathe Thy Life, and spread Thy Light!
Loving Spirit, God of Peace!
Great Distributor of grace!
  Rest upon this congregation,
  Hear, O hear our supplication!

From that height which knows no measure,
  As a gracious shower descend,
Bringing down the richest treasure
  Men can wish, or God can send!
O Thou Glory, shining down
From the Father and the Son,
  Grant us Thy illumination!
  Rest upon this congregation!

Known to Thee are all recesses
  Of the earth and spreading skies;
Every sand the shore possesses
  Thy Omniscient Mind descries.
Holy Fountain! wash us clean
Both from error and from sin!
  Make us fly what Thou refusest,
  And delight in what Thou choosest!

Manifest Thy love for ever;
  Fence us in on every side;
In distress be our reliever,
  Guard and teach, support and guide!
Let Thy kind effectual grace
Turn our feet from evil ways;
  Show Thyself our new Creator,
  And conform us to Thy Nature!

Be our Friend on each occasion,
  God! omnipotent to save!
When we die, be our salvation,
  When we're buried, be our grave!
And, when from the grave we rise,
Take us up above the skies,
  Seat us with Thy saints in glory,
  There for ever to adore Thee!

Variation by Augustus M. Toplady. 1776.
From John Christian Jacobi. 1722.

CI.

Holy Spirit, in my breast
Grant that lively Faith may rest,
And subdue each rebel thought
To believe what Thou hast taught.

When around my sinking soul
Gathering waves of sorrow roll,
Spirit blest, the tempest still,
And with Hope my bosom fill.

Holy Spirit, from my mind
Thought and wish and will unkind,
Deed and word unkind remove,
And my bosom fill with love.

Faith, and Hope, and Charity,
Comforter, descend from Thee;
Thou the Anointing Spirit art,
These Thy gifts to us impart.

Till our faith be lost in sight,
Hope be swallowed in delight,
And love return to dwell with Thee,
In the threefold Deity!
Bishop Richard Mant. 1837.

CII.

Full of weakness and of sin,
  We look to Thee for life:
Lord, Thy gracious work begin,
  And calm the inward strife!

Though our hearts are prone to stray,
  Be Thou a constant Friend:
Though we know not how to pray,
  Thy saving mercy send!

Let Thy Spirit, gracious Lord,
  Our souls with love inspire,
Strength and confidence afford,
  And breathe celestial fire!

Teach us first to feel our need,
  Then all that need supply;
When we hunger, deign to feed,
  And hear us when we cry!

When we cleave to earthly things,
　　Send Thy reviving grace;
Raise our souls, and give them wings,
　　To reach Thy holy place!
　　　　　William Hiley Bathurst. 1831.

CIII.

There is a River, deep and broad,
　　Its course no mortal knows;
It fills with joy the Church of God,
　　And widens as it flows.

Clearer than crystal is the stream,
　　And bright with endless day;
The waves with every blessing teem,
　　And life and health convey.

Where'er they flow, contentions cease,
　　And love and meekness reign;
The Lord Himself commands the peace,
　　And foes conspire in vain.

Along the shores, angelic bands
　　Watch every moving wave;
With holy joy their breast expands,
　　When men the waters crave.

To them distressèd souls repair,
　　The Lord invites them nigh;
They leave their cares and sorrows there,
　　They drink, and never die.

Flow on, sweet Stream, more largely flow,
　　The earth with glory fill;
Flow on, till all the Saviour know,
　　And all obey His will.
　　　　　William Hurn. 1813.

CIV.

There is a Stream, which issues forth
    From God's eternal Throne,
And from the Lamb, a living stream
    Clear as the crystal stone.

The stream doth water Paradise;
    It makes the angels sing;
One cordial drop revives my heart;
    Hence all my joys do spring.

Such joys as are unspeakable,
    And full of glory too;
Such hidden manna, hidden pearls,
    As worldlings do not know.

Eye hath not seen, nor ear hath heard,
    From fancy 'tis concealed,
What Thou, Lord, hast laid up for Thine,
    And hast to me revealed.

I see Thy face, I hear Thy voice,
    I taste Thy sweetest love:
My soul doth leap: but O for wings,
    The wings of Noah's dove!

Then should I flee far hence away,
    Leaving this world of sin!
Then should my Lord put forth His hand,
    And kindly take me in!

Then should my soul with angels feast
    On joys that always last!
Blest be my God, the God of joy,
    Who gives me here a taste.

John Mason. 1683.

CV.

Ye sons of earth, prepare the plough,
    Break up your fallow ground;
The Sower is gone forth to sow,
    And scatter blessings round.

The seed that finds a stony soil
    Shoots forth a hasty blade;
But ill repays the sower's toil,
    Soon wither'd, scorch'd, and dead.

The thorny ground is sure to balk
    All hopes of harvest there;
We find a tall and sickly stalk,
    But not the fruitful ear.

The beaten path and highway side
    Receive the trust in vain;
The watchful birds the spoil divide,
    And pick up all the grain.

But when the Lord of grace and power
    Has bless'd the happy field,
How plenteous is the golden store
    The deep-wrought furrows yield!

Father of mercies! we have need
    Of Thy preparing grace:
Let the same Hand, that gives the seed,
    Provide a fruitful place!
        William Cowper. 1779.

CVI.

Psalm XIX.

Behold, the morning sun
Begins his glorious way;
His beams through all the nations run,
And life and light convey.

But where the gospel comes,
It spreads diviner light,
It calls dead sinners from their tombs,
And gives the blind their sight.

How perfect is Thy word!
And all Thy judgments just!
For ever sure Thy promise, Lord;
And men securely trust.

While with my heart and tongue
I spread Thy praise abroad,
Accept the worship and the song,
My Saviour and my God!

Isaac Watts. 1719.

CVII.

Psalm XIX.

The starry firmament on high,
And all the glories of the sky,
Yet shine not to Thy praise, O Lord,
So brightly as Thy written word;
The hopes that holy word supplies,
Its truths divine, and precepts wise,
In each a heavenly beam I see,
And every beam conducts to Thee.

When, taught by painful proof to know
That all is vanity below,
The sinner roams from comfort far,
And looks in vain for sun or star;
Soft gleaming then those lights divine
Through all the cheerless darkness shine,
And sweetly to the ravish'd eye
Disclose the Day-spring from on high.

The heart, in sensual fetters bound,
And barren as the wintry ground,
Confesses, Lord, Thy quickening ray;
Thy word can charm the spell away;
With genial influence can beguile
The frozen wilderness to smile;
Bid living waters o'er it flow,
And all be paradise below.

Almighty Lord, the sun shall fail,
The moon forget her nightly tale,
And deepest silence hush on high
The radiant chorus of the sky;
But, fix'd for everlasting years,
Unmoved amid the wreck of spheres,
Thy word shall shine in cloudless day,
When heaven and earth have pass'd away.
Sir Robert Grant. [1839.]

IX.

THE HOLY CATHOLIC CHURCH.

"*And I believe one Catholic and Apostolic Church.*"

CVIII.

Jerusalem, my happy home,
   When shall I come to thee?
When shall my sorrows have an end,
   Thy joys when shall I see?

O happy harbour of the saints!
   O sweet and pleasant soil!
In thee no sorrow may be found,
   No grief, no care, no toil.

There lust and lucre cannot dwell,
   There envy bears no sway;
There is no hunger, heat, nor cold,
   But pleasure every way.

Thy walls are made of precious stones,
   Thy bulwarks diamonds square;
Thy gates are of right orient pearl,
   Exceeding rich and rare.

Thy turrets and thy pinnacles
   With carbuncles do shine;
Thy very streets are paved with gold,
   Surpassing clear and fine.

Ah, my sweet home, Jerusalem,
   Would God I were in thee!
Would God my woes were at an end,
   Thy joys that I might see!

Thy saints are crown'd with glory great;
    They see God face to face;
They triumph still, they still rejoice,
    Most happy is their case.

We that are here in banishment
    Continually do moan,
We sigh, and sob, we weep, and wail,
    Perpetually we groan.

Our sweet is mix'd with bitter gall,
    Our pleasure is but pain,
Our joys scarce last the looking on,
    Our sorrows still remain.

But there they live in such delight,
    Such pleasure and such play,
As that to them a thousand years
    Doth seem as yesterday.

Thy gardens and thy gallant walks
    Continually are green,
There grow such sweet and pleasant flowers
    As nowhere else are seen.

Quite through the streets, with silver sound,
    The flood of Life doth flow;
Upon whose banks on every side
    The wood of Life doth grow.

There trees for evermore bear fruit,
    And evermore do spring;
There evermore the angels sit,
    And evermore do sing.

Jerusalem, my happy home,
  Would God I were in thee !
Would God my woes were at an end,
  Thy joys that I might see !
Anon. "*F. B. P.*" [1616.]

CIX.

Sweet place, sweet place alone !
The court of God most High,
The Heaven of Heavens' Throne,
Of spotless majesty !
  O happy place !
    When shall I be,
    My God, with Thee,
  To see Thy face ?

The stranger homeward bends,
And fighteth for his rest:
Heaven is my home, my friends
Lodge there in Abraham's breast:
  O happy place !
    When shall I be,
    My God, with Thee,
  To see Thy face ?

Earth's but a sorry tent
Pitch'd for a few frail days,
A short leas'd tenement ;
Heaven's still my song, my praise.
  O happy place !
    When shall I be,
    My God, with Thee,
  To see Thy face ?

No tears from any eyes
Drop in that holy quire;
But Death itself there dies,
And sighs themselves expire.
  O happy place!
    When shall I be,
      My God, with Thee,
  To see Thy face?

There should temptation cease,
My frailties there should end;
There should I rest in peace
In the arms of my best Friend.
  O happy place!
    When shall I be,
      My God, with Thee,
  To see Thy face?

Jerusalem on high
My song and City is,
My home whene'er I die,
The centre of my bliss:
  O happy place!
    When shall I be,
      My God, with Thee,
  To see Thy face?

Thy walls, sweet city, thine,
With pearls are garnishèd;
Thy gates with praises shine,
Thy streets with gold are spread;
  O happy place!
    When shall I be,
      My God, with Thee,
  To see Thy face?

No sun by day shines there,
No moon by silent night;
Oh no! these needless are;
The Lamb's the city's Light:
  O happy place!
    When shall I be,
    My God, with Thee,
  To see Thy face?

There dwells my Lord, my King,
Judged here unfit to live;
There angels to Him sing,
And lovely homage give:
  O happy place!
    When shall I be,
    My God, with Thee,
  To see Thy face?

The Patriarchs of old
There from their travels cease;
The Prophets there behold
Their long'd-for Prince of Peace:
  O happy place!
    When shall I be,
    My God, with Thee,
  To see Thy face?

The Lamb's Apostles there
I might with joy behold,
The Harpers I might hear
Harping on harps of gold:
  O happy place!
    When shall I be,
    My God, with Thee,
  To see Thy face?

The bleeding Martyrs, they
Within these courts are found,
Clothèd in pure array,
Their scars with glory crown'd:
   O happy place!
     When shall I be,
      My God, with Thee,
   To see Thy face?

Ah me! Ah me! that I
In Kedar's tents here stay!
No place like this on high!
Thither, Lord! guide my way!
   O happy place!
     When shall I be,
      My God, with Thee,
   To see Thy face?
         Samuel Crossman. 1664.

CX.

Jerusalem, my happy home,
  Name ever dear to me!
When shall my labours have an end,
  In joy and peace, and thee?

When shall these eyes thy heaven-built walls,
  And pearly gates behold?
Thy bulwarks with salvation strong,
  And streets of shining gold?

There happier bowers than Eden's bloom,
  Nor sin nor sorrow know:
Blest seats! through rude and stormy scenes
  I onward press to you.

Why should I shrink from pain and woe,
    Or feel at death dismay?
I've Canaan's goodly land in view,
    And realms of endless day.

Apostles, martyrs, prophets, there
    Around my Saviour stand;
And soon my friends in Christ below
    Will join the glorious band.

Jerusalem, my happy home!
    My soul still pants for thee:
Then shall my labours have an end,
    When I thy joys shall see.

Anon. [1801.]

CXI.

REV. VII. 13—17.

What are these in bright array,
    This innumerable throng,
Round the altar, night and day,
    Hymning one triumphant song?
"Worthy is the Lamb, once slain,
    Blessing, honour, glory, power,
Wisdom, riches, to obtain,
    New dominion every hour."

These through fiery trials trod;
    These from great affliction came;
Now, before the Throne of God,
    Seal'd with His Almighty Name,
Clad in raiment pure and white,
    Victor-palms in every hand,
Through their dear Redeemer's might,
    More than conquerors they stand.

Hunger, thirst, disease unknown,
  On immortal fruits they feed;
Them the Lamb amidst the Throne
  Shall to living fountains lead:
Joy and gladness banish sighs;
  Perfect love dispels all fear;
And for ever from their eyes
  God shall wipe away the tear.

James Montgomery. 1819.

CXII.
Rev. VII. 13—17.

Exalted high at God's right hand,
Nearer the throne than cherubs stand,
With glory crown'd, in white array,
My wondering soul says, who are they?

These are the saints beloved of God,
Wash'd are their robes in Jesus' blood,
More spotless than the purest white
They shine in uncreated light.

Brighter than angels, lo! they shine,
Their glories great, and all divine:
Tell me their origin, and say,
Their order what, and whence came they?

Through tribulation great they came,
They bore the cross, and scorn'd the shame:
Within the Living Temple blest,
In God they dwell, and on Him rest.

And does the cross thus prove their gain?
And shall they thus for ever reign,
Seated on sapphire thrones, to praise
The wonders of Redeeming grace?

Hunger they ne'er shall feel again,
Nor burning thirst shall they sustain :
To wells of living water led,
By God the Lamb for ever fed.

Unknown to mortal ears, they sing
The secret glories of their King :
Tell me the subject of their lays,
And whence their loud exalted praise?

Jesus, the Saviour, is their theme ;
They sing the wonders of His Name ;
To Him ascribing power and grace,
Dominion, and eternal praise.

Amen ! they cry, to Him alone,
Who dares to fill His Father's throne ;
They give Him glory, and again
Repeat His praise, and say, Amen !
Rowland Hill. 1783.

CXIII.

O happy saints, who dwell in light,
And walk with Jesus, clothed in white ;
Safe landed on that peaceful shore,
Where pilgrims meet to part no more.

Released from sin, and toil, and grief,
Death was their gate to endless life ;
An open'd cage, to let them fly
And build their happy nest on high.

And now they range the heavenly plains,
And sing their hymns in melting strains ;
And now their souls begin to prove
The heights and depths of Jesus' love.

He cheers them with eternal smile;
They sing hosannas all the while;
Or, overwhelm'd with rapture sweet,
Sink down adoring at His feet.

Ah! Lord! with tardy steps I creep,
And sometimes sing, and sometimes weep;
Yet strip me of this house of clay,
And I will sing as loud as they.
John Berridge. 1785.

CXIV.

REV. VII. 13—17.

How bright these glorious spirits shine:
   Whence all their white array?
How came they to the blissful seats
   Of everlasting day?

Lo! these are they from sufferings great
   Who came to realms of light;
And in the blood of Christ have wash'd
   Those robes which shine so bright.

Now with triumphal palms they stand
   Before the throne on high,
And serve the God they love, amidst
   The glories of the sky.

His presence fills each heart with joy,
   Tunes every mouth to sing;
By day, by night, the sacred courts
   With glad hosannas ring.

Hunger and thirst are felt no more,
　　Nor suns with scorching ray ;
God is their Sun, whose cheering beams
　　Diffuse eternal day.

The Lamb, which dwells amidst the throne,
　　Shall o'er them still preside,
Feed them with nourishment divine,
　　And all their footsteps guide.

'Mong pastures green He'll lead His flock,
　　Where living streams appear ;
And God the Lord from every eye
　　Shall wipe off every tear.
　　　　　　　William Cameron. 1770.
　　　(*Variation from Isaac Watts.* 1709.)

CXV.

Rev. VII. 13—17.

Palms of glory, raiment bright,
Crowns that never fade away,
Gird and deck the saints in light,
Priests, and kings, and conquerors they.

Yet the conquerors bring their palms
To the Lamb amidst the throne,
And proclaim in joyful psalms
Victory through His cross alone.

Kings for harps their crowns resign,
Crying, as they strike the chords,
" Take the kingdom, it is Thine,
King of kings, and Lord of lords ! "

Round the altar priests confess,
If their robes are white as snow,
'Twas the Saviour's righteousness,
And His blood, that made them so.

Who were these? on earth they dwelt;
Sinners once, of Adam's race;
Guilt, and fear, and suffering felt;
But were saved by sovereign grace.

They were mortal, too, like us:
Ah! when we, like them, must die,
May our souls, translated thus,
Triumph, reign, and shine on high!
James Montgomery. [1853.]

CXVI.

PSALM LXXXVII.

Glorious things of thee are spoken,
   Zion, city of our God;
He, whose word cannot be broken,
   Form'd thee for His own abode:
On the Rock of Ages founded,
   What can shake thy sure repose?
With salvation's walls surrounded,
   Thou mayst smile at all thy foes.

See, the streams of living waters,
   Springing from eternal love,
Well supply thy sons and daughters,
   And all fear of want remove:
Who can faint, while such a river
   Ever flows their thirst to assuage;
Grace, which, like the Lord the giver,
   Never fails from age to age?

Round each habitation hovering,
   See the cloud and fire appear,
For a glory and a covering;
   Showing that the Lord is near.
Thus deriving from their banner
   Light by night, and shade by day,
Safe they feed upon the manna,
   Which He gives them when they pray.

Saviour, if of Zion's city
   I, through grace, a member am,
Let the world deride or pity,
   I will glory in Thy Name:
Fading is the worldling's pleasure,
   All his boasted pomp and show;
Solid joys and lasting treasure
   None but Zion's children know.

John Newton. 1779.

CXVII.

The Son of God goes forth to war,
   A kingly crown to gain;
His blood-red banner streams afar:
   Who follows in His train?

Who best can drink His cup of woe,
   Triumphant over pain,
Who patient bears His cross below,
   He follows in his train.

The martyr, first, whose eagle eye
   Could pierce beyond the grave;
Who saw his Master in the sky,
   And call'd on Him to save.

Like Him, with pardon on his tongue,
  In midst of mortal pain,
He prayed for them that did the wrong :
  Who follows in his train ?

A glorious band, the chosen few,
  On whom the Spirit came ;
Twelve valiant saints, their hope they knew,
  And mock'd the cross and flame.

They met the tyrant's brandish'd steel,
  The lion's gory mane ;
They bow'd their necks the death to feel :
  Who follows in their train ?

A noble army, men and boys,
  The matron and the maid,
Around the Saviour's throne rejoice,
  In robes of light arrayed.

They climb'd the steep ascent of heaven,
  Through peril, toil, and pain ;
O God ! to us may grace be given
  To follow in their train !
            Bishop Reginald Heber. 1827.

CXVIII.

Ye servants of the Lord,
  Each in his office wait,
Observant of His heavenly word,
  And watchful at His gate.

Let all your lamps be bright,
  And trim the golden flame ;
Gird up your loins, as in His sight,
  For awful is His name.

Watch; 'tis your Lord's command;
  And, while we speak, He's near;
Mark the first signal of His hand,
  And ready all appear.

O happy servant he,
  In such a posture found!
He shall his Lord with rapture see,
  And be with honour crown'd.

Christ shall the banquet spread
  With His own Royal hand;
And raise that favourite servant's head
  Amid the angelic band.
             Philip Doddridge. 1755.

CXIX.

A soldier's course, from battles won
  To new-commencing strife;
A pilgrim's, restless as the sun;
  Behold the Christian's life!

Prepared the trumpet's call to greet,
  Soldier of Jesus, stand!
Pilgrim of Christ, with ready feet
  Await thy Lord's command.

The hosts of Satan pant for spoil;
  How can thy warfare close?
Lonely, thou tread'st a foreign soil;
  How canst thou hope repose?

Seek, soldier! pilgrim! seek thine home,
  Reveal'd in sacred lore;
The land, whence pilgrims never roam,
  Where soldiers war no more:

Where grief shall never wound, nor death
  Disturb the Saviour's reign;
Nor sin, with pestilential breath,
  His holy realm profane:

The land, where, (suns and moons unknown,
  And night's alternate sway,)
Jehovah's ever-burning throne
  Upholds unbroken day:

The land, (for Heaven its bliss unseen
  Bids earthly types suggest,)
Where healing leaves and fadeless green
  Fruit-laden groves invest:

Where founts of life their treasures yield
  In streams that never cease;
Where everlasting mountains shield
  Vales of eternal peace:

Where they who meet shall never part;
  Where grace achieves its plan;
And God, uniting every heart,
  Dwells face to face with man.
              Thomas Gisborne. 1803.

CXX.

Hark, 'tis a martial sound!
  To arms, ye saints, to arms!
  Your foes are gathering round,
  And peace has lost its charms:
Prepare the helmet, sword, and shield;
The trumpet calls you to the field.

  No common foes appear
    To dare you to the fight,
  But such as own no fear
    And glory in their might:

The Powers of Darkness are at hand ;
Resist, or bow to their command.

   An arm of flesh must fail
   In such a strife as this ;
   He only can prevail
   Whose arm immortal is :
'Tis Heaven itself the strength must yield,
And weapons fit for such a field.

   And Heaven supplies them too :
   The Lord, who never faints,
   Is greater than the foe,
   And He is with His saints :
Thus arm'd, they venture to the fight ;
Thus arm'd, they put their foes to flight.

   And, when the conflict's past,
   On yonder peaceful shore
   They shall repose at last,
   And see their foes no more ;
The fruits of victory enjoy,
And never more their arms employ.
Thomas Kelly. 1809

CXXI.

O Israel, to thy tents repair :
   Why thus secure on hostile ground ?
Thy King commands thee to beware,
   For many foes thy camp surround.

The trumpet gives a martial strain :
   O Israel, gird thee for the fight !
Arise, the combat to maintain,
   And put thine enemies to flight !

Thou shouldst not sleep, as others do ;
   Awake ; be vigilant ; be brave !
The coward, and the sluggard too,
   Must wear the fetters of the slave.

A nobler lot is cast for thee ;
   A kingdom waits thee in the skies :
With such a hope; shall Israel flee,
   Or yield, through weariness, the prize ?

No ! let a careless world repose
   And slumber on through life's short day,
While Israel to the conflict goes,
   And bears the glorious prize away !
                Thomas Kelly. 1806.

CXXII.

Much in sorrow, oft in woe,
Onward, Christians, onward go ;
Fight the fight, and, worn with strife,
Steep with tears the Bread of Life.

Onward, Christians, onward go ;
Join the war, and face the foe ;
Faint not ! much doth yet remain ;
Dreary is the long campaign.

Shrink not, Christians ! will ye yield ?
Will ye quit the painful field ?
Will ye flee in danger's hour ?
Know ye not your Captain's power ?

Let your drooping hearts be glad ;
March, in heavenly armour clad ;
Fight, nor think the battle long ;
Victory soon shall tune your song.

Let not sorrow dim your eye,
Soon shall every tear be dry;
Let not woe your course impede;
Great your strength, if great your need.

Onward then to battle move;
More than conquerors ye shall prove;
Though opposed by many a foe,
Christian soldiers, onward go.
  Fragment by Henry Kirke White. 1806.
Completed by Fanny Fuller Maitland. 1827.

CXXIII.

Come, we that love the Lord,
 And let our joys be known;
Join in a song with sweet accord,
 And thus surround the throne.

Let those refuse to sing
 That never knew our God;
But favourites of the Heavenly King
 May speak their joys abroad.

The men of grace have found
 Glory begun below;
Celestial fruits on earthly ground
 From faith and hope may grow.

The hill of Zion yields
 A thousand sacred sweets,
Before we reach the heavenly fields,
 Or walk the golden streets.

Then let our songs abound,
 And every tear be dry:
We're marching through Emmanuel's ground
 To fairer worlds on high.
    Isaac Watts. 1709.

CXXIV.

From Egypt lately come,
  Where death and darkness reign,
We seek our new, our better home,
  Where we our rest shall gain.
      Hallelujah!
      We are on our way to God!

To Canaan's sacred bound
  We haste with songs of joy,
Where peace and liberty are found,
  And sweets that never cloy.
      Hallelujah!
      We are on our way to God!

There sin and sorrow cease,
  And every conflict's o'er;
There we shall dwell in endless peace,
  And never hunger more:
      Hallelujah!
      We are on our way to God!

There in celestial strains
  Enraptured myriads sing;
There love in every bosom reigns,
  For God Himself is King.
      Hallelujah!
      We are on our way to God!

We soon shall join the throng,
  Their pleasures we shall share,
And sing the everlasting song
  With all the ransom'd there.
      Hallelujah!
      We are on our way to God!

How sweet the prospect is!
It cheers the pilgrim's breast!
We're journeying through the wilderness,
But soon shall gain our rest!
Hallelujah!
We are on our way to God!
Thomas Kelly. 1812.

CXXV.

When Israel, by Divine command,
  The pathless desert trod,
They found, though 'twas a barren land,
  A sure resource in God.

A cloudy pillar mark'd their road,
  And screen'd them from the heat;
From the hard rocks their water flow'd,
  And manna was their meat.

Like them, we have a rest in view,
  Secure from adverse powers;
Like them, we pass a desert too;
  And Israel's God is ours.

His Word a light before us spreads
  By which our path we see;
His Love, a banner o'er our heads,
  From harm preserves us free.

Jesus, the Bread of Life, is given
  To be our daily food;
We drink a wondrous stream from Heaven,
  'Tis water, wine, and blood.

Lord! 'tis enough! I ask no more,
  These blessings are Divine;
I envy not the worldling's store,
  If Christ and Heaven are mine.
John Newton. 1779.

CXXVI.

Children of the Heavenly King,
As ye journey, sweetly sing;
Sing your Saviour's worthy praise,
Glorious in His works and ways!

We are travelling home to God,
In the way the Fathers trod;
They are happy now; and we
Soon their happiness shall see.

O ye banish'd seed, be glad!
Christ our Advocate is made;
Us to save, our flesh assumes;
Brother to our souls becomes.

Shout, ye little flock, and blest!
You on Jesus' Throne shall rest;
There your seat is now prepared,
There your kingdom and reward.

Lift your eyes, ye sons of Light!
Zion's city is in sight:
There our endless home shall be,
There our Lord we soon shall see.

Fear not, brethren; joyful stand
On the borders of your land;
Jesus Christ, your Father's Son,
Bids you undismayed go on.

Lord! obediently we go,
Gladly leaving all below:
Only Thou our Leader be,
And we still will follow Thee!

Seal our love, our labours end;
Let us to Thy bliss ascend;
Let us to Thy kingdom come;
Lord! we long to be at home.

John Cennick. 1742.

CXXVII.

Awake, and sing the song
  Of Moses and the Lamb,
Wake every heart and every tongue
  To praise the Saviour's Name.

Sing of His dying love;
  Sing of His rising power;
Sing how He intercedes above
  For those whose sins He bore.

'Sing, till we feel our hearts
  Ascending with our tongues;
Sing, till the love of sin departs,
  And grace inspires our songs.

Sing on your heavenly way,
  Ye ransom'd sinners, sing;
Sing on, rejoicing every day
  In Christ the eternal King.

Soon shall ye hear Him say,
  Ye blessed children, come;
Soon will He call you hence away,
  And take his wanderers home.

Variation from William Hammond. 1745.
By Martin Madan. 1760.

CXXVIII.

" Te læta, mundi Conditor."

Thou, great Creator, art possest,
And Thou alone, of endless rest;
To angels only it belongs
To lift to Thee their ceaseless songs.

But we must toil and toil again
With ceaseless woe and endless pain;
How then can we, in exile drear,
Lift the glad song of glory here!

Oh Thou, who wilt forgiving be
To all who truly turn to Thee,
Grant us to mourn the heavy cause
Of all our woe, Thy broken laws:

Then to such salutary grief
Let Faith and Hope bring due relief;
And we, too, soon shall be possest
Of ceaseless songs and endless rest.
John Chandler. 1837.

CXXIX.

Praise to the radiant Source of bliss,
   Who gives the blind their sight,
And scatters round their wond'ring eyes
   A flood of sacred light.

In paths unknown He leads them on
   To His Divine abode,
And shows new miracles of grace
   Through all the heavenly road.

The ways all rugged and perplex'd
  He renders smooth and straight,
And strengthens every feeble knee
  To march to Zion's gate.

Through all the path I'll sing His Name,
  Till I the Mount ascend,
Where toils and storms are known no more,
  And anthems never end!
Philip Doddridge. 1755.

X.

THE COMMUNION OF SAINTS.

"*The Communion of Saints*" (*Apostles' Creed*).

CXXX.

When Christ the Lord would come on earth,
  His messenger before Him went,
The greatest born of mortal birth
  And charged with words of deep intent.

The least of all that here attend
  Hath honour greater far than he;
He was the Bridegroom's joyful friend,
  His Body and His Spouse are we.

A higher race, the sons of light,
  Of water and the Spirit born;
He the last star of parting night,
  And we the children of the morn.

And, as he boldly spake Thy word,
    And joyed to hear the Bridegroom's voice,
Thus may Thy pastors teach, O Lord !
    And thus Thy hearing Church rejoice.
Henry Alford. 1845.

CXXXI.

How rich Thy favours, God of grace,
    How various and Divine !
Full as the ocean they are pour'd,
    And bright as Heaven they shine.

He to eternal glory calls,
    And leads the wondrous way
To His own Palace, where He reigns
    In uncreated day.

Jesus, the Herald of His love,
    Displays the radiant prize,
And shows the purchase of His Blood
    To our admiring eyes.

He perfects what His hand begins,
    And stone on stone he lays,
Till firm and fair the building rise
    A temple to His praise.

The songs of everlasting years
    That mercy shall attend,
Which leads, through sufferings of an hour,
    To joys that never end.
Philip Doddridge. 1755.

CXXXII.

PSALM LXXXIV.

Pleasant are Thy courts above
In the land of light and love;
Pleasant are thy courts below
In this land of sin and woe.
O, my spirit longs and faints
For the converse of Thy saints,
For the brightness of Thy face,
For Thy fulness, God of grace!

Happy birds that sing and fly
Round Thy altars, O Most High!
Happier souls that find a rest
In a Heavenly Father's breast!
Like the wandering dove, that found
No repose on earth around,
They can to their ark repair,
And enjoy it ever there.

Happy souls! their praises flow
Even in this vale of woe;
Waters in the desert rise,
Manna feeds them from the skies:
On they go from strength to strength,
Till they reach Thy throne at length,
At Thy feet adoring fall,
Who hast led them safe through all.

Lord! be mine this prize to win!
Guide me through a world of sin:
Keep me by Thy saving grace;
Give me at Thy side a place:

Sun and Shield alike Thou art;
Guide and guard my erring heart!
Grace and glory flow from Thee;
Shower, O shower them, Lord, on me!
Henry Francis Lyte. 1834.

CXXXIII.
Psalm LXXXIV.

Lord of the worlds above,
How pleasant and how fair
The dwellings of Thy love,
Thy earthly temples, are!
   To Thine abode
     My heart aspires
     With warm desires
   To see my God.

O happy souls that pray
Where God appoints to hear!
O happy men that pay
Their constant service there!
   They praise Thee still;
     And happy they
     That love the way
   To Sion's hill.

They go from strength to strength
Through this dark vale of tears,
Till each arrives at length,
Till each in Heaven appears:
   O glorious seat,
     When God our King
     Shall thither bring
   Our willing feet!
Isaac Watts. 1719.

CXXXIV.

'Tis Heaven begun below
To hear Christ's praises flow
In Zion, where His Name is known:
  What will it be above
  To sing redeeming love,
And cast our crowns before His throne!

  When we adore Him there,
  We shall be void of fear,
Nor faith, nor hope, nor patience need:
  Love will absorb us quite,
  Love in the midst of light,
On God's eternal love shall feed.

  Oh! what sweet company
  We then shall hear and see!
What harmony will there abound!
  When souls unnumber'd sing
  The praise of Zion's King,
Nor one dissenting voice is found!

  With everlasting joy,
  Such as will never cloy,
We shall be fill'd, nor wish for more;
  Bright as meridian day,
  Calm as the evening ray,
Full as a sea without a shore.

  Till that blest period come,
  Zion shall be my home;
And may I never thence remove,
  Till from the Church below
  To heaven at once I go,
And there commune in perfect love!

Joseph Swain.   1792.

CXXXV.

Lo! God is here! Let us adore,
  And own, how dreadful is this place!
Let all within us feel His power,
  And silent bow before His face!
Who know His power, His grace who prove,
Serve Him with awe, with reverence love.

Lo! God is here! Him day and night
  Th' united quires of angels sing:
To Him, enthroned above all height,
  Heaven's hosts their noblest praises bring:
Disdain not, Lord, our meaner song,
Who praise Thee with a stammering tongue!

Gladly the toys of earth we leave,
  Wealth, pleasure, fame, for Thee alone:
To Thee our will, soul, flesh, we give;
  O take, O seal them for Thine own!
Thou art the God! Thou art the Lord!
Be Thou by all Thy works adored!

Being of beings, may our praise
  Thy courts with grateful fragrance fill;
Still may we stand before Thy face,
  Still hear and do Thy sovereign will!
To Thee may all our thoughts arise,
Ceaseless, accepted sacrifice!

In Thee we move; all things of Thee
  Are full, Thou source and life of all!
Thou vast, unfathomable Sea!
  Fall prostrate, lost in wonder fall,
Ye sons of men; for God is Man!
All may we lose, so Thee we gain!

As flowers their opening leaves display,
   And glad drink in the solar fire,
So may we catch Thy every ray,
   So may Thy influence us inspire;
Thou Beam of the eternal Beam,
Thou purging Fire; Thou quickening Flame!

John Wesley. 1739.
From Gerhard Tersteegen.

CXXXVI.

Jesus, where'er Thy people meet,
There they behold Thy mercy-seat;
Where'er they seek Thee, Thou art found,
And every place is hallowed ground.

For Thou, within no walls confined,
Inhabitest the humble mind;
Such ever bring Thee where they come,
And going take Thee to their home.

Dear Shepherd of Thy chosen few,
Thy former mercies here renew;
Here to our waiting hearts proclaim
The sweetness of Thy saving Name.

Here may we prove the power of prayer
To strengthen faith, and sweeten care,
To teach our faint desires to rise,
And bring all Heaven before our eyes.

Behold, at Thy commanding word,
We stretch the curtain and the cord;
Come Thou, and fill this wider space,
And bless us with a large increase.

Lord, we are few, but Thou art near;
Nor short Thine arm, nor deaf Thine ear;
O rend the heavens, come quickly down,
And make a thousand hearts Thine own!
William Cowper. 1779.

CXXXVII.

The heaven of heavens cannot contain
   The Universal Lord;
Yet He in humble hearts will deign
   To dwell and be adored.

Where'er ascends the sacrifice
   Of fervent praise and prayer,
Or on the earth, or in the skies,
   The Heaven of God is there.

His presence there is spread abroad
   Through realms, through worlds unknown;
Who seeks the mercies of his God
   Is ever near His Throne.
William Drennan. 1815.

CXXXVIII.

How blest the sacred tie that binds,
In union sweet, according minds;
How swift the heavenly course they run,
Whose hearts, whose faith, whose hopes are one!

To each the soul of each how dear!
What jealous love, what holy fear!
How doth the generous flame within
Refine from earth, and cleanse from sin!

Their streaming tears together flow
For human guilt and mortal woe;
Their ardent prayers together rise
Like mingling flames in sacrifice.

Together both they seek the place
Where God reveals His awful face;
How high, how strong, their raptures swell,
There's none but kindred souls can tell.

Nor shall the glowing flame expire,
When nature droops her sickening fire;
Then shall they meet in realms above;
A heaven of joy, a heaven of love.
Anna Lætitia Barbauld. [1825.]

CXXXIX.

O quam juvat fratres, Deus.

O Lord, how joyful 'tis to see
The brethren join in love to Thee;
On Thee alone their heart relies,
Their only strength Thy grace supplies.

How sweet, within Thy holy place,
With one accord to sing Thy grace,
Besieging Thine attentive ear
With all the force of fervent prayer.

O may we love the house of God,
Of peace and joy the blest abode;
O may no angry strife destroy
That sacred peace, that holy joy.

The world without may rage, but we
Will only cling more close to Thee,
With hearts to Thee more wholly given,
More wean'd from earth, more fix'd on Heaven.

Lord, shower upon us from above
The sacred gift of mutual love;
Each other's wants may we supply,
And reign together in the sky.

John Chandler. 1837.

CXL.

Come, let us join our friends above,
    That have obtain'd the prize,
And on the eagle wings of love
    To joy celestial rise.
Let all the saints terrestrial sing
    With those to glory gone,
For all the servants of our King,
    In earth and Heaven, are one.

One family, we dwell in Him,
    One Church, above, beneath,
Though now divided by the stream,
    The narrow stream of death.
One army of the living God,
    To His command we bow;
Part of His host hath cross'd the flood,
    And part is crossing now.

Ten thousand to their endless home
    This solemn moment fly;
And we are to the margin come,
    And we expect to die;
His militant embodied host
    With wishful looks we stand,
And long to see that happy coast,
    And reach that heavenly land.

Our old companions in distress
    We haste again to see,
And eager long for our release
    And full felicity:
Even now by faith we join our hands
    With those that went before,
And greet the blood-besprinkled bands
    On the eternal shore.

Our spirits too shall quickly join,
    Like theirs with glory crown'd,
And shout to see our Captain's sign,
    To hear His trumpet sound.
Oh! that we now might grasp our Guide!
    Oh! that the word were given!
Come, Lord of hosts! the waves divide,
    And land us all in Heaven!

Charles Wesley. 1759.

CXLI.

Hosanna to the Living Lord!
Hosanna to the Incarnate Word!
To Christ, Creator, Saviour, King,
Let earth, let Heaven, Hosanna sing.
    Hosanna! Lord! Hosanna in the highest!

"Hosanna," Lord, Thine angels cry;
"Hosanna," Lord, Thy saints reply:
Above, beneath us, and around,
The dead and living swell the sound.
    Hosanna! Lord! Hosanna in the highest!

O Saviour, with protecting care
Return to this Thy house of prayer,
Assembled in Thy sacred Name,
Where we Thy parting promise claim.
    Hosanna! Lord! Hosanna in the highest!

But, chiefest, in our cleansèd breast,
Eternal, bid Thy Spirit rest;
And make our secret soul to be
A temple pure, and worthy Thee.
    Hosanna! Lord! Hosanna in the highest!

So, in the last and dreadful day,
When earth and Heaven shall melt away,
Thy flock, redeem'd from sinful stain,
Shall swell the sound of praise again.
    Hosanna! Lord! Hosanna in the highest!
        Bishop Reginald Heber. 1827.

XI.
THE FORGIVENESS OF SINS.

" I acknowledge one Baptism for the Remission of Sins."

CXLII.

PSALM CIII.

    My soul, repeat His praise
    Whose mercies are so great,
Whose anger is so slow to rise,
    So ready to abate.

    High as the heavens are raised
    Above the ground we tread,
So far the riches of His grace
    Our highest thoughts exceed.

    His power subdues our sins;
    And His forgiving love,
Far as the east is from the west,
    Doth all our guilt remove.

The pity of the Lord
To those that fear His Name,
Is such as tender parents feel;
He knows our feeble frame.

Our days are as the grass,
Or like the morning flower;
If one sharp blast sweep o'er the field,
It withers in an hour.

But Thy compassions, Lord,
To endless years endure,
And children's children ever find
Thy words of promise sure.
Isaac Watts. 1719

CXLIII.

There is a fountain fill'd with blood
Drawn from Emmanuel's veins;
And sinners, plunged beneath that flood,
Lose all their guilty stains.

The dying thief rejoiced to see
That fountain in his day;
And there have I, as vile as he,
Wash'd all my sins away.

Dear dying Lamb! Thy precious Blood
Shall never lose its power,
Till all the ransom'd Church of God
Be saved, to sin no more.

E'er since, by faith, I saw the stream
Thy flowing wounds supply,
Redeeming love has been my theme,
And shall be till I die.

Then in a nobler, sweeter song
   I'll sing Thy power to save,
When this poor lisping, stammering tongue
   Lies silent in the grave.

Lord, I believe Thou hast prepared,
   Unworthy though I be,
For me a blood-bought free reward,
   A golden harp for me:

'Tis strung, and tuned for endless years,
   And form'd by power divine,
To sound in God the Father's ears,
   No other Name but Thine.
              William Cowper. 1779.

CXLIV.

Jesu, Thou art my Righteousness,
   For all my sins were Thine;
Thy death hath bought of God my peace,
   Thy life hath made Him mine.

Spotless and just in Thee I am;
   I feel my sins forgiven;
I taste salvation in Thy Name,
   And antedate my heaven.

For ever here my rest shall be,
   Close to Thy bleeding side;
This all my hope, and all my plea,
   For me the Saviour died!

My dying Saviour and my God,
   Fountain for guilt and sin,
Sprinkle me ever with Thy Blood,
   And cleanse and keep me clean!

Wash me, and make me thus Thine own;
  Wash me, and mine Thou art!
Wash me, but not my feet alone:
  My hands, my head, my heart!

Th' atonement of Thy Blood apply,
  Till faith to sight improve;
Till hope in full fruition die,
  And all my soul be love.

Charles Wesley. 1740.

CXLV.

Rock of Ages, cleft for me,
Let me hide myself in Thee!
Let the water and the blood,
From Thy riven side which flowed,
Be of sin the double cure,
Cleanse me from its guilt and power.

Not the labours of my hands
Can fulfil Thy law's demands;
Could my zeal no respite know,
Could my tears for ever flow,
All for sin could not atone;
Thou must save, and Thou alone.

Nothing in my hand I bring;
Simply to Thy Cross I cling;
Naked, come to Thee for dress;
Helpless, look to Thee for grace;
Foul, I to the Fountain fly;
Wash me, Saviour, or I die!

While I draw this fleeting breath,
When my eyestrings break in death,
When I soar through tracts unknown,
See Thee on Thy judgment-throne;
Rock of Ages, cleft for me,
Let me hide myself in Thee!
  Augustus Montague Toplady. 1776.

CXLVI.

God of my salvation, hear,
 And help me to believe;
Simply do I now draw near,
 Thy blessing to receive.
Full of guilt, alas! I am,
But to Thy wounds for refuge flee;
 Friend of sinners! spotless Lamb!
 Thy Blood was shed for me.

Standing now as newly slain,
 To Thee I lift mine eye;
Balm of all my grief and pain,
 Thy Blood is always nigh;
Now as yesterday the same
Thou art, and wilt for ever be;
 Friend of sinners! spotless Lamb!
 Thy Blood was shed for me.

Nothing have I, Lord, to pay,
 Nor can Thy grace procure;
Empty send me not away,
 For I, Thou know'st, am poor:
Dust and ashes is my name,
My all is sin and misery;
 Friend of sinners! spotless Lamb!
 Thy Blood was shed for me.

No good work, or word, or thought,
    Bring I to gain Thy grace ;
Pardon I accept unbought,
    Thy proffer I embrace ;
Coming, as at first I came,
To take, and not bestow on Thee ;
    Friend of sinners ! spotless Lamb !
    Thy Blood was shed for me.

Saviour ! from Thy wounded side
    I never will depart ;
Here will I my spirit hide
    When I am pure in heart :
Till my place above I claim,
This only shall be all my plea,
    Friend of sinners ! spotless Lamb !
    Thy Blood was shed for me.
Charles Wesley. 1742.

CXLVII.

Just as I am, without one plea
But that Thy Blood was shed for me,
And that Thou bidd'st me come to Thee,
    O Lamb of God, I come !

Just as I am, and waiting not
To rid my soul of one dark blot,
To Thee, whose Blood can cleanse each spot,
    O Lamb of God, I come !

Just as I am, though toss'd about
With many a conflict, many a doubt,
Fightings and fears within, without,
    O Lamb of God, I come !

Just as I am, poor, wretched, blind,
Sight, riches, healing of the mind,
Yea, all I need, in Thee to find,
   O Lamb of God, I come!

Just as I am, Thou wilt receive,
Wilt welcome, pardon, cleanse, relieve!
Because Thy promise I believe,
   O Lamb of God, I come!

Just as I am, (Thy Love unknown
Has broken every barrier down,)
Now, to be Thine, yea, Thine alone,
   O Lamb of God, I come!

Just as I am, of that free love
The breadth, length, depth, and height to prove,
Here for a season, then above,
   O Lamb of God, I come!
              Charlotte Elliott. 1836.

CXLVIII.

When wounded sore the stricken soul
   Lies bleeding and unbound,
One only hand, a piercèd hand,
   Can salve the sinner's wound.

When sorrow swells the laden breast,
   And tears of anguish flow,
One only heart, a broken heart,
   Can feel the sinner's woe.

When penitence has wept in vain
   Over some foul dark spot,
One only stream, a stream of blood,
   Can wash away the blot.

'Tis Jesus' blood that washes white,
   His hand that brings relief,

His heart that's touch'd with all our joys
    And feeleth for our grief.

Lift up Thy bleeding hand, O Lord ;
    Unseal that cleansing tide ;
We have no shelter from our sin,
    But in Thy wounded side.
Cecil Frances Alexander. 1858.

XII.

RESURRECTION AND ETERNAL LIFE.

"And I look for the Resurrection of the dead, and the Life of the world to come. Amen."

CXLIX.

Earth to earth, and dust to dust,
Lord, we own the sentence just ;
Head and tongue, and hand and heart,
All in guilt have borne their part ;
Righteous is the common doom,
All must moulder in the tomb.

Like the seed in spring-time sown,
Like the leaves in autumn strown,
Low these goodly frames must lie,
All our pomp and glory die ;
Soon the Spoiler seeks his prey,
Soon he bears us all away.

Yet the seed, upraised again,
Clothes with green the smiling plain ;
Onward as the seasons move,
Leaves and blossoms deck the grove ;
And shall we forgotten lie,
Lost for ever, when we die ?

Lord, from Nature's gloomy night
Turn we to the Gospel's light;
Thou didst triumph o'er the grave,
Thou wilt all Thy people save;
Ransom'd by Thy Blood, the just
Rise immortal from the dust.
John Hampden Gurney. 1851.

CL.

O God, Thy grace and blessing give
    To us, who on thy Name attend,
That we this mortal life may live
    Regardful of our journey's end.

Teach us to know that Jesus died,
    And rose again, our souls to save;
Teach us to take Him as our Guide,
    Our Help from childhood to the grave.

Then shall not death with terror come,
    But welcome as a bidden guest,
The herald of a better home,
    The messenger of peace and rest.

And, when the awful signs appear
    Of Judgment, and the Throne above,
Our hearts still fix'd, we shall not fear,
    God is our trust; and God is Love.
Anon. [1853.]

CLI.

Dearest of names, our Lord, our King!
Jesus, Thy praise we humbly sing:
In cheerful songs we'll spend our breath,
And in Thee triumph over death.

Death is no more among our foes,
Since Christ, the mighty Conqueror, rose;
Both power and sting the Saviour broke;
He died, and gave the finish'd stroke.

Saints die, and we should gently weep;
Sweetly in Jesus' arms they sleep;
Far from this world of sin and woe,
Nor sin, nor pain, nor grief, they know.

Death no terrific foe appears;
An angel's lovely form he wears;
A friendly messenger he proves
To every soul whom Jesus loves.

Death is a sleep; and O! how sweet
To souls prepared its stroke to meet!
Their dying beds, their graves are blest,
For all to them is peace and rest.

Their bodies sleep; their souls take wing,
Uprise to Heaven, and there they sing
With joy before the Saviour's face,
Triumphant in victorious grace.

Soon shall the earth's remotest bound
Feel the Archangel's trumpet sound;
Then shall the grave's dark caverns shake,
And joyful all the saints shall wake.

Bodies and souls shall then unite,
Arrayed in glory, strong and bright;
And all His saints will Jesus bring
His face to see, His love to sing.

O may I live, with Jesus nigh,
And sleep in Jesus when I die !
Then, joyful, when from death I wake,
I shall eternal bliss partake.
Samuel Medley. 1800.

CLII.

We sing His love, Who once was slain,
Who soon o'er death revived again,
That all His saints through Him might have
Eternal conquests o'er the grave.
    Soon shall the trumpet sound, and we
    Shall rise to immortality.

The saints who now with Jesus sleep,
His own Almighty power shall keep,
Till dawns the bright illustrious day
When death itself shall die away :
    Soon shall the trumpet sound, and we
    Shall rise to immortality.

How loud shall our glad voices sing,
When Christ His risen saints shall bring
From beds of dust, and silent clay,
To realms of everlasting day !
    Soon shall the trumpet sound, and we
    Shall rise to immortality.

When Jesus we in glory meet,
Our utmost joys shall be complete ;
When landed on that heavenly shore,
Death and the curse will be no more :
    Soon shall the trumpet sound, and we
    Shall rise to immortality.

Hasten, dear Lord, the glorious day,
And this delightful scene display,
When all Thy saints from death shall rise
Raptured in bliss beyond the skies!
  Soon shall the trumpet sound, and we
  Shall rise to immortality.
Rowland Hill. 1796.

CLIII.

My life's a shade, my days
Apace to death decline;
My Lord is Life, He'll raise
My dust again, ev'n mine.
      Sweet truth to me!
      I shall arise,
      And with these eyes
      My Saviour see.

My peaceful grave shall keep
My bones till that sweet day;
I wake from my long sleep
And leave my bed of clay.
      Sweet truth to me!
      I shall arise,
      And with these eyes
      My Saviour see.

My Lord His angels shall
Their golden trumpets sound,
At whose most welcome call
My grave shall be unbound.
      Sweet truth to me!
      I shall arise,
      And with these eyes
      My Saviour see.

I said sometimes with tears,
Ah me! I'm loth to die!
Lord, silence Thou these fears:
My life's with Thee on high.
  Sweet truth to me!
  I shall arise,
  And with these eyes
  My Saviour see.

What means my trembling heart,
To be thus shy of death?
My Life and I sha'nt part,
Though I resign my breath.
  Sweet truth to me!
  I shall arise,
  And with these eyes
  My Saviour see.

Then welcome, harmless grave!
By thee to heaven I'll go:
My Lord His death shall save
Me from the flames below.
  Sweet truth to me!
  I shall arise,
  And with these eyes
  My Saviour see.
    Samuel Crossman. 1664.

CLIV.

Why do we mourn departing friends,
 Or shake at death's alarms?
'Tis but the voice that Jesus sends
 To call them to His arms.

Are we not tending upward too,
    As fast as time can move?
Nor would we wish the hours more slow
    To keep us from our love.

Why should we tremble to convey
    Their bodies to the tomb?
There the dear flesh of Jesus lay,
    And left a long perfume.

The graves of all His saints He bless'd,
    And softened every bed:
Where should the dying members rest,
    But with the dying Head?

Thence He arose, ascending high,
    And showed our feet the way;
Up to the Lord our flesh shall fly
    At the great rising day.

Then let the last loud trumpet sound,
    And bid our kindred rise:
Awake, ye nations under ground!
    Ye saints, ascend the skies!
                    Isaac Watts. 1709.

CLV.

Spirit! leave thine house of clay!
    Lingering dust, resign thy breath!
Spirit! cast thy chains away!
    Dust, be thou dissolved in death!
Thus the Almighty Saviour speaks,
    While the faithful Christian dies;
Thus the bonds of life he breaks,
    And the ransomed captive flies.

Prisoner, long detained below;
  Prisoner, now with freedom blest;
Welcome from a world of woe,
  Welcome to a Land of Rest!
Thus the choir of angels sing,
  As they bear the soul on high,
While with hallelujahs ring
  All the regions of the sky.

Grave, the guardian of our dust!
  Grave, the treasury of the skies!
Every atom of thy trust
  Rests in hope again to rise.
Hark! the Judgment trumpet calls:
  Soul, rebuild thy house of clay,
Immortality thy walls,
  And Eternity thy day!

Variation. [1812.]
From James Montgomery. 1803

CLVI.

Deathless principle, arise!
Soar, thou native of the skies;
Pearl of price, by Jesus bought,
To His glorious likeness wrought!

Go, to shine before His throne;
Deck his mediatorial crown;
Go, His triumphs to adorn;
Made for God, to God return!

Lo, He beckons from on high!
Fearless to His presence fly!
Thine the merit of His Blood;
Thine the Righteousness of God.

Angels, joyful to attend ;
Hovering round thy pillow, bend ;
Wait to catch the signal given,
And escort thee quick to Heaven.

Is thy earthly house distrest,
Willing to retain her guest ?
'Tis not thou, but she, must die ;
Fly, celestial tenant, fly !

Burst thy shackles, drop thy clay,
Sweetly breathe thyself away ;
Singing, to thy crown remove,
Swift of wing, and fired with love.

Shudder not to pass the stream ;
Venture all thy care on Him :
Him, whose dying love and power
Still'd its tossing, hush'd its roar.

Safe is the expanded wave,
Gentle as a summer's eve ;
Not one object of His care
Ever suffered shipwreck there.

See the haven full in view ;
Love Divine shall bear thee through ;
Trust to that propitious gale ;
Weigh thy anchor, spread thy sail.

Saints, in glory perfect made,
Wait thy passage through the shade :
Ardent for thy coming o'er,
See, they throng the blissful shore !

Mount, their transports to improve ;
Join the longing choir above ;
Swiftly to their wish be given ;
Kindle higher joy in Heaven !

Such the prospects that arise
To the dying Christian's eyes ;
Such the glorious vista faith
Opens through the shades of death.
  Augustus Montague Toplady. 1777.

CLVII.

Happy soul ! thy days are ended,
 All thy mourning days below ;
Go, by angel guards attended,
 To the sight of Jesus go !
Waiting to receive thy spirit,
 Lo, the Saviour stands above,
Shews the purchase of His merit,
 Reaches out the crown of love !

Struggle through thy latest passion
 To thy dear Redeemer's breast,
To His uttermost salvation,
 To His everlasting rest !
For the joy He sets before thee,
 Bear a momentary pain ;
Die, to live the life of glory ;
 Suffer, with thy Lord to reign !
   Charles Wesley. 1749.

CLVIII.

The waves of trouble, how they rise,
    How loud the tempests roar !
But death shall land our weary souls
    Safe on the heavenly shore.

There, to fulfil His sweet commands,
    Our speedy feet shall move ;
No sin shall clog our wingèd zeal,
    Or cool our burning love.

There shall we sit, and sing, and tell
    The wonders of His grace,
Till heavenly raptures fire our hearts,
    And smile in every face.

For ever His dear sacred Name
    Shall dwell upon our tongue,
And Jesus and salvation be
    The close of every song.
                  Isaac Watts. 1709.

CLIX.

Ye golden lamps of heaven, farewell,
    With all your feeble light :
Farewell, thou ever-changing moon,
    Pale empress of the night.

And thou, refulgent orb of day,
    In brighter flames array'd ;
My soul, that springs beyond thy sphere,
    No more demands thine aid.

Ye stars are but the shining dust
  Of my divine abode,
The pavement of those heavenly courts
  Where I shall reign with God.

The Father of eternal light
  Shall there His beams display,
Nor shall one moment's darkness mix
  With that unvaried day.

No more the drops of piercing grief
  Shall swell into mine eyes;
Nor the meridian sun decline
  Amid those brighter skies.

There all the millions of His saints
  Shall in one song unite,
And each the bliss of all shall view
  With infinite delight.
Philip Doddridge. 1755.

CLX.

Far from these narrow scenes of night
  Unbounded glories rise,
And realms of infinite delight,
  Unknown to mortal eyes.

Fair distant land; could mortal eyes
  But half its joys explore,
How would our spirits long to rise,
  And dwell on earth no more!

There pain and sickness never come,
  And grief no more complains :
Health triumphs in immortal bloom,
  And endless pleasure reigns.

No cloud those blissful regions know,
  For ever bright and fair ;
For sin, the source of mortal woe,
  Can never enter there.

There no alternate night is known,
  Nor sun's faint sickly ray ;
But glory from the sacred Throne
  Spreads everlasting day.

The glorious monarch there displays
  His beams of wondrous grace ;
His happy subjects sing His praise,
  And bow before His face.

O may the heavenly prospect fire
  Our hearts with ardent love,
Till wings of faith and strong desire
  Bear every thought above!

Prepare us, Lord, by grace divine,
  For Thy bright courts on high ;
Then bid our spirits rise, and join
  The chorus of the sky.

Anne Steele. 1760.

CLXI.

There is a land of pure delight,
   Where saints immortal reign,
Infinite day excludes the night,
   And pleasures banish pain.

There everlasting spring abides,
   And never withering flowers;
Death, like a narrow sea, divides
   This heavenly land from ours.

Sweet fields beyond the swelling flood
   Stand dress'd in living green:
So to the Jews old Canaan stood,
   While Jordan roll'd between.

But timorous mortals start and shrink
   To cross this narrow sea,
And linger shivering on the brink,
   And fear to launch away.

O! could we make our doubts remove,
   These gloomy doubts that rise,
And see the Canaan that we love
   With unbeclouded eyes;

Could we but climb where Moses stood,
   And view the landscape o'er;
Not Jordan's stream, nor death's cold flood,
   Should fright us from the shore.

               Isaac Watts. 1709.

CLXII.

There is a blessed Home
  Beyond this land of woe,
Where trials never come,
  Nor tears of sorrow flow;
Where faith is lost in sight,
  And patient hope is crown'd,
And everlasting light
  Its glory throws around.

There is a land of peace,
  Good angels know it well;
Glad songs that never cease
  Within its portals swell;
Around its glorious Throne
  Ten thousand saints adore
Christ, with the Father One,
  And Spirit, evermore.

O joy all joys beyond,
  To see the Lamb who died,
And count each sacred wound
  In hands, and feet, and side;
To give to Him the praise
  Of every triumph won,
And sing through endless days
  The great things He hath done.

Look up, ye saints of God,
  Nor fear to tread below
The path your Saviour trod
  Of daily toil and woe;
Wait but a little while
  In uncomplaining love,
His own most gracious smile
  Shall welcome you above.

Sir Henry Baker. 1861.

CLXIII.

The roseate hues of early dawn,
  The brightness of the day,
The crimson of the sunset sky,
  How fast they fade away!
Oh! for the pearly gates of heaven!
  Oh! for the golden floor!
Oh! for the Sun of Righteousness
  That setteth nevermore!

The highest hopes we cherish here,
  How fast they tire and faint!
How many a spot defiles the robe
  That wraps an earthly saint!
Oh! for a heart that never sins!
  Oh! for a soul wash'd white!
Oh! for a voice to praise our King,
  Nor weary day or night!

Here faith is ours, and heavenly hope,
  And grace to lead us higher:
But there are perfectness and peace
  Beyond our best desire.
Oh! by Thy love and anguish, Lord!
  Oh! by Thy life laid down!
Oh! that we fall not from Thy grace,
  Nor cast away our crown!

Cecil Frances Alexander. [1853.]

CLXIV.

Friend after friend departs;
  Who hath not lost a friend?
There is no union here of hearts,

That finds not here an end:
Were this frail world our only rest,
Living or dying, none were blest.

Beyond the flight of time,
  Beyond this vale of death,
There surely is some blessed clime,
  Where life is not a breath,
Nor life's affections transient fire,
Whose sparks fly upwards to expire.

There is a world above,
  Where parting is unknown;
A whole eternity of love,
  Form'd for the good alone:
And faith beholds the dying here
Translated to that happier sphere.

Thus star by star declines
  Till all are pass'd away,
As morning high and higher shines
  To pure and perfect day;
Nor sink those stars in empty night;
They hide themselves in heaven's own light.
              James Montgomery. 1824.

CLXV.

Rise, my soul, and stretch thy wings,
  Thy better portion trace;
Rise from transitory things
  Towards Heaven, thy native place.
Sun and moon and stars decay;
Time shall soon this earth remove;
Rise, my soul, and haste away
  To seats prepared above.

Rivers to the ocean run,
   Nor stay in all their course;
Fire ascending seeks the sun;
   Both speed them to their source:
So my soul, derived from God,
Pants to view His glorious face,
Forward tends to His abode,
   To rest in His embrace.

Fly me Riches, fly me Cares,
   Whilst I that coast explore;
Flattering world, with all thy snares,
   Solicit me no more!
Pilgrims fix not here their home;
Strangers tarry but a night;
When the last dear morn is come,
   They'll rise to joyful light.

Cease, ye pilgrims, cease to mourn;
   Press onward to the prize;
Soon our Saviour will return
   Triumphant in the skies.
Yet a season, and you know
Happy entrance will be given,
All our sorrows left below,
   And earth exchanged for heaven.

Robert Seagrave. 1748.

CLXVI.

We seek a rest beyond the skies,
    In everlasting day;
Through floods and flames the passage lies,
    But Jesus guards the way:
The swelling flood, and raging flame,
    Hear and obey His word;
Then let us triumph in His Name;
    Our Saviour is the Lord!

John Newton. 1779.

CLXVII.

There is an hour, when I must part
    With all I hold most dear;
And life, with its best hopes, will then
    As nothingness appear.

There is an hour, when I must lie
    Low on affliction's bed,
And anguish, pain, and tears become
    My bitter daily bread.

There is an hour, when I must sink
    Beneath the stroke of death,
And yield to Him, who gave it first,
    My struggling vital breath.

There is an hour, when I must stand
    Before the judgment seat,
And all my sins, and all my foes,
    In awful vision meet.

There is an hour, when I must look
    On one eternity,
And nameless woe, or blissful life,
    My endless portion be.

O Saviour, then, in all my need,
    Be near, be near to me;
And let my soul, in stedfast faith,
    Find life and Heaven in Thee!
               Andrew Reed. 1842.

CLXVIII.

Psalm XC.

Our God, our help in ages past,
    Our hope for years to come,
Our shelter from the stormy blast,
    And our eternal home:

Under the shadow of Thy Throne
    Thy saints have dwelt secure;
Sufficient is Thine arm alone,
    And our defence is sure.

Before the hills in order stood,
    Or earth received her frame,
From everlasting Thou art God,
    To endless years the same.

A thousand ages in Thy sight
    Are like an evening gone;
Short as the watch that ends the night
    Before the rising sun.

The busy tribes of flesh and blood,
   With all their lives and cares,
Are carried downwards by Thy flood,
   And lost in following years.

Time, like an ever-rolling stream,
   Bears all its sons away;
They fly forgotten, as a dream
   Dies at the opening day.

Our God, our help in ages past;
   Our hope for years to come;
Be Thou our guard while troubles last,
   And our eternal home!

Isaac Watts. 1719.

END OF PART I.

PART II.

HYMNS ARRANGED ACCORDING TO THE SUBJECTS OF THE LORD'S PRAYER.

The Book of Praise.

PART THE SECOND.

"LORD, TEACH US TO PRAY."
(*Luke* xi. 1.)

CLXIX.

Prayer is the soul's sincere desire,
   Utter'd, or unexpress'd;
The motion of a hidden fire
   That trembles in the breast.

Prayer is the burthen of a sigh,
   The falling of a tear,
The upward glancing of the eye,
   When none but God is near.

Prayer is the simplest form of speech
   That infant lips can try;
Prayer the sublimest strains that reach
   The Majesty on high.

Prayer is the contrite sinner's voice
   Returning from his ways,
While angels in their songs rejoice,
   And cry, Behold, he prays!

Prayer is the Christian's vital breath,
  The Christian's native air;
His watchword at the gates of death;
  He enters Heaven with prayer.

The saints, in prayer, appear as one
  In word, and deed, and mind;
While with the Father and the Son
  Sweet fellowship they find.

Nor prayer is made by man alone:
  The Holy Spirit pleads;
And Jesus, on the eternal Throne,
  For mourners intercedes.

O Thou, by Whom we come to God!
  The Life, the Truth, the Way!
The path of prayer Thyself hast trod:
  Lord! teach us how to pray!
                    James Montgomery. 1819.

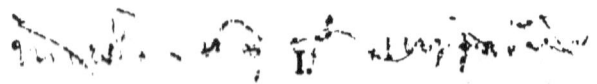

"OUR FATHER, WHICH ART IN HEAVEN;
HALLOWED BE THY NAME."

CLXX.

Psalm LXIII.

O God, Thou art my God alone;
  Early to Thee my soul shall cry;
A pilgrim in a land unknown,
  A thirsty land whose springs are dry.

Oh! that it were as it hath been!
  When, praying in the holy place,
Thy power and glory I have seen,
  And marked the footsteps of Thy grace!

Yet, through this rough and thorny maze,
  I follow hard on Thee, my God:
Thine hand unseen upholds my ways;
  I safely tread where Thou hast trod.

Thee, in the watches of the night,
  When I remember on my bed,
Thy Presence makes the darkness light,
  Thy guardian wings are round my head.

Better than life itself Thy love,
  Dearer than all beside to me:
For whom have I in Heaven above,
  Or what on earth compared to Thee?

Praise with my heart, my mind, my voice,
  For all Thy mercy I will give;
My soul shall still in God rejoice;
  My tongue shall bless Thee while I live.
              James Montgomery. 1822.

CLXXI.

Psalm CXLV.

My God, my King, Thy various praise
Shall fill the remnant of my days;
Thy grace employ my humble tongue,
Till death and glory raise the song.

The wings of every hour shall bear
Some thankful tribute to Thine ear,
And every setting sun shall see
New works of duty done for Thee.

Thy truth and justice I'll proclaim;
Thy bounty flows, an endless stream;
Thy mercy swift, Thine anger slow,
But dreadful to the stubborn foe.

But who can speak Thy wondrous deeds?
Thy greatness all our thoughts exceeds;
Vast and unsearchable Thy ways,
Vast and immortal be Thy praise!
Isaac Watts. 1719.

CLXXII.
Psalm CXXXIX.

Lord, Thou hast form'd mine every part,
    Mine inmost thought is known to Thee;
Each word, each feeling of my heart,
    Thine ear doth hear, Thine eye can see.

Though I should seek the shades of night,
    And hide myself in guilty fear,
To Thee the darkness seems as light,
    The midnight as the noonday clear.

The heavens, the earth, the sea, the sky,
    All own Thee ever present there;
Where'er I turn, Thou still art nigh,
    Thy Spirit dwelling everywhere.

Oh may that Spirit, ever blest,
    Upon my soul in radiance shine,
Till, welcomed to eternal rest,
    I taste Thy Presence, Lord Divine!
Robert Allan Scott. 1839.

CLXXIII.

When all Thy mercies, O my God,
   My rising soul surveys,
Transported with the view, I'm lost
   In wonder, love, and praise.

O how shall words with equal warmth
   The gratitude declare,
That glows within my ravish'd heart!
   But Thou canst read it there.

Thy Providence my life sustain'd,
   And all my wants redrest,
When in the silent womb I lay,
   And hung upon the breast.

To all my weak complaints and cries
   Thy mercy lent an ear,
Ere yet my feeble thoughts had learnt
   To form themselves in prayer.

Unnumbered comforts to my soul
   Thy tender care bestowed,
Before my infant heart conceived
   From whence these comforts flowed.

When in the slippery paths of youth
   With heedless steps I ran,
Thine arm, unseen, conveyed me safe,
   And led me up to man.

Through hidden dangers, toils, and death,
    It gently clear'd my way;
And through the pleasing snares of vice,
    More to be fear'd than they.

When worn with sickness, oft hast Thou
    With health renew'd my face;
And, when in sins and sorrows sunk,
    Revived my soul with grace.

Thy bounteous hand with worldly bliss
    Has made my cup run o'er;
And in a kind and faithful friend
    Has doubled all my store.

Ten thousand thousand precious gifts
    My daily thanks employ;
Nor is the least a cheerful heart
    That tastes those gifts with joy.

Through every period of my life
    Thy goodness I'll pursue;
And after death, in distant worlds,
    The glorious theme renew.

When nature fails, and day and night
    Divide thy works no more,
My ever-grateful heart, O Lord,
    Thy mercy shall adore.

Through all eternity to Thee
    A joyful song I'll raise:
But O! eternity's too short
    To utter all Thy praise!

                Joseph Addison. 1728.

II.
"THY KINGDOM COME."

CLXXIV.

Lord! come away!
Why dost Thou stay?
Thy road is ready; and Thy paths made straight
 With longing expectation wait
The consecration of Thy beauteous feet!
Ride on triumphantly! Behold, we lay
 Our lusts and proud wills in Thy way!

Hosanna! Welcome, to our hearts! Lord, here
Thou hast a temple too; and full as dear
As that of Sion, and as full of sin:
Nothing but thieves and robbers dwell therein:
Enter, and chase them forth, and cleanse the floor!
Crucify them, that they may never more
 Profane that holy place
 Where Thou hast chose to set Thy face!
And then, if our stiff tongues shall be
Mute in the praises of Thy Deity,
 The stones out of the temple wall
 Shall cry aloud, and call
Hosanna! and Thy glorious footsteps greet! Amen!
Bishop Jeremy Taylor. 1655.

CLXXV.

Jesus, Thy Church with longing eyes
 For Thy expected coming waits;
When will the promised light arise,
 And glory beam from Zion's gates?

Ev'n now, when tempests round us fall,
    And wintry clouds o'ercast the sky,
Thy words with pleasure we recall,
    And deem that our redemption's nigh.

Come, gracious Lord, our hearts renew,
    Our foes repel, our wrongs redress,
Man's rooted enmity subdue,
    And crown Thy Gospel with success.

O come, and reign o'er every land;
    Let Satan from his throne be hurl'd;
All nations bow to Thy command,
    And grace revive a dying world!

Yes, Thou wilt speedily appear!
    The smitten earth already reels;
And not far off we seem to hear
    The thunder of Thy chariot wheels.

Teach us in watchfulness and prayer
    To wait for the appointed hour;
And fit us by Thy grace to share
    The triumphs of Thy conquering power.
        William Hiley Bathurst. 1831.

CLXXVI.

Light of the lonely pilgrim's heart,
    Star of the coming day!
Arise, and with Thy morning beams
    Chase all our griefs away!

Come, blessed Lord! let every shore
 And answering island sing
The praises of Thy royal name,
 And own Thee as their King.

Bid the whole earth, responsive now
 To the bright world above,
Break forth in sweetest strains of joy
 In memory of Thy love.

Jesus! Thy fair creation groans,
 The air, the earth, the sea,
In unison with all our hearts,
 And calls aloud for Thee.

Thine was the Cross, with all its fruits
 Of grace and peace divine:
Be Thine the crown of glory now,
 The palm of victory Thine!

Anon. [1852.]

CLXXVII.

O Saviour! is Thy promise fled?
 Nor longer might Thy grace endure
To heal the sick, and raise the dead,
 And preach the Gospel to the poor?

Come, Jesus, come! return again;
 With brighter beam Thy servants bless,
Who long to feel Thy perfect reign,
 And share Thy kingdom's happiness!

A feeble race, by passion driven,
 In darkness and in doubt we roam,
And lift our anxious eyes to Heaven,
 Our hope, our harbour, and our home.

Yet, 'mid the wild and wintry gale,
  When death rides darkly o'er the sea,
And strength and earthly daring fail,
  Our prayers, Redeemer! rest on Thee.

Come, Jesus, come! and as of yore
  The prophet went to clear Thy way,
A harbinger Thy feet before,
  A dawning to Thy brighter day;

So now may grace, with heavenly shower,
  Our stony hearts for truth prepare;
Sow in our souls the seed of power,
  Then come, and reap Thy harvest there!
Bishop Reginald Heber. 1827.

CLXXVIII.

O Spirit of the living God!
  In all Thy plenitude of grace,
Where'er the foot of man hath trod,
  Descend on our apostate race!

Give tongues of fire and hearts of love
  To preach the reconciling word;
Give power and unction from above,
  Whene'er the joyful sound is heard.

Be darkness, at Thy coming, Light;
  Confusion, order in Thy path;
Souls without strength inspire with might;
  Bid mercy triumph over wrath.

O Spirit of the Lord! prepare
  All the round earth her God to meet;
Breathe Thou abroad like morning air,
  Till hearts of stone begin to beat.

Baptize the nations far and nigh;
　The triumphs of Thy Cross record;
The name of Jesus glorify,
　　Till every kindred call Him Lord.
　　　　　　James Montgomery. 1825.

CLXXIX.

Speed Thy servants, Saviour, speed them!
　Thou art Lord of winds and waves:
They were bound, but Thou hast freed them;
　Now they go to free the slaves:
　　Be Thou with them!
'Tis Thine arm alone that saves.

Friends and home and all forsaking,
　Lord! they go, at Thy command;
As their stay Thy promise taking,
　While they traverse sea and land:
　　O be with them!
Lead them safely by the hand!

Speed them through the mighty ocean,
　In the dark and stormy day,
When the waves in wild commotion
　Fill all others with dismay:
　　Be Thou with them!
Drive their terrors far away.

When they reach the land of strangers,
　And the prospect dark appears,
Nothing seen but toils and dangers,
　Nothing felt but doubts and fears;
　　Be Thou with them!
Hear their sighs, and count their tears.

When they think of home, now dearer
   Than it ever seem'd before,
Bring the promised glory nearer;
   Let them see that peaceful shore,
     Where Thy people
   Rest from toil, and weep no more!

Where no fruit appears to cheer them,
   And they seem to toil in vain,
Then in mercy, Lord, draw near them,
   Then their sinking hopes sustain:
     Thus supported,
   Let their zeal revive again!

In the midst of opposition
   Let them trust, O Lord, in Thee:
When success attends their mission,
   Let Thy servants humbler be:
     Never leave them,
   Till Thy face in Heaven they see;

There to reap, in joy for ever,
   Fruit that grows from seed here sown;
There to be with Him, Who never
   Ceases to preserve His own,
     And with triumph
   Sing a Saviour's grace alone!

Thomas Kelly. 1836.

CLXXX.

Thou, Whose Almighty word
Chaos and darkness heard,
   And took their flight;
Hear us, we humbly pray;
And, where the gospel's day
Sheds not its glorious ray,
   Let there be light!

Thou, Who didst come to bring
On Thy redeeming wing
   Healing and sight,
Health to the sick in mind,
Sight to the inly blind,
Oh, now to all mankind
   Let there be light!

Spirit of truth and love,
Life-giving, holy Dove,
   Speed forth Thy flight!
Move on the waters' face
Bearing the lamp of grace,
And in earth's darkest place
   Let there be light!

Holy and blessed Three,
Glorious Trinity,
   Wisdom, Love, Might!
Boundless as ocean's tide
Rolling in fullest pride,
Through the earth, far and wide,
   Let there be light!

John Marriott. 1816.

III.

"THY WILL BE DONE."

"Thy will be done, in earth, as it is in Heaven."

CLXXXI.

Come, my soul, Thy suit prepare;
Jesus loves to answer prayer:
He Himself has bid thee pray,
Therefore will not say thee nay.

Thou art coming to a King,
Large petitions with thee bring;
For his grace and power are such,
None can ever ask too much.

With my burden I begin;
Lord, remove this load of sin;
Let Thy blood, for sinners spilt,
Set my conscience free from guilt.

Lord, I come to Thee for rest;
Take possession of my breast;
There Thy blood-bought right maintain,
And without a rival reign.

As the image in the glass
Answers the beholder's face,
Thus unto my heart appear,
Print Thine own resemblance there.

While I am a pilgrim here,
Let Thy love my spirit cheer;
As my Guide, my Guard, my Friend,
Lead me to my journey's end.

"*Thy Will be done.*"

Shew me what I have to do;
Every hour my strength renew;
Let me live a life of faith;
Let me die Thy people's death.

John Newton. 1779.

CLXXXII.

My faith looks up to Thee,
Thou Lamb of Calvary,
   Saviour divine!
Now hear me while I pray;
Take all my guilt away;
O let me from this day
   Be wholly Thine!

May Thy rich grace impart
Strength to my fainting heart,
   My zeal inspire!
As Thou hast died for me,
O may my love to Thee
Pure, warm, and changeless be,
   A living fire!

While life's dark maze I tread,
And griefs around me spread,
   Be Thou my Guide!
Bid darkness turn to day,
Wipe sorrow's tears away,
Nor let me ever stray
   From Thee aside.

When ends life's transient dream,
When death's cold sullen stream
    Shall o'er me roll;
Blest Saviour! then in love
Fear and distrust remove;
O bear me safe above,
    A ransom'd soul!

Ray Palmer. [1840.]

CLXXXIII.

PSALM CXVI.

Redeem'd from guilt, redeem'd from fears,
My soul enlarged, and dried my tears,
What can I do, O Love Divine,
What, to repay such gifts as Thine?

What can I do, so poor, so weak,
But from Thy hands new blessings seek,
A heart to feel Thy mercies more,
A soul to know Thee, and adore?

O teach me at Thy feet to fall,
And yield Thee up myself, my all!
Before Thy saints my debts to own,
And live and die to Thee alone!

Thy Spirit, Lord, at large impart,
Expand and raise and fill my heart!
So may I hope my life shall be
Some faint return, O Lord, to Thee.

Henry Francis Lyte. 1834.

CLXXXIV.

Psalm CI.

Lord, when I lift my voice to Thee,
    To whom all praise belongs,
Thy justice and Thy love shall be
    The subject of my songs.

Let wisdom o'er my heart preside,
    To lead my steps aright,
And make Thy perfect law my guide,
    Thy service my delight.

All sinful ways I will abhor,
    All wicked men forsake;
And only those, who love Thy law,
    For my companions take.

Lord! that I may not go astray,
    Thy constant grace impart:
When wilt Thou come to point my way,
    And fix my roving heart?
        William Hiley Bathurst. 1831.

CLXXXV.

Forth in Thy Name, O Lord, I go,
    My daily labour to pursue,
Thee, only Thee, resolved to know,
    In all I think, or speak, or do.

The task Thy wisdom hath assign'd
    O let me cheerfully fulfil;
In all my works Thy presence find,
    And prove Thine acceptable will.

Preserve me from my calling's snare,
   And hide my simple heart above,
Above the thorns of choking care,
   The gilded baits of worldly love.

Thee may I set at my right hand,
   Whose eyes mine inmost substance see,
And labour on at Thy command,
   And offer all my works to Thee.

Give me to bear Thy easy yoke,
   And every moment watch and pray;
And still to things eternal look,
   And hasten to Thy glorious day.

For Thee delightfully employ
   Whate'er Thy bounteous grace hath given,
And run my course with even joy,
   And closely walk with Thee to Heaven.
              Charles Wesley. 1749.

CLXXXVI.

Now it belongs not to my care
   Whether I die or live;
To love and serve Thee is my share,
   And this Thy grace must give.

If death shall bruise this springing seed
   Before it come to fruit,
The will with Thee goes for the deed,
   Thy life was in the root.

Would I long bear my heavy load,
   And keep my sorrows long?
Would I long sin against my God,
   And His dear mercy wrong?

How much is sinful flesh my foe,
   That doth my soul pervert
To linger here in sin and woe,
   And steals from God my heart!

Christ leads me through no darker rooms
   Than He went through before;
He that unto God's Kingdom comes
   Must enter by this door.

Come, Lord, when grace hath made me meet
   Thy blessed face to see;
For, if Thy work on earth be sweet,
   What will Thy glory be?

Then I shall end my sad complaints,
   And weary sinful days,
And join with the triumphant saints
   That sing Jehovah's praise.

My knowledge of that life is small;
   The eye of faith is dim;
But it's enough that Christ knows all,
   And I shall be with Him.
               Richard Baxter. 1681.

CLXXXVII.

O Thou, who camest from above,
   The pure celestial fire to impart,
Kindle a flame of sacred love
   On the mean altar of my heart.

There let it for Thy glory burn
   With inextinguishable blaze ;
And, trembling, to its source return,
   In humble prayer and fervent praise.

Jesus! confirm my heart's desire
   To work, and speak, and think for Thee ;
Still let me guard the holy fire ;
   And still stir up Thy gift in me ;

Ready for all Thy perfect will,
   My acts of faith and love repeat ;
Till death Thy endless mercies seal,
   And make my sacrifice complete.
Charles Wesley. 1762.

CLXXXVIII.

Psalm XXXI.

My spirit on Thy care,
   Blest Saviour, I recline ;
Thou wilt not leave me to despair,
   For Thou art Love divine.

In Thee I place my trust,
   On Thee I calmly rest ;
I know Thee good, I know Thee just,
   And count Thy choice the best.

Whate'er events betide,
   Thy will they all perform ;
Safe in Thy breast my head I hide,
   Nor fear the coming storm.

Let good or ill befal,
   It must be good for me;
Secure of having Thee in all,
   Of having all in Thee.
             Henry Francis Lyte. 1834.

CLXXXIX.

Blest be Thy love, dear Lord,
   That taught us this sweet way,
Only to love Thee for Thyself,
   And for that love obey.

O Thou, our souls' chief hope!
   We to Thy mercy fly;
Where'er we are, Thou canst protect,
   Whate'er we need, supply.

Whether we sleep or wake,
   To Thee we both resign;
By night we see, as well as day,
   If Thy light on us shine.

Whether we live or die,
   Both we submit to Thee;
In death we live, as well as life,
   If Thine in death we be.
             John Austin. 1668.

CXC.

O Lord, my best desire fulfil,
   And help me to resign
Life, health, and comfort to Thy will,
   And make Thy pleasure mine.

Why should I shrink from Thy command,
   Whose love forbids my fears,
Or tremble at the gracious hand
   That wipes away my tears?

No, rather let me freely yield
   What most I prize to Thee,
Who never hast a good withheld,
   Or wilt withhold, from me.

Thy favour, all my journey through,
   Thou art engaged to grant;
What else I want, or think I do,
   'Tis better still to want.

But ah! my inward spirit cries,
   Still bind me to Thy sway!
Else the next cloud that veils the skies,
   Drives all these thoughts away.
William Cowper. 1779.

CXCI.

O for an heart to praise my God,
   An heart from sin set free!
An heart that always feels Thy Blood,
   So freely spilt for me!

An heart resign'd, submissive, meek,
   My dear Redeemer's throne;
Where only Christ is heard to speak,
   Where Jesus reigns alone.

An humble, lowly, contrite heart,
   Believing, true, and clean:
Which neither life nor death can part
   From Him that dwells within:

"Thy Will be done."

An heart in every thought renew'd,
   And full of love divine ;
Perfect, and right, and pure, and good,
   A copy, Lord, of Thine.

Thy nature, gracious Lord, impart ;
   Come quickly from above ;
Write Thy new Name upon my heart,
   Thy new, best Name of Love.

Charles Wesley. 1742.

CXCII.

Oh what, if we are Christ's,
   Is earthly shame or loss ?
Bright shall the crown of glory be,
   When we have borne the cross.

Keen was the trial once,
   Bitter the cup of woe,
When martyr'd saints, baptized in blood,
   Christ's sufferings shared below.

Bright is their glory now,
   Boundless their joy above,
Where, on the bosom of their God,
   They rest in perfect love.

Lord ! may that grace be ours ;
   Like them in faith to bear
All that of sorrow, grief, or pain,
   May be our portion here !

Enough, if Thou at last
   The word of blessing give,
And let us rest beneath Thy feet,
   Where saints and angels live !

All glory, Lord, to Thee,
  Whom Heaven and earth adore;
To Father, Son, and Holy Ghost,
  One God for evermore.
              Sir Henry Baker. [1857.]

CXCIII.

My God and Father, while I stray
Far from my home, on life's rough way,
O teach me from my heart to say,
    Thy will be done!

Though dark my path and sad my lot,
Let me be still and murmur not,
Or breathe the prayer divinely taught,
    Thy will be done!

What though in lonely grief I sigh
For friends beloved, no longer nigh,
Submissive still would I reply,
    Thy will be done!

Though Thou hast call'd me to resign
What most I prized, it ne'er was mine,
I have but yielded what was Thine;
    Thy will be done!

Should grief or sickness waste away
My life in premature decay,
My Father! still I strive to say,
    Thy will be done.

Let but my fainting heart be blest
With Thy sweet Spirit for its guest,
My God, to Thee I leave the rest;
    Thy will be done!

Renew my will from day to day;
Blend it with Thine; and take away
All that now makes it hard to say,
    Thy will be done!

Then, when on earth I breathe no more,
The prayer, oft mix'd with tears before,
I'll sing upon a happier shore,
    Thy will be done!
               Charlotte Elliott. 1836.

CXCIV.

O Lord, Thy heavenly grace impart,
And fix my frail inconstant heart;
Henceforth my chief desire shall be
To dedicate myself to Thee,
    To Thee, my God, to Thee!

Whate'er pursuits my time employ,
One thought shall fill my soul with joy;
That silent, secret thought shall be,
That all my hopes are fix'd on Thee,
    On Thee, my God, on Thee!

Thy glorious eye pervadeth space;
Thou'rt present, Lord, in every place;
And, wheresoe'er my lot may be,
Still shall my spirit cleave to Thee,
    To Thee, my God, to Thee!

Renouncing every worldly thing,
Safe 'neath the covert of Thy wing,
My sweetest thought henceforth shall be,
That all I want I find in Thee,
    In Thee, my God, in Thee!
          Mrs. Daniel Wilson. 1830.
          From John Frederic Oberlin.

CXCV.

When I survey life's varied scene,
   Amid the darkest hours
Sweet rays of comfort shine between,
   And thorns are mix'd with flowers.

Lord, teach me to adore Thy hand,
   From whence my comforts flow,
And let me in this desert land
   A glimpse of Canaan know.

And O! whate'er of earthly bliss
   Thy sovereign hand denies,
Accepted at Thy throne of grace
   Let this petition rise:

Give me a calm, a thankful heart,
   From every murmur free;
The blessings of Thy grace impart,
   And let me live to Thee.

Let the sweet hope, that Thou art mine,
   My path of life attend,
Thy presence through my journey shine,
   And bless its happy end!
Anne Steele. 1760.

CXCVI.

Father of Love, our Guide and Friend,
  Oh lead us gently on,
Until life's trial-time shall end,
  And heavenly peace be won!
We know not what the path may be
  As yet by us untrod;
But we can trust our all to Thee,
  Our Father and our God!

If call'd, like Abraham's child, to climb
  The hill of sacrifice,
Some angel may be there in time;
  Deliverance shall arise:
Or, if some darker lot be good,
  Oh, teach us to endure
The sorrow, pain, or solitude,
  That make the spirit pure!

Christ by no flowery pathway came;
  And we, His followers here,
Must do Thy will and praise Thy Name,
  In hope, and love, and fear.
And, till in Heaven we sinless bow,
  And faultless anthems raise,
O Father, Son, and Spirit, now
  Accept our feeble praise!
          William Joseph Irons. 1853.

CXCVII.

Thy way, not mine, O Lord,
  However dark it be!
Lead me by Thine own hand,
  Choose out the path for me.

Smooth let it be or rough,
  It will be still the best;
Winding or straight, it leads
  Right onward to Thy rest.

I dare not choose my lot;
  I would not, if I might;
Choose Thou for me, my God;
  So shall I walk aright.

The kingdom that I seek
  Is Thine; so let the way
That leads to it be Thine;
  Else I must surely stray.

Take Thou my cup, and it
  With joy or sorrow fill,
As best to Thee may seem;
  Choose Thou my good and ill;

Choose Thou for me my friends,
  My sickness or my health;
Choose Thou my cares for me,
  My poverty or wealth.

Not mine, not mine the choice,
  In things or great or small;
Be Thou my guide, my strength,
  My wisdom, and my all!

Horatius Bonar. 1856.

CXCVIII.

Father, I know that all my life
   Is portion'd·out for me,
And the changes that are sure to come
   I do not fear to see;
But I ask Thee for a present mind,
   Intent on pleasing Thee.

I ask Thee for a thoughtful love,
   Through constant watching wise,
To meet the glad with joyful smiles
   And wipe the weeping eyes;
And a heart at leisure from itself,
   To soothe and sympathize.

I would not have the restless will
   That hurries to and fro;
Seeking for some great thing to do,
   Or secret thing to know:
I would be treated as a child,
   And guided where I go.

Wherever in the world I am,
   In whatsoe'er estate,
I have a fellowship with hearts
   To keep and cultivate,
And a work of lowly love to do,
   For the Lord on whom I wait.

So I ask Thee for the daily strength
   To none that ask denied,
And a mind to blend with outward life,
   While keeping at Thy side;
Content to fill a little space,
   If Thou be glorified.

And if some things I do not ask
  In my cup of blessing be,
I would have my spirit fill'd the more
  With grateful love to Thee;
More careful, not to serve Thee much,
  But to please Thee perfectly.

There are briars besetting every path,
  That call for patient care;
There is a cross in every lot,
  And an earnest need for prayer;
But a lowly heart, that leans on Thee,
  Is happy anywhere.

In a service which Thy will appoints
  There are no bonds for me;
For my inmost heart is taught the Truth
  That makes Thy children free;
And a life of self-renouncing love
  Is a life of liberty.
Anna Lætitia Waring. 1850—1860.

CXCIX.

Psalm CXXXI.

Quiet, Lord, my froward heart,
  Make me teachable and mild,
Upright, simple, free from art,
  Make me as a weanèd child,
From distrust and envy free,
Pleased with all that pleases Thee.

"*Thy Will be done.*"

What Thou shalt to-day provide,
    Let me as a child receive;
What to-morrow may betide
    Calmly to thy wisdom leave:
'Tis enough that Thou wilt care;
Why should I the burden bear?

As a little child relies
    On a care beyond his own,
Knows he's neither strong nor wise,
    Fears to stir a step alone;
Let me thus with Thee abide,
As my Father, Guard, and Guide.

Thus, preserv'd from Satan's wiles,
    Safe from dangers, free from fears,
May I live upon Thy smiles
    Till the promised hour appears,
When the sons of God shall prove
All their Father's boundless love!
John Newton. 1779.

CC.
Psalm CXXXI.

Jesus, cast a look on me;
Give me sweet simplicity,
Make me poor and keep me low,
Seeking only Thee to know.

Weanèd from my lordly self
Weanèd from the miser's pelf,
Weanèd from the scorner's ways,
Weanèd from the lust of praise.

All that feeds my busy pride,
Cast it evermore aside;
Bid my will to Thine submit;
Lay me humbly at Thy feet.

Make me like a little child,
Of my strength and wisdom spoil'd,
Seeing only in Thy light,
Walking only in Thy might,

Leaning on Thy loving breast,
Where a weary soul may rest;
Feeling well the peace of God
Flowing from Thy precious Blood!

In this posture let me live,
And hosannas daily give;
In this temper let me die,
And hosannas ever cry!
John Berridge. 1785.

CCI.

Lord, I feel a carnal mind
  That hangs about me still,
Vainly though I strive to bind
  My own rebellious will;
Is not haughtiness of heart
The gulph between my God and me?
Meek Redeemer! now impart
  Thine own humility!

"Thy Will be done."

Fain would I my Lord pursúe,
  Be all my Saviour taught,
Do as Jesus bade me do,
  And think as Jesus thought:
But 'tis Thou must change my heart;
The perfect gift must come from Thee;
  Meek Redeemer! now impart
    Thine own humility!

Lord, I cannot, must not rest,
  Till I Thy mind obtain,
Chase presumption from my breast,
  And all Thy mildness gain:
Give me, Lord, Thy gentle heart;
Thy lowly mind my portion be:
  Meek Redeemer! now impart
    Thine own humility!

Let Thy cross my will control;
  Conform me to my Guide!
In the manger lay my soul,
  And crucify my pride!
Give me, Lord, a contrite heart,
An heart that always looks to Thee:
  Meek Redeemer! now impart
    Thine own humility!

Tear away my every boast;
  My stubborn mind abase;
Saviour, fix my only trust
  In Thy redeeming grace!
Give me a submissive heart,
From pride and self-dependence free;
  Meek Redeemer! now impart
    Thine own humility!
      Augustus Montague Toplady. 1759.

CCII.

Gracious Spirit, dwell with me;
I myself would gracious be,
And with words that help and heal
Would Thy life in mine reveal,
And with actions bold and meek
Would for Christ my Saviour speak.

Truthful Spirit, dwell with me;
I myself would truthful be,
And with wisdom kind and clear
Let Thy life in mine appear,
And with actions brotherly
Speak my Lord's sincerity.

Tender Spirit, dwell with me;
I myself would tender be,
Shut my heart up like a flower
At temptation's darksome hour,
Open it when shines the sun,
And His love by fragrance own.

Silent Spirit, dwell with me;
I myself would quiet be,
Quiet as the growing blade
Which through earth its way has made,
Silently, like morning light,
Putting mists and chills to flight.

Mighty Spirit, dwell with me;
I myself would mighty be,
Mighty so as to prevail
Where unaided man must fail,
Ever by a mighty hope
Pressing on and bearing up.

Holy Spirit, dwell with me;
I myself would holy be;
Separate from sin, I would
Choose and cherish all things good,
And whatever I can be
Give to Him, who gave me Thee!

    Thomas Toke Lynch. 1855.

CCIII.

MATT. V. 3—10.

There is a dwelling-place above;
Thither, to meet the God of love,
  The poor in spirit go;
There is a paradise of rest;
For contrite hearts and souls distrest
  Its streams of comfort flow.

There is a goodly heritage,
Where earthly passions cease to rage;
  The meek that haven gain:
There is a board, where they who pine,
Hungry, athirst, for grace divine,
  May feast, nor crave again.

There is a voice to mercy true;
To them who mercy's path pursue
  That voice shall bliss impart;
There is a sight from man concealed;
That sight, the face of God revealed;
  Shall bless the pure in heart.

There is a name, in heaven bestow'd;
That name, which hails them sons of God,
    The friends of peace shall know:
There is a kingdom in the sky,
Where they shall reign with God on high,
    Who serve Him best below.

Lord! be it mine like them to choose
The better part, like them to use
    The means Thy love hath given!
Be holiness my aim on earth,
That death be welcomed as a birth
    To life and bliss in Heaven!
          Bishop Richard Mant. 1831.

CCIV.

MATTHEW V. 3—10.

Blest are the humble souls that see
Their emptiness and poverty;
Treasures of grace to them are given,
And crowns of joy laid up in Heaven.

Blest are the men of broken heart
Who mourn for sin with inward smart;
The Blood of Christ divinely flows,
A healing balm for all their woes.

Blest are the meek, who stand afar
From rage and passion, noise and war;
God will secure their happy state,
And plead their cause against the great.

"Thy Will be done."

Blest are the souls that thirst for grace,
Hunger and long for righteousness;
They shall be well supplied and fed
With living streams and living bread.

Blest are the men whose bowels move
And melt with sympathy and love;
From Christ the Lord shall they obtain
Like sympathy and love again.

Blest are the pure, whose hearts are clean
From the defiling power of sin;
With endless pleasure they shall see
A God of spotless purity.

Blest are the men of peaceful life,
Who quench the coals of growing strife;
They shall be call'd the heirs of bliss,
The sons of God, the God of peace.

Blest are the sufferers, who partake
Of pain and shame for Jesus' sake;
Their souls shall triumph in the Lord,
Glory and joy are their reward.
Isaac Watts. 1709.

IV.

"GIVE US THIS DAY OUR DAILY BREAD."

CCV.

Lord of my life, whose tender care
    Hath led me on till now,
Here lowly at the hour of prayer
    Before Thy throne I bow;
I bless Thy gracious hand, and pray
Forgiveness for another day.

Oh! may I daily, hourly, strive
    In heavenly grace to grow;
To Thee and to Thy glory live,
    Dead else to all below;
Tread in the path my Saviour trod,
Though thorny, yet the path to God!

With prayer my humble praise I bring
    For mercies day by day;
Lord, teach my heart Thy love to sing,
    Lord, teach me how to pray!
All that I have, I am, to Thee
I offer through Eternity!

Anon. [1853.]

CCVI.

Lord, in the day Thou art about
    The paths wherein I tread;
And in the night, when I lie down,
    Thou art about my bed.

While others in God's prisons lie,
   Bound with affliction's chain,
I walk at large, secure and free
   From sickness and from pain.

'Tis Thou dost crown my hopes and plans
   With good success each day;
This crown, together with myself,
   At Thy blest feet I lay.

O let my house a temple be,
   That I and mine may sing
Hosanna to Thy Majesty,
   And praise our heavenly King!
Cento by John Hampden Gurney. 1851.
From John Mason. 1683.

CCVII.

Shine on our souls, eternal God,
   With rays of beauty shine!
O let Thy favour crown our days,
   And all their round be thine!

Did we not raise our hands to Thee,
   Our hands might toil in vain;
Small joy success itself could give,
   If Thou Thy love restrain.

With Thee let every week begin,
   With Thee each day be spent;
For Thee each fleeting hour improv'd,
   Since each by Thee is lent.

Thus cheer us through this desert road,
  Till all our labours cease,
And Heaven refresh our weary souls
  With everlasting peace!

Philip Doddridge. 1755.

CCVIII.

O how kindly hast Thou led me,
  Heavenly Father, day by day!
Found my dwelling, clothed and fed me,
  Furnish'd friends to cheer my way!
Didst Thou bless me, didst Thou chasten,
  With Thy smile, or with Thy rod,
'Twas that still my step might hasten
  Homeward, heavenward, to my God!

O how slowly have I often
  Follow'd where Thy hand would draw!
How Thy kindness fail'd to soften!
  How Thy chastening fail'd to awe!
Make me for Thy rest more ready
  As Thy path is longer trod;
Keep me in Thy friendship steady,
  Till Thou call me home, my God!

Thomas Grinfield. 1836.

CCIX.

Heavenly Father, to Whose eye
Future things unfolded lie,
Through the desert where I stray,
Let Thy counsels guide my way.

"Give us this day our Daily Bread."

Lord, uphold me day by day;
Shed a light upon my way;
Guide me through perplexing snares;
Care for me in all my cares.

All I ask for is, enough;
Only, when the way is rough,
Let Thy rod and staff impart
Strength and courage to my heart.

Should Thy wisdom, Lord, decree
Trials long and sharp for me,
Pain or sorrow, care or shame,
Father! glorify Thy Name!

Let me neither faint nor fear,
Feeling still that Thou art near,
In the course my Saviour trod,
Tending still to Thee, my God.
Josiah Conder. 1856.

CCX.

Sovereign Ruler of the skies,
Ever gracious, ever wise,
All my times are in Thy hand,
All events at Thy command.

His decree, who form'd the earth,
Fix'd my first and second birth;
Parents, native place, and time,
All appointed were by Him.

The Book of Praise.

He that form'd me in the womb,
He shall guide me to the tomb;
All my times shall ever be
Order'd by His wise decree.

Times of sickness, times of health,
Times of penury and wealth;
Times of trial and of grief,
Times of triumph and relief.

Times the Tempter's power to prove,
Times to taste a Saviour's love;
All must come, and last, and end,
As shall please my heavenly Friend.

Plagues and deaths around me fly;
Till He bids, I cannot die:
Not a single shaft can hit
Till the God of love sees fit.

O Thou Gracious, Wise, and Just!
In Thy hands my life I trust:
Have I something dearer still?
I resign it to Thy will.

May I always own Thy hand;
Still to the surrender stand;
Know, that Thou art God alone;
I and mine are all Thy own.

Thee at all times will I bless;
Having Thee, I all possess;
How can I bereavèd be,
Since I cannot part with Thee?

John Ryland. 1777.

CCXI.

O Lord, I would delight in Thee,
   And on Thy care depend;
To Thee in every trouble flee,
   My best, my only Friend.

When all created streams are dried,
   Thy fulness is the same;
May I with this be satisfied,
   And glory in Thy Name!

Why should the soul a drop bemoan,
   Who has a fountain near;
A fountain, which will ever run
   With waters sweet and clear?

No good in creatures can be found,
   But may be found in Thee;
I must have all things, and abound,
   While God is God to me.

Oh! that I had a stronger faith,
   To look within the veil!
To credit what my Saviour saith,
   Whose word can never fail!

He that has made my heaven secure,
   Will here all good provide;
While Christ is rich, can I be poor?
   What can I want beside?

O Lord, I cast my care on Thee;
   I triumph and adore:
Henceforth my great concern shall be
   To love and please Thee more.

John Ryland. 1777.

CCXII.

How gentle God's commands,
　How kind His precepts are!
Come, cast your burdens on the Lord,
　And trust His constant care.

While Providence supports,
　Let saints securely dwell;
That Hand, which bears all Nature up,
　Shall guide His children well.

Why should this anxious load
　Press down your weary mind?
Haste to your heavenly Father's throne,
　And sweet refreshment find.

His goodness stands approved
　Down to the present day:
I'll drop my burden at His feet,
　And bear a song away.
　　　　　　Philip Doddridge. 1755.

CCXIII.

O God of Bethel, by whose hand
　Thy people still are fed,
Who through this weary pilgrimage
　Hast all our fathers led;

Our vows, our prayers, we now present
　Before Thy throne of grace;
God of our fathers! be the God
　Of their succeeding race.

Through each perplexing path of life
   Our wandering footsteps guide ;
Give us each day our daily bread,
   And raiment fit provide.

O spread Thy covering wings around
   Till all our wanderings cease,
And at our Father's loved abode
   Our souls arrive in peace !

Such blessings from Thy gracious hand
   Our humble prayers implore ;
And Thou shalt be our chosen God,
   And portion evermore.
              Variation by John Logan. 1770.
              From Philip Doddridge. 1755.

CCXIV.

O King of earth, and air, and sea !
The hungry ravens cry to Thee ;
To Thee the scaly tribes, that sweep
The bosom of the boundless deep :
To Thee the lions roaring call ;
The common Father, kind to all :
Then grant Thy servants, Lord, we pray,
Our daily bread from day to day.

The fishes may for food complain,
The ravens spread their wings in vain,
The roaring lions lack and pine ;
But, God, Thou carest still for Thine :
Thy bounteous hand with food can bless
The bleak and lonely wilderness ;
And Thou hast taught us, Lord, to pray
For daily bread from day to day.

And oh! when through the wilds we roam
That part us from our heavenly home;
When, lost in danger, want, and woe,
Our faithless tears begin to flow;
Do Thou the gracious comfort give,
By which alone the soul may live;
And grant Thy servants, Lord, we pray,
The bread of life from day to day!

Bishop Reginald Heber. 1827.

CCXV.

Jesus, the Shepherd of the sheep,
Thy little flock in safety keep,
The flock for which Thou cam'st from Heaven,
The flock for which Thy life was given.

Thou saw'st them wandering far from Thee
Secure, as if from danger free;
Thy love did all their wanderings trace,
And brought them to a wealthy place.

O guard Thy sheep from beasts of prey,
And guide them that they never stray;
Cherish the young, sustain the old,
Let none be feeble in Thy fold!

Secure them from the scorching beam,
And lead them to the living stream;
In verdant pastures let them lie,
And watch them with a Shepherd's eye!

Oh, may Thy sheep discern Thy voice,
And in its sacred sound rejoice;
From strangers may they ever flee,
And know no other guide but Thee!

Lord, bring Thy sheep that wander yet,
And let the number be complete:
Then let Thy flock from earth remove,
And occupy the fold above.
Thomas Kelly. 1804-1836.

CCXVI.
Psalm XXIII.

The Lord my pasture shall prepare,
And feed me with a Shepherd's care;
His presence shall my wants supply,
And guard me with a watchful eye;
My noon-day walks He shall attend,
And all my midnight hours defend.

When in the sultry glebe I faint,
Or on the thirsty mountain pant,
To fertile vales and dewy meads
My weary, wandering steps He leads,
Where peaceful rivers, soft and slow,
Amid the verdant landscape flow.

Though in the paths of death I tread,
With gloomy horrors overspread,
My stedfast heart shall fear no ill,
For Thou, O Lord, art with me still;
Thy friendly crook shall give me aid,
And guide me through the dreadful shade.

Though in a bare and rugged way,
Through devious lonely wilds I stray,
Thy bounty shall my wants beguile;
The barren wilderness shall smile
With sudden greens and herbage crown'd,
And streams shall murmur all around.
Joseph Addison. 1728.

CCXVII.
Psalm XXIII.

My Shepherd will supply my need,
   Jehovah is His Name ;
In pastures fresh He makes me feed
   Beside the living stream.

He brings my wandering spirit back
   When I forsake His ways,
And leads me, for His mercy's sake,
   In paths of truth and grace.

When I walk through the shades of death,
   Thy presence is my stay :
A word of Thy supporting breath
   Drives all my fears away.

Thy hand, in spite of all my foes,
   Doth still my table spread ;
My cup with blessings overflows,
   Thine oil anoints my head.

The sure provisions of my God
   Attend me all my days ;
O may Thy house be mine abode,
   And all my work be praise !

There would I find a settled rest,
   While others go and come ;
No more a stranger or a guest,
   But like a child at home.

                  Isaac Watts. 1719.

CCXVIII.
Psalm XXIII.

The Lord my Shepherd is,
  I shall be well supplied;
Since He is mine, and I am His,
  What can I want beside?

He leads me to the place
  Where heavenly pasture grows,
Where living waters gently pass,
  And full salvation flows.

If e'er I go astray,
  He doth my soul reclaim,
And guides me in His own right way
  For His most holy Name.

While He affords His aid,
  I cannot yield to fear;
Though I should walk through death's dark shade,
  My Shepherd's with me there.

In spite of all my foes
  Thou dost my table spread;
My cup with blessings overflows,
  And joy exalts my head.

The bounties of Thy love
  Shall crown my following days;
Nor from Thy house will I remove,
  Nor cease to speak Thy praise.

Isaac Watts. 1719.

V.

AND FORGIVE US OUR TRESPASSES.

"And forgive us our trespasses; as we forgive them that trespass against us."

CCXIX.

Approach, my soul, the mercy-seat
  Where Jesus answers prayer;
There humbly fall before His feet,
  For none can perish there.

Thy promise is my only plea,
  With this I venture nigh;
Thou callest burden'd souls to Thee,
  And such, O Lord, am I.

Bow'd down beneath a load of sin,
  By Satan sorely prest,
By war without, and fears within,
  I come to Thee for rest.

Be Thou my shield and hiding-place,
  That, shelter'd near Thy side,
I may my fierce accuser face,
  And tell him, Thou hast died!

O wondrous love! to bleed and die,
  To bear the cross and shame,
That guilty sinners, such as I,
  Might plead Thy gracious Name!

John Newton. 1779.

"*And forgive us our Trespasses.*"

CCXX.

Almighty God, Thy piercing eye
   Strikes through the shades of night;
And our most secret actions lie
   All open to Thy sight.

There's not a sin that we commit,
   Nor wicked word we say,
But in Thy dreadful book 'tis writ
   Against the judgment-day.

And must the crimes that I have done
   Be read and publish'd there,
Be all expos'd before the sun,
   While men and angels hear?

Lord! at Thy foot ashamed I lie,
   Upward I dare not look;
Pardon my sins before I die,
   And blot them from Thy book!

Remember all the dying pains
   That my Redeemer felt,
And let His Blood wash out my stains,
   And answer for my guilt!
              Isaac Watts. 1720.

CCXXI.

Mercy alone can meet my case;
   For mercy, Lord, I cry:
Jesus! Redeemer! show Thy face
   In mercy, or I die.

Save me, for none beside can save;
   At Thy command I tread
With failing step life's stormy wave;
   The wave goes o'er my head.

I perish, and my doom were just;
   But wilt Thou leave me? No:
I hold Thee fast, my hope, my trust;
   I will not let Thee go!

Still sure to me Thy promise stands,
   And ever must abide;
Behold it written on Thy hands,
   And graven in Thy side!

To this, this only, will I cleave;
   Thy word is all my plea;
Thy word is truth, and I believe:
   Have mercy, Lord, on me!
                James Montgomery. 1825.

CCXXII.

O Jesus, Saviour of the lost,
   My Rock and Hiding-place,
By storms of sin and sorrow tost,
   I seek Thy sheltering grace.

Guilty, forgive me, Lord! I cry;
   Pursued by foes I come;
A sinner, save me, or I die;
   An outcast, take me home.

Once safe in Thine almighty arms,
   Let storms come on amain;
There danger never, never harms;
   There death itself is gain.

And when I stand before Thy throne,
   And all Thy glory see,
Still be my righteousness alone
   To hide myself in Thee.
        Edward Henry Bickersteth. 1858.

CCXXIII.

When at Thy footstool, Lord, I bend,
   And plead with Thee for mercy there,
Think of the sinner's dying friend,
   And for His sake receive my prayer.

O think not of my shame and guilt,
   My thousand stains of deepest dye;
Think of the blood which Jesus spilt,
   And let that blood my pardon buy.

Think, Lord, how I am still Thy own,
   The trembling creature of Thy hand;
Think how my heart to sin is prone,
   And what temptations round me stand.

O think upon Thy holy word,
   And every plighted promise there;
How prayer should evermore be heard,
   And how Thy glory is to spare.

O think not of my doubts and fears,
   My strivings with Thy grace Divine:
Think upon Jesus' woes and tears,
   And let His merits stand for mine.

Thine eye, Thine ear, they are not dull;
   Thine arm can never shorten'd be;
Behold me here; my heart is full;
   Behold, and spare, and succour me!
        Henry Francis Lyte. 1833.

CCXXIV.

As o'er the past my memory strays,
   Why heaves the secret sigh?
'Tis that I mourn departed days,
   Still unprepared to die.

The world, and worldly things beloved,
   My anxious thoughts employed,
And time unhallow'd, unimproved,
   Presents a fearful void.

Yet, holy Father, wild despair
   Chase from my labouring breast!
Thy grace it is, which prompts the prayer;
   That grace can do the rest.

My life's brief remnant all be Thine!
   And, when Thy sure decree
Bids me this fleeting breath resign,
   O, speed my soul to Thee!
Bishop Thomas Fanshaw Middleton. [1831

CCXXV.

Forth from the dark and stormy sky,
Lord! to Thine altar's shade we fly:
Forth from the world, its hope and fear,
Saviour! we seek Thy shelter here:
Weary and weak, Thy grace we pray:
Turn not, O Lord, Thy guests away!

Long have we roam'd in want and pain;
Long have we sought Thy rest in vain;
Wilder'd in doubt, in darkness lost,
Long have our souls been tempest-tost:
Low at Thy feet our sins we lay;
Turn not, O Lord, Thy guests away!
          Bishop Reginald Heber. 1827.

CCXXVI.

O Lord, turn not Thy face away
   From them that lowly lie,
Lamenting sore their sinful life
   With tears and bitter cry;
Thy mercy-gates are open wide
   To them that mourn their sin;
O shut them not against us, Lord,
   But let us enter in.

We need not to confess our fault,
   For surely Thou canst tell;
What we have done, and what we are,
   Thou knowest very well;
Wherefore, to beg and to entreat,
   With tears we come to Thee,
As children that have done amiss
   Fall at their father's knee.

And need we then, O Lord, repeat
   The blessing which we crave,
When Thou dost know, before we speak,
   The thing that we would have?
Mercy, O Lord, mercy we ask,
   This is the total sum;
For mercy, Lord, is all our prayer;
   O let Thy mercy come!

   Variation by Bishop Reginald Heber. 1827.
        From John Mardley. 1562.

VI.

"AND LEAD US NOT INTO TEMPTATION; BUT DELIVER US FROM EVIL."

CCXXVII.

Lead us, heavenly Father, lead us
  O'er the world's tempestuous sea;
Guard us, guide us, keep us, feed us,
  For we have no help but Thee;
    Yet possessing
    Every blessing,
If our God our Father be.

Saviour, breathe forgiveness o'er us;
  All our weakness Thou dost know;
Thou didst tread this earth before us,
  Thou didst feel its keenest woe;
    Lone and dreary,
    Faint and weary,
Through the desert Thou didst go.

Spirit of our God, descending,
  Fill our hearts with heavenly joy;
Love with every passion blending,
  Pleasure that can never cloy:
    Thus provided,
    Pardon'd, guided,
Nothing can our peace destroy.

James Edmeston. 1820.

CCXXVIII.

Jesu! guide our way
To eternal day!
So shall we, no more delaying,
Follow Thee, Thy voice obeying;
   Lead us by Thy hand
   To our Father's land!

When we danger meet,
Stedfast make our feet!
Lord, preserve us uncomplaining
'Mid the darkness round us reigning!
   Through adversity
   Lies our way to Thee.

Order all our way
Through this mortal day;
In our toil with aid be near us;
In our need with succour cheer us;
   When life's course is o'er,
   Open Thou the door!

Arthur Tozer Russell. 1851.
From Louis, Count Zinzendorf.

CCXXIX.

Star of morn and even,
Sun of Heaven's heaven,
   Saviour high and dear,
   Toward us turn Thine ear;
   Through whate'er may come,
   Thou canst lead us home.

Though the gloom be grievous,
Those we leant on leave us,
  Though the coward heart
  Quit its proper part,
  Though the Tempter come,
  Thou wilt lead us home.

Saviour pure and holy,
Lover of the lowly,
  Sign us with Thy sign,
  Take our hands in Thine,
  Take our hands and come,
  Lead Thy children home!

Star of morn and even,
Shine on us from Heaven,
  From Thy glory-throne
  Hear Thy very own!
  Lord and Saviour, come,
  Lead us to our home!
        Francis Turner Palgrave. 1862.

CCXXX.

O Thou, to whose all-searching sight
The darkness shineth as the light,
Search, prove my heart; it pants for Thee;
O, burst these bands, and set it free!

Wash out its stains, refine its dross;
Nail my affections to the cross;
Hallow each thought; let all within
Be clean, as Thou, my Lord, art clean.

If in this darksome wild I stray,
Be Thou my Light, be Thou my Way;
No foes, no violence I fear,
No fraud, while Thou, my God, art near.

When rising floods my soul o'erflow,
When sinks my heart in waves of woe,
Jesu, Thy timely aid impart,
And raise my head, and cheer my heart.

Saviour! where'er Thy steps I see,
Dauntless, untired, I follow Thee:
O let Thy hand support me still,
And lead me to Thy holy hill!

If rough and thorny be the way,
My strength proportion to my day;
Till toil, and grief, and pain shall cease
Where all is calm and joy and peace.
    John Wesley. 1739—1743.
     From the German.

CCXXXI.

Guide me, O Thou great Jehovah!
 Pilgrim through this barren land;
I am weak, but Thou art mighty;
 Hold me with Thy powerful hand!
  Bread of Heaven! Bread of Heaven!
Feed me now and evermore!

Open now the crystal Fountain,
 Whence the healing streams do flow;
Let the fiery cloudy pillar
 Lead me all my journey through;
  Strong Deliverer! Strong Deliverer!
Be Thou still my Strength and Shield!

When I tread the verge of Jordan,
   Bid my anxious fears subside;
Death of death, and Hell's Destruction,
   Land me safe on Canaan's side;
     Songs of praises, Songs of praises,
I will ever give to Thee!
William Williams. 1774.

CCXXXII.

Jesus! lead us with Thy power
   Safe unto the promised Rest;
Hide our souls within Thy bosom;
   Let us slumber on Thy breast;
Feed us with the heavenly manna,
   Bread that angels eat above;
Let us drink from the holy Fountain
   Draughts of everlasting Love!

Throughout the desert wild conduct us
   With a glorious pillar bright,
In the day a cooling comfort,
   And a cheering fire by night;
Be our guide in every peril,
   Watch us hourly night and day;
Otherwise we'll err and wander
   From Thy Spirit far away.

In Thy Presence we are happy;
   In Thy Presence we're secure;
In Thy Presence all afflictions
   We will easily endure;
In Thy Presence we can conquer,
   We can suffer, we can die;
Far from Thee, we faint and languish:
   Lord, our Saviour, keep us nigh!
William Williams. 1772.

CCXXXIII.

PSALM CXXI.

Up to the hills I lift mine eyes,
The eternal hills beyond the skies;
Thence all her help my soul derives,
There my Almighty Refuge lives.

He lives, the everlasting God,
That built the world, that spread the flood;
The heavens with all their hosts He made,
And the dark regions of the dead.

He guides our feet, He guards our way;
His morning smiles bless all the day;
He spreads the evening veil, and keeps
The silent hours while Israel sleeps.

Israel, a name divinely blest,
May rise secure, securely rest;
Thy holy Guardian's wakeful eyes
Admit no slumber nor surprise.

No sun shall smite thy head by day,
Nor the pale moon with sickly ray
Shall blast thy couch; no baleful star
Dart his malignant fire so far.

Should earth and hell with malice burn,
Still thou shalt go, and still return,
Safe in the Lord; His heavenly care
Defends thy life from every snare.

On thee foul spirits have no power;
And, in thy last departing hour,
Angels, that trace the airy road,
Shall bear thee homeward to thy God.

Isaac Watts. 1719.

CCXXXIV.
Psalm CXXI.

To Heaven I lift mine eye,
  To Heaven, Jehovah's throne,
For there my Saviour sits on high,
And thence shall strength and aid supply
  To all He calls His own.

He will not faint nor fail,
  Nor cause thy feet to stray:
For Him no weary hours assail,
Nor evening darkness spreads her veil
  O'er His eternal day.

Beneath that light divine
  Securely shalt thou move;
The sun with milder beams shall shine,
And eve's still queen her lamp incline
  Benignant from above.

For He, thy God and Friend,
  Shall keep thy soul from harm,
In each sad scene of doubt attend,
And guide thy life, and bless thine end,
  With His Almighty arm.

John Bowdler. 1814.

CCXXXV.
Psalm XI.

My trust is in the Lord,
  What foe can injure me?
Why bid me like a bird
  Before the fowler flee?
The Lord is on His heavenly throne,
And He will shield and save His own.

"*But deliver us from Evil.*"

 The wicked may assail,
 The Tempter sorely try,
 All earth's foundations fail,
 All nature's springs be dry;
Yet God is in His holy shrine,
And I am strong while He is mine.

 His flock to Him is dear,
 He watches them from high;
 He sends them trials here
 To form them for the sky;
But safely will He tend and keep
The humblest, feeblest, of His sheep.

 His foes a season here
 May triumph and prevail;
 But ah! the hour is near
 When all their hopes must fail;
While, like the sun, His saints shall rise,
And shine with Him above the skies.
Henry Francis Lyte. 1834.

CCXXXVI.

Psalm XLVI.

God is our Refuge, tried and proved,
 Amid a stormy world;
We will not fear, though earth be moved,
 And hills in ocean hurled.

The waves may roar, the mountains shake,
 Our comforts shall not cease;
The Lord His saints will not forsake,
 The Lord will give us peace.

A gentle stream of hope and love
    To us shall ever flow;
It issues from His throne above,
    It cheers His Church below.

When earth and hell against us came,
    He spake, and quell'd their powers;
The Lord of hosts is still the same;
    The God of grace is ours.
Henry Francis Lyte. 1834

CCXXXVII.

PSALM XCI.

There is a safe and secret place
    Beneath the wings divine,
Reserved for all the heirs of grace;
    O, be that refuge mine!

The least and feeblest there may bide,
    Uninjured and unawed;
While thousands fall on every side,
    He rests secure in God.

The angels watch him on his way,
    And aid with friendly arm;
And Satan, roaring for His prey,
    May hate, but cannot harm.

He feeds in pastures large and fair
    Of love and truth divine:
O child of God, O glory's heir,
    How rich a lot is thine!

A hand Almighty to defend,
   An ear for every call,
An honour'd life, a peaceful end,
   And Heaven to crown it all!
               Henry Francis Lyte. 1834.

CCXXXVIII.

Oh help us, Lord! each hour of need,
   Thy heavenly succour give;
Help us in thought, and word, and deed,
   Each hour on earth we live!

Oh, help us when our spirits bleed
   With contrite anguish sore;
And when our hearts are cold and dead,
   Oh, help us, Lord, the more!

Oh, help us, through the prayer of faith,
   More firmly to believe;
For still, the more the servant hath,
   The more shall he receive.

If strangers to Thy fold we call,
   Imploring at Thy feet
The crumbs that from Thy table fall,
   'Tis all we dare entreat.

But be it, Lord of mercy, all,
   So Thou wilt grant but this:
The crumbs that from Thy table fall
   Are light, and life, and bliss.

Oh, help us, Jesus, from on high !
  We know no help but Thee :
Oh, help us so to live and die,
  As Thine in Heaven to be !

Henry Hart Milman. 1827.

CCXXXIX.

O Thou, from whom all goodness flows,
  I lift my heart to Thee ;
In all my sorrows, conflicts, woes,
  Dear Lord, remember me !

When groaning on my burden'd heart
  My sins lie heavily,
My pardon speak, new peace impart,
  In love remember me !

Temptations sore obstruct my way ;
  And ills I cannot flee :
Oh, give me strength, Lord, as my day ;
  For good remember me !

Distrest in pain, disease, and grief,
  This feeble body see !
Grant patience, rest, and kind relief ;
  Hear, and remember me !

If on my face, for Thy dear Name,
  Shame and reproaches be ;
All hail reproach, and welcome shame,
  If Thou remember me !

"*But deliver us from Evil.*"

The hour is near; consign'd to death
   I own the just decree:
"Saviour!" with my last parting breath,
   I'll cry, "Remember me!"
Thomas Haweis. 1792.

CCXL.

Jesu, lover of my soul,
   Let me to Thy bosom fly,
While the nearer waters roll,
   While the tempest still is high!
Hide me, O my Saviour, hide,
   Till the storm of life is past,
Safe into the haven guide;
   O receive my soul at last!

Other refuge have I none;
   Hangs my helpless soul on Thee;
Leave, ah! leave me not alone,
   Still support and comfort me!
All my trust on Thee is stay'd,
   All my help from Thee I bring:
Cover my defenceless head
   With the shadow of Thy wing!

Wilt Thou not regard my call?
   Wilt Thou not accept my prayer?
Lo! I sink, I faint, I fall!
   Lo! on Thee I cast my care!
Reach me out Thy gracious hand!
   While I of Thy strength receive,
Hoping against hope I stand,
   Dying, and behold I live!

Thou, O Christ, art all I want;
  More than all in Thee I find:
Raise the fallen, cheer the faint,
  Heal the sick, and lead the blind!
Just and holy is Thy Name;
  I am all unrighteousness;
False and full of sin I am,
  Thou art full of truth and grace.

Plenteous grace with Thee is found,
  Grace to cover all my sin;
Let the healing streams abound;
  Make and keep me pure within!
Thou of Life the Fountain art,
  Freely let me take of Thee;
Spring Thou up within my heart!
  Rise to all eternity!

Charles Wesley. 1740.

CCXLI.

Now may He, who from the dead
  Brought the Shepherd of the sheep,
Jesus Christ, our King and Head,
  All our souls in safety keep!

May He teach us to fulfil
  What is pleasing in His sight,
Perfect us in all His will,
  And preserve us day and night!

To that dear Redeemer's praise
  Who the covenant seal'd with blood,
Let our hearts and voices raise
  Loud thanksgivings to our God!

John Newton. 1779.

CCXLII.

O most merciful,
O most bountiful,
God the Father Almighty!
By the Redeemer's
Sweet intercession,
Hear us, help us, when we cry!

Bishop Reginald Heber. 1827.

VII.

FOR THINE IS THE KINGDOM, THE POWER,
AND THE GLORY, FOR EVER AND EVER.
AMEN."

CCXLIII.

Now to Him, who loved us, gave us
  Every pledge that love could give,
Freely shed His Blood to save us,
  Gave His life that we might live:
Be the kingdom, and dominion,
  And the glory, evermore!

Variation. [1851.]
From Samuel Miller Waring. 1827.

CCXLIV.

Worship, honour, glory, blessing,
  Be to Him who reigns above!
Young and old Thy Name confessing,
  Saviour! let us share Thy love!
As the saints in Heaven adore Thee,
  We would bow before Thy throne;
As Thine angels bow before Thee,
  So on earth Thy will be done!

Anon. [1851.]

CCXLV.

Psalm CXVII.

From all that dwell below the skies
Let the Creator's praise arise ;
Let the Redeemer's Name be sung
Through every land, by every tongue !

Eternal are Thy mercies, Lord !
Eternal truth attends Thy word :
Thy praise shall sound from shore to shore.
Till suns shall rise and set no more.
Isaac Watts. 1719.

END OF PART II.

PART III.

HYMNS FOR NATURAL AND SACRED SEASONS.

The Book of Praise.

PART THE THIRD.

HYMNS FOR NATURAL AND SACRED SEASONS.

I.

DAY AND NIGHT.

CCXLVI.

Morning.

Awake, my soul, and with the sun
Thy daily stage of duty run;
Shake off dull sloth, and joyful rise
To pay Thy morning sacrifice.

Thy precious time mis-spent redeem;
Each present day thy last esteem;
Improve thy talent with due care;
For the great day thyself prepare.

In conversation be sincere;
Keep conscience as the noontide clear;
Think how All-seeing God thy ways
And all thy secret thoughts surveys.

By influence of the light divine
Let thy own light to others shine;
Reflect all Heaven's propitious rays,
In ardent love and cheerful praise.

Wake and lift up thyself, my heart,
And with the angels bear thy part,
Who, all night long, unwearied sing
High praise to the Eternal King.

Awake! awake! Ye heavenly choir,
May your devotion me inspire,
That I, like you, my age may spend,
Like you may on my God attend!

May I, like you, in God delight,
Have all day long my God in sight,
Perform like you my Maker's will!
O may I never more do ill!

Had I your wings, to Heaven I'd fly;
But God shall that defect supply;
And my soul, wing'd with warm desire,
Shall all day long to Heaven aspire.

All praise to Thee, who safe hast kept,
And hast refresh'd me whilst I slept!
Grant, Lord, when I from death shall wake,
I may of endless light partake!

I would not wake, nor rise again,
Ev'n Heaven itself I would disdain,
Wert Thou not there to be enjoy'd,
And I in hymns to be employ'd!

Heaven is, dear Lord, where'er Thou art;
O never then from me depart!
For, to my soul, 'tis hell to be
But for one moment void of Thee.

Lord, I my vows to Thee renew;
Disperse my sins as morning dew;

Guard my first springs of thought and will,
And with Thyself my spirit fill.

Direct, control, suggest, this day,
All I design, or do, or say ;
That all my powers, with all their might,
In Thy sole glory may unite.

Praise God, from whom all blessings flow ;
Praise Him, all creatures here below !
Praise Him above, ye heavenly host ;
Praise Father, Son and Holy Ghost !
    Bishop Thomas Ken. 1700.

CCXLVII.

Morning.

God of the morning, at whose voice
 The cheerful sun makes haste to rise,
And like a giant doth rejoice
 To run his journey through the skies ;

From the fair chambers of the east
 The circuit of his race begins ;
And, without weariness or rest,
 Round the whole earth he flies and shines :

O, like the sun, may I fulfil
 Th' appointed duties of the day,
With ready mind and active will
 March on, and keep my heavenly way !

But I shall rove and lose the race,
 If God, my sun, should disappear,
And leave me in this world's wide maze
 To follow every wandering star.

Lord! Thy commands are clean and pure,
    Enlightening our beclouded eyes;
Thy threatenings just, Thy promise sure;
    Thy Gospel makes the simple wise.

Give me Thy counsel for my guide,
    And then receive me to Thy bliss:
All my desires and hopes beside
    Are faint and cold, compared with this!

Isaac Watts. 1719.

CCXLVIII.

Morning.

O timely happy, timely wise,
Hearts that with rising morn arise!
Eyes that the beam celestial view,
Which evermore makes all things new!

New every morning is the love
Our wakening and uprising prove,
Through sleep and darkness safely brought,
Restored to life, and power, and thought.

New mercies, each returning day,
Hover around us while we pray;
New perils past, new sins forgiven,
New thoughts of God, new hopes of Heaven.

If, on our daily course, our mind
Be set to hallow all we find,
New treasures still, of countless price,
God will provide for sacrifice.

Old friends, old scenes, will lovelier be,
As more of Heaven in each we see;
Some softening gleam of love and prayer
Shall dawn on every cross and care.

Day and Night.

As for some dear familiar strain
Untired we ask, and ask again;
Ever, in its melodious store,
Finding a spell unheard before;

Such is the bliss of souls serene,
When they have sworn, and steadfast mean,
Counting the cost, in all t' espy
Their God, in all themselves deny.

O could we learn that sacrifice,
What lights would all around us rise!
How would our hearts with wisdom talk
Along life's dullest dreariest walk!

We need not bid, for cloister'd cell,
Our neighbour and our work farewell,
Nor strive to wind ourselves too high
For sinful man beneath the sky:

The trivial round, the common task,
Will furnish all we ought to ask;
Room to deny ourselves; a road
To bring us, daily, nearer God.

Seek we no more: content with these,
Let present rapture, comfort, ease,
As Heaven shall bid them, come and go;
The secret this of rest below.

Only, O Lord, in Thy dear love
Fit us for perfect rest above;
And help us, this and every day,
To live more nearly as we pray!

John Keble. 1827.

CCXLIX.

Morning.

Since Thou hast added now, O God!
    Unto my life another day,
And giv'st me leave to walk abroad,
    And labour in my lawful way;
My walks and works with me begin,
Conduct me forth, and bring me in.

In every power my soul enjoys
    Internal virtues to improve;
In every sense that she employs
    In her external works to move;
Bless her, O God! and keep me sound
From outward harm and inward wound.

Let sin nor Satan's fraud prevail
    To make mine eye of reason blind,
Or faith, or hope, or love to fail,
    Or any virtues of the mind;
But more and more let them increase,
And bring me to mine end in peace.

Lewd courses let my feet forbear;
    Keep Thou my hands from doing wrong;
Let not ill counsels pierce mine ear,
    Nor wicked words defile my tongue;
And keep the windows of each eye
That no strange lust climb in thereby.

But guard Thou safe my heart in chief;
    That neither hate, revenge, nor fear,
Nor vain desire, vain joy, or grief,
    Obtain command or dwelling there:
And, Lord! with every saving grace,
Still true to Thee maintain that place!

So till the evening of this morn
  My time shall then so well be spent,
That when the twilight shall return
  I may enjoy it with content,
And to Thy praise and honour say,
That this hath proved a happy day.
George Wither. 1641.

CCL.

Morning.

Christ, whose glory fills the skies,
  Christ, the true, the only Light,
Sun of Righteousness, arise,
  Triumph o'er the shades of night!
Day-spring from on high, be near!
Day-star, in my heart appear!

Dark and cheerless is the morn
  Unaccompanied by Thee;
Joyless is the day's return,
  Till Thy mercy's beams I see;
Till they inward light impart,
Glad my eyes, and warm my heart.

Visit then this soul of mine,
  Pierce the gloom of sin and grief!
Fill me, Radiancy Divine,
  Scatter all my unbelief!
More and more Thyself display,
Shining to the perfect day!
Charles Wesley. 1740.

CCLI.

Morning.

"Splendor Paternæ Gloriæ."

O Jesu, Lord of heavenly grace,
Thou brightness of Thy Father's face,
Thou Fountain of eternal light,
Whose beams disperse the shades of night!

Come, holy Sun of heavenly love,
Shower down Thy radiance from above,
And to our inward hearts convey
The Holy Spirit's cloudless ray!

And we the Father's help will claim,
And sing the Father's glorious Name;
His powerful succour we implore,
That we may stand, to fall no more.

May He our actions deign to bless,
And loose the bonds of wickedness;
From sudden falls our feet defend,
And bring us to a prosperous end!

May faith, deep rooted in the soul,
Subdue our flesh, our minds control;
May guile depart, and discord cease,
And all within be joy and peace!

And Christ shall be our daily food,
Our daily drink His precious blood;
And thus the Spirit's calm excess
Shall fill our souls with holiness.

O hallowed be the approaching day!
Let meekness be our morning ray;
And faithful love our noonday light;
And hope our sunset, calm and bright!

O Christ! with each returning morn
Thine image to our hearts is borne:
O, may we ever clearly see
Our Saviour and our God in Thee!
John Chandler. 1837.
From St. Ambrose.

CCLII.

Morning.

Lord God of morning and of night,
We thank Thee for Thy gift of light:
As in the dawn the shadows fly,
We seem to find Thee now more nigh.

Fresh hopes have waken'd in our hearts,
Fresh energy to do our parts;
Thy thousand sleeps our strength restore,
A thousand fold to serve Thee more.

Yet whilst Thy will we would pursue,
Oft what we would we cannot do;
The sun may stand in zenith skies,
But on the soul thick midnight lies.

O Lord of lights! 'tis Thou alone
Canst make our darken'd hearts Thine own:
Though this new day with joy we see,
O Dawn of God! we cry for Thee!

Praise God, our Maker and our Friend!
Praise Him through time, till time shall end!
Till psalm and song His Name adore
Through Heaven's great day of Evermore!
Francis Turner Palgrave. 1862.

CCLIII.

Mid-day.

When at mid-day my task I ply
With labouring hand or watchful eye,
I need the timely aid of prayer
To guard my soul from worldly care.

Thou, Lord, didst consecrate this hour
To mind us of Thy saving power,
Thy living water's heavenly spell,
The mystery of Jacob's well.

There, about noon, with toil oppress'd,
Feebly Thy voice its plaint express'd,
"Give Me to drink!" O wondrous woe!
God thirsts, from whom all blessings flow!

He needed not, by whom we live,
And only ask'd, that He might give:
A mightier want He felt within;
The thirst to save a soul from sin.

Lord, in our pilgrimage of grace,
Thy weary footsteps oft we trace;
And in the inner man renew
The grief, Thy sacred body knew.

Our spirits faint upon the way,
We bear the burden of the day:
'Tis then for strength to Thee we turn,
Sit at Thy feet, and wisdom learn.

We ask of Thee, the gift of God,
Pure water from the vital flood,
To cure our feverish thirst of sin,
A well of water deep within.

Day and Night.

'Twas at mid-day, on blood intent,
Saul to Damascus raging went :
A light from heaven upon him came,
Putting that mid-day sun to shame.

The sudden glorious burst appals ;
Dash'd to the earth he headlong falls :
A Voice reproves ; a Form appears ;
Aghast he sees and trembling hears.

Now streams that light with mellow'd glow
Around our path, where'er we go ;
Inviting us at noon to raise
Our hearts to God in prayer and praise.

And calmly now we hear that word ;
It bids us rise and meet the Lord :
What hour He cometh, none can say ;
At dead of night, or at mid-day.

O ! rise thou then, and strive, my soul,
To reach the beatific goal !
Thy every nerve and sinew strain,
The crown of glory to obtain !

For see, in all this noon-tide heat,
How worldlings labour for the meat
That perishes and comes to nought,
Like shadow, when we think 'tis caught.

And wilt thou then refuse thy pains
For heaven's imperishable gains ?
Or canst thou grudge thy utmost toil
For treasures, none can steal or spoil ?

The sun has its meridian past;
Soon will its beams oblique be cast;
And twilight pale will rise t' enshroud
Their radiance in the western cloud.

Yet, for a time, 'tis bright and glad;
But coming night is dark and sad:
The day to man for toil was given;
And none at night can work for Heaven.

Sun of my soul, Thyself display!
Quicken me, Lord, and cheer my way!
Till, borne upon Thy healing wing,
Upward I soar Thy praise to sing.

E'en now, when far from Thy bless'd light,
At morn and eve, at noon and night,
I tune my heart betimes, to join,
Where angels in Thy presence shine.

Yet angels, in their loftiest song,
Fail in their flight, and do Thee wrong;
Like as their veil'd adoring face
Tells of a Glory, none can trace!

And now, my mid-day homage paid,
Life's busy path again I tread;
Yet happier far its task I ply
From surer trust that Thou art nigh;

Nigh to defend, assist, and bless,
Making my cares and dangers less;
And daily duteous toil the road,
That leads to perfect peace in God:

Peace, through the grace of Christ our Lord;
Rest, in the Father's love restor'd;
Joy, by the Spirit's union given;
The peace, the rest, the joy of Heaven!
James Ford. 1856.

CCLIV.

Evening.

The day, O Lord, is spent;
　Abide with us, and rest;
Our hearts' desires are fully bent
　On making Thee our guest.

We have not reach'd that land,
　That happy land, as yet,
Where holy angels round Thee stand,
　Whose sun can never set.

Our sun is sinking now;
　Our day is almost o'er:
O Sun of Righteousness, do Thou
　Shine on us evermore!
John Mason Neale. 1854.

CCLV.

Evening.

Behold the sun, that seem'd but now
　Enthronèd overhead,
Beginneth to decline below
　The globe whereon we tread;
And he, whom yet we look upon
　With comfort and delight,
Will quite depart from hence anon,
　And leave us to the night.

Thus time, unheeded, steals away
    The life which nature gave;
Thus are our bodies every day
    Declining to the grave:
Thus from us all our pleasures fly
    Whereon we set our heart;
And when the night of death draws nigh,
    Thus will they all depart.

Lord! though the sun forsake our sight,
    And mortal hopes are vain;
Let still Thine everlasting light
    Within our souls remain!
And in the nights of our distress
    Vouchsafe those rays divine,
Which from the Sun of Righteousness
    For ever brightly shine!
              George Wither. 1641.

CCLVI.

Evening.

Accept, my God, my evening song,
    Like incense let it fragrant rise;
Stir up my heart, and tune my tongue,
    And let the music reach the skies.

Thou hast my kind protector been
    Through all the dangers of the day;
My guardian to defend from sin,
    My guide to choose me out my way.

The flowing spring of all my good,
    Still pouring blessings from on high;
Thine hand hath dealt me out my food,
    For every want a kind supply.

Unceasing, Lord, Thy bounty flow'd;
  Each moment brought me in fresh aid;
But what returns of love to God
  Have I for all His kindness made?

What have I done for Him that died
  To save my soul from endless woe?
How much have I His patience tried
  From whom all my enjoyments flow!

Fast as my flying minutes pass,
  My faults augment the former sum!
Forgive the past, and by Thy grace
  Prevent the like for time to come!

Dear Saviour, to Thy cross I'll fly,
  And there my guilty head recline,
And my whole soul, that sin may die,
  Yield up to influence divine!

Then, sprinkled with atoning blood,
  I'll lay me down and take my rest,
Trust the protection of my God,
  And sleep as on my Saviour's breast.
            Variation from Isaac Watts. 1709.
                By Simon Browne. 1720.

CCLVII.

Evening.

All praise to Thee, my God, this night,
For all the blessings of the light;
Keep me, oh keep me, King of kings,
Beneath Thine own Almighty wings!

The Book of Praise.

Forgive me, Lord, for Thy dear Son,
The ill that I this day have done;
That with the world, myself, and Thee,
I, ere I sleep, at peace may be.

Teach me to live, that I may dread
The grave as little as my bed!
To die, that this vile body may
Rise glorious at the awful day!

O may my soul on Thee repose;
And may sweet sleep mine eyelids close;
Sleep, that may me more vig'rous make
To serve my God when I awake!

When in the night I sleepless lie,
My soul with heavenly thoughts supply!
Let no ill dreams disturb my rest,
No powers of darkness me molest!

Dull sleep, of sense me to deprive!
I am but half my time alive:
Thy faithful lovers, Lord, are griev'd
To lie so long of Thee bereav'd.

But though sleep o'er my frailty reigns,
Let it not hold me long in chains!
And now and then let loose my heart,
Till it an hallelujah dart!

The faster sleep the senses binds,
The more unfetter'd are our minds;
O may my soul, from matter free,
Thy loveliness unclouded see!

O when shall I, in endless day,
For ever chase dark sleep away,
And hymns with the supernal choir
Incessant sing, and never tire?

O may my Guardian, while I sleep,
Close to my bed his vigils keep;
His love angelical instil;
Stop all the avenues of ill:

May he celestial joy rehearse,
And thought to thought with me converse;
Or in my stead, all the night long,
Sing to my God a grateful song!

Praise God, from whom all blessings flow,
Praise Him, all creatures here below!
Praise Him above, ye heavenly host!
Praise Father, Son, and Holy Ghost!
Bishop Thomas Ken. 1700.

CCLVIII.
Evening.

O Lord, another day is flown;
  And we, a lonely band,
Are met once more before Thy throne
  To bless Thy fostering hand.

And wilt Thou lend a listening ear
  To praises low as ours?
Thou wilt! for Thou dost love to hear
  The song which meekness pours.

And, Jesus, Thou Thy smiles wilt deign
  As we before Thee pray;
For Thou didst bless the infant train,
  And we are less than they.

O let Thy grace perform its part,
   And let contention cease ;
And shed abroad in every heart
   Thine everlasting peace!

Thus chastened, cleansed, entirely Thine,
   A flock by Jesus led,
The Sun of holiness shall shine
   In glory on our head.

And Thou wilt turn our wandering feet,
   And Thou wilt bless our way,
Till worlds shall fade, and faith shall greet
   The dawn of lasting day!
              Henry Kirke White. 1803.

CCLIX.

Evening.

Sun of my soul, Thou Saviour dear,
It is not night if thou be near ;
Oh! may no earth-born cloud arise
To hide Thee from Thy servant's eyes !

When round Thy wondrous works below
My searching rapturous glance I throw,
Tracing out wisdom, power, and love,
In earth or sky, in stream or grove ;

Or, by the light Thy words disclose,
Watch time's full river as it flows,
Scanning Thy gracious Providence,
Where not too deep for mortal sense ;

When with dear friends sweet talk I hold,
And all the flowers of life unfold ;
Let not my heart within me burn,
Except in all I Thee discern !

Day and Night.

When the soft dews of kindly sleep
My wearied eyelids gently steep,
Be my last thought, how sweet to rest
For ever on my Saviour's breast!

Abide with me from morn till eve,
For without Thee I cannot live!
Abide with me when night is nigh,
For without Thee I dare not die!

Thou Framer of the light and dark,
Steer through the tempest Thine own ark!
Amid the howling wintry sea
We are in port if we have Thee.

The rulers of this Christian land,
'Twixt Thee and us ordain'd to stand,
Guide Thou their course, O Lord, aright!
Let all do all as in Thy sight!

Oh! by Thine own sad burthen, borne
So meekly up the hill of scorn,
Teach Thou Thy priests their daily cross,
To bear as Thine, nor count it loss!

If some poor wandering child of Thine
Have spurn'd, to-day, the voice divine;
Now, Lord, the gracious work begin;
Let him no more lie down in sin!

Watch by the sick, enrich the poor
With blessings from Thy boundless store!
Be every mourner's sleep to-night
Like infant's slumbers, pure and light!

Come near and bless us when we wake,
Ere through the world our way we take :
Till, in the ocean of Thy love,
We lose ourselves in Heaven above !

John Keble. 1827.

CCLX.

Night.

Hear my prayer, O heavenly Father,
   Ere I lay me down to sleep :
Bid Thy angels, pure and holy,
   Round my bed their vigil keep.

Great my sins are, but Thy mercy
   Far outweighs them every one ;
Down before Thy cross I cast them,
   Trusting in Thy help alone.

Keep me, through this night of peril,
   Underneath its boundless shade ;
Take me to Thy rest, I pray Thee,
   When my pilgrimage is made !

None shall measure out Thy patience
   By the span of human thought ;
None shall bound the tender mercies
   Which Thy Holy Son hath wrought.

Pardon all my past transgressions ;
   Give me strength for days to come ;
Guide and guard me with Thy blessing,
   Till Thine angels bid me home !

Thomas Park. 1797.

CCLXI.

Night.

God, that madest earth and heaven,
   Darkness and light;
Who the day for toil hast given,
   For rest the night;
May Thine angel guards defend us!
Slumber sweet Thy mercy send us!
Holy dreams and hopes attend us,
   This live-long night!
         Bishop Reginald Heber. 1827.

CCLXII.

Night.

Through the day Thy love hath spared us:
   Now we lay us down to rest;
Through the silent watches guard us!
   Let no foe our peace molest!
Jesus, Thou our Guardian be!
Sweet it is to trust in Thee.

Pilgrims here on earth, and strangers;
   Dwelling in the midst of foes:
Us and ours preserve from dangers
   In Thine arms may we repose!
And, when life's sad day is past
Rest with Thee in Heaven at last!
         Thomas Kelly. 1806.

CCLXIII.

Night.

All praise to Him who dwells in bliss,
   Who made both day and night;
Whose throne is darkness, in th' abyss
   Of uncreated light!

Each thought and deed His piercing eyes
   With strictest search survey;
The deepest shades no more disguise
   Than the full blaze of day.

Whom Thou dost guard, O King of kings,
   No evil shall molest:
Under the shadow of Thy wings
   Shall they securely rest.

Thy angels shall around their beds
   Their constant stations keep;
Thy faith and truth shall shield their heads,
   For Thou dost never sleep.

May we, with calm and sweet repose,
   And heavenly thoughts refresh'd,
Our eyelids with the morn unclose,
   And bless the Ever-bless'd!
               Charles Wesley. 1741.

CCLXIV.

Night.

Interval of grateful shade,
Welcome to my weary head:
Welcome slumber to mine eyes,
Tired with glaring vanities.

Day and Night.

My great Master still allows
Needful periods of repose;
By my Heavenly Father blest,
Thus I give my powers to rest.

Heavenly Father! gracious Name!
Night and day His love the same!
Far be each suspicious thought,
Every anxious care forgot.

Thou, my ever bounteous God,
Crown'st my days with various good;
Thy kind eye, that cannot sleep,
These defenceless hours shall keep.

What though downy slumbers flee,
Strangers to my couch and me?
Sleepless, well I know to rest,
Lodged within my Father's breast.

While the empress of the night
Scatters mild her silver light,
While the vivid planets stray
Various through their mystic way,

While the stars unnumbered roll
Round the ever constant pole,
Far above these spangled skies
All my soul to God shall rise.

Mid the silence of the night
Mingling with those angels bright,
Whose harmonious voices raise
Ceaseless love and ceaseless praise,

Through the throng His gentle ear
Shall my tuneless accents hear;
From on high doth He impart
Secret comfort to my heart.

He in these serenest hours
Guides my intellectual powers,
And His Spirit doth diffuse,
Sweeter far than midnight dews,

Lifting all my thoughts above
On the wings of faith and love:
Blest alternative to me,
Thus to sleep, or wake with Thee!

What if death my sleep invade?
Should I be of death afraid?
Whilst encircled by Thine arm,
Death may strike, but cannot harm.

What if beams of opening day
Shine around my breathless clay?
Brighter visions from on high
Shall regale my mental eye.

Tender friends awhile may mourn
Me from their embraces torn;
Dearer, better friends I have
In the realms beyond the grave.

See the guardian angels nigh
Wait to waft my soul on high!
See the golden gates displayed!
See the crown to grace my head!

Day and Night.

See a flood of sacred light,
Which no more shall yield to night!
Transitory world, farewell!
Jesus calls, with Him to dwell!

With Thy heavenly presence blest,
Death is life, and labour rest;
Welcome sleep or death to me,
Still secure, for still with Thee!
Philip Doddridge. 1755.

CCLXV.

Midnight.

My God, now I from sleep awake,
The sole possession of me take;
From midnight terrors me secure,
And guard my heart from thoughts impure!

Bless'd angels! while we silent lie,
You hallelujahs sing on high;
You joyful hymn the Ever-blest
Before the Throne, and never rest.

I with your choir celestial join
In offering up a hymn divine;
With you in Heaven I hope to dwell,
And bid the night and world farewell.

My soul, when I shake off this dust,
Lord, in Thy arms I will entrust:
O make me Thy peculiar care;
Some mansion for my soul prepare!

Give me a place at Thy saints' feet,
Or some fall'n angel's vacant seat!
I'll strive to sing as loud as they,
Who sit above in brighter day.

O may I always ready stand
With my lamp burning in my hand:
May I in sight of Heaven rejoice,
Whene'er I hear the Bridegroom's voice!

All praise to Thee in light array'd,
Who light Thy dwelling-place hast made;
A boundless ocean of bright beams
From Thy all-glorious Godhead streams.

The Sun in its meridian height
Is very darkness in Thy sight!
My soul O lighten and inflame,
With thought and love of Thy great Name!

Bless'd Jesu, Thou, on Heaven intent,
Whole nights hast in devotion spent;
But I, frail creature, soon am tired,
And all my zeal is soon expired.

My soul, how canst thou weary grow
Of antedating bliss below,
In sacred hymns, and heavenly love,
Which will eternal be above?

Shine on me, Lord, new life impart!
Fresh ardours kindle in my heart!
One ray of Thy all-quickening light
Dispels the sloth and clouds of night.

Lord, lest the tempter me surprise,
Watch over Thine own sacrifice!

All loose, all idle thoughts cast out,
And make my very dreams devout!

Praise God from whom all blessings flow,
Praise Him, all creatures here below!
Praise Him above, ye heavenly host;
Praise Father, Son, and Holy Ghost!
Bishop Thomas Ken. 1700.

CCLXVI.

Midnight.

Awake, my soul, awake to prayer;
Thy vigil of the night prepare:
Now all around is dark and still,
Angels defending us from ill.

The time to sacred thought is dear,
When Thou alone, good Lord, art near;
Hush'd is the world's external din,
That we may hear Thy voice within.

It seems to plead with gentle breath;
" Sad child of frailty, heir of death,
" Its rest thy wearied body knows;
" O! let thy soul on Me repose!

" I came to suffer in thy stead;
" I had not where to lay My head:
" Think on the love, that could provide
" Blessings for man, to God denied!"

Thus silent hours of darkness prove
Remembrancers of Jesu's love;
While constancy in prayer we learn
From each succeeding night's return.

Day without night the Angels sing,
Nor rest upon the drooping wing;
Teaching our souls betimes to ascend,
Where hallelujahs never end.

David awaked his harp and voice,
And all within him, to rejoice,
God's love to praise at morning light,
And tell of all His truth at night.

Jacob in prayer nocturnal strove;
No stern repulse his prayer could move:
In vain the Angel-man did say,
"Dismiss Me; for 'tis break of day!"

See how, in galling fetters laid,
At midnight Paul and Silas pray'd;
Their gory wounds still smarting sore,
And cold the prison's rugged floor.

They sang the praises of the Lord;
So loud they sang, the prisoners heard:
And yet they thought that death was nigh;
And clouds obscured their morning sky.

How shall I then Thy praise decline,
When health, and friends, and home are mine?
My dawn of day is clear and calm;
No foes oppress, no fears alarm.

Are these Thy mercies, Lord, to me?
O! let me then Thy servant be!
Submitting to Thy just control,
And loving Thee with all my soul.

So shall I find Thee strong to save,
When my last bed shall be the grave;
The Grave shall own my Saviour's might,
And darkness vanish at Thy sight!

Only my soul must now awake
From sleep of sin, for Thy dear sake!
And then my body shall arise
From sleep of death to yonder skies.

'Tis there I hope Thy Face to see,
The crown of all felicity;
'Tis there I hope that rest to gain,
Which here I seek, but seek in vain.

As endless ages roll along,
Endless shall be my grateful song:
And Heaven itself shall pass away,
Before I cease my vows to pay.

Glory to God, who Israel keeps,
Who never slumbers, never sleeps!
Almighty Power no weakness knows;
Unwearied Love asks no repose.

And now, my midnight musings o'er,
Thy wonted mercies, Lord, restore:
Let sleep again my eyelids fill,
And Angels guard my soul from ill.

Praise to the Father, and the Son,
And th' Holy Ghost, Bless'd Three in One!
Praise to the Lord, our God, be giv'n
By all on earth, by all in heaven!

James Ford. 1856.

II.

SEED TIME AND HARVEST.

CCLXVII.

Eternal source of every joy,
Well may Thy praise our lips employ,
While in Thy temple we appear,
Whose goodness crowns the circling year.

The flowery spring at Thy command
Embalms the air and paints the land;
The summer rays with vigour shine,
To raise the corn, and cheer the vine.

Thy hand in autumn richly pours
Through all our coasts redundant stores,
And winters, soften'd by Thy care,
No more a face of horror wear.

Seasons and months and weeks and days
Demand successive songs of praise;
Still be the cheerful homage paid
With opening light and evening shade!

Oh! may our more harmonious tongues
In worlds unknown pursue the songs;
And in those brighter courts adore,
Where days and years revolve no more!
Philip Doddridge. 1755

CCLXVIII.

Fountain of mercy! God of love!
  How rich Thy bounties are!
The rolling seasons, as they move,
  Proclaim Thy constant care.

When in the bosom of the earth
    The sower hid the grain,
Thy goodness mark'd its secret birth,
    And sent the early rain.

The spring's sweet influence was Thine,
    The plants in beauty grew;
Thou gav'st refulgent suns to shine,
    And mild refreshing dew.

These various mercies from above,
    Matur'd the swelling grain;
A yellow harvest crowns Thy love,
    And plenty fills the plain.

Seed-time and harvest, Lord, alone
    Thou dost on man bestow;
Let him not then forget to own
    From whom his blessings flow!

Fountain of love! our praise is Thine;
    To Thee our songs we'll raise,
And all created Nature join
    In sweet harmonious praise!
            Anne Flowerdew. 1811.

CCLXIX.

Lord, in Thy Name Thy servants plead,
    And Thou hast sworn to hear;
Thine is the harvest, Thine the seed,
    The fresh and fading year.

Our hope, when autumn winds blew wild,
    We trusted, Lord, with Thee;
And now, that spring has on us smiled,
    We wait on Thy decree.

The former and the latter rain,
  The summer sun and air,
The green ear, and the golden grain,
  All Thine, are ours by prayer.

Thine too by right, and ours by grace,
  The wondrous growth unseen,
The hopes that soothe, the fears that brace,
  The love that shines serene!

So grant the precious things brought forth
  By sun and moon below,
That Thee, in Thy new heaven and earth,
  We never may forego!

To Father, Son, and Holy Ghost,
  The God whom we adore,
Be glory, as it was, is now,
  And shall be evermore!
        Amen!

John Keble. 1857.

CCLXX.

Praise, O praise our God and King,
Hymns of adoration sing,
    For His mercies still endure,
    Ever faithful, ever sure.

Praise Him that He made the sun
Day by day his course to run,
    For His mercies still endure,
    Ever faithful, ever sure.

And the silver moon by night,
Shining with her gentle light,
    For His mercies still endure,
    Ever faithful, ever sure.

Praise Him that He gave the rain
To mature the swelling grain,
    For His mercies still endure,
    Ever faithful, ever sure.

And hath bid the fruitful field
Crops of precious increase yield;
    For His mercies still endure,
    Ever faithful, ever sure.

Praise Him for our harvest-store;
He hath fill'd the garner-floor;
    For His mercies still endure,
    Ever faithful, ever sure.

And for richer food than this,
Pledge of everlasting bliss;
    For His mercies still endure,
    Ever faithful, ever sure.

Glory to our bounteous King!
Glory let Creation sing!
    Glory to the Father, Son,
    And blest Spirit, Three in One!
              Sir Henry Baker. 1861.

CCLXXI.

Praise to God, immortal praise,
For the love that crowns our days!
Bounteous source of every joy,
Let Thy praise our tongues employ.

For the blessings of the field,
For the stores the gardens yield;
For the vine's exalted juice,
For the generous olive's use:

Flocks that whiten all the plain;
Yellow sheaves of ripen'd grain;
Clouds that drop their fattening dews;
Suns that temperate warmth diffuse:

All that Spring with bounteous hand
Scatters o'er the smiling land;
All that liberal Autumn pours
From her rich o'erflowing stores:

These to Thee, my God, we owe,
Source whence all our blessings flow;
And for these my soul shall raise
Grateful vows and solemn praise.

Yet, should rising whirlwinds tear
From its stem the ripening ear;
Should the fig-tree's blasted shoot
Drop her green untimely fruit;

Should the vine put forth no more,
Nor the olive yield her store;
Though the sickening flocks should fall,
And the herds desert the stall;

Should Thine alter'd hand restrain
The early and the latter rain;
Blast each opening bud of joy,
And the rising year destroy;

Yet to Thee my soul should raise
Grateful vows and solemn praise;
And, when every blessing's flown,
Love Thee for Thyself alone!
Anna Lætitia Barbauld. [1825.]

CCLXXII.

Lord of the harvest! Thee we hail;
Thine ancient promise doth not fail;
The varying seasons haste their round,
With goodness all our years are crown'd;
    Our thanks we pay
    This holy day;
O let our hearts in tune be found!

If Spring doth wake the song of mirth;
If Summer warms the fruitful earth;
When Winter sweeps the naked plain,
Or Autumn yields its ripen'd grain;
    Still do we sing
    To Thee, our King;
Through all their changes Thou dost reign.

But chiefly when Thy liberal hand
Scatters new plenty o'er the land,
When sounds of music fill the air,
As homeward all their treasures bear;
    We too will raise
    Our hymn of praise,
For we Thy common bounties share.

Lord of the harvest! all is Thine!
The rains that fall, the suns that shine,
The seed once hidden in the ground,
The skill that makes our fruits abound!
    New, every year,
    Thy gifts appear;
New praises from our lips shall sound!
        John Hampden Gurney. 1851.

CCLXXIII.

Lord of the harvest! once again
We thank Thee for the ripen'd grain;
For crops safe carried, sent to cheer
Thy servants through another year;
For all sweet holy thoughts supplied
By seed-time, and by harvest-tide.

The bare dead grain, in autumn sown,
Its robe of vernal green puts on;
Glad from its wintry grave it springs,
Fresh garnish'd by the King of kings:
So, Lord, to those who sleep in Thee
Shall new and glorious bodies be.

Nor vainly of Thy Word we ask
A lesson from the reaper's task;
So shall Thine angels issue forth;
The tares be burnt; the just of earth,
Playthings of sun and storm no more,
Be gather'd to their Father's store.

Daily, O Lord, our prayers be said,
As Thou hast taught, for daily bread;
But not alone our bodies feed;
Supply our fainting spirits' need!
O Bread of Life! from day to day,
Be Thou their Comfort, Food, and Stay!
Joseph Anstice. [1836.]

CCLXXIV.

Come, ye thankful people, come,
Raise the song of Harvest-Home!
All is safely gather'd in,
Ere the winter-storms begin;

Seed Time and Harvest.

God, our Maker, doth provide
For our wants to be supplied;
Come to God's own temple, come,
Raise the song of Harvest-Home!

We ourselves are God's own field,
Fruit unto His praise to yield;
Wheat and tares together sown,
Unto joy or sorrow grown:
First the blade, and then the ear,
Then the full corn shall appear:
Grant, O harvest Lord, that we
Wholesome grain and pure may be!

For the Lord our God shall come,
And shall take His harvest home!
From His field shall purge away
All that doth offend, that day;
Give His Angels charge at last
In the fire the tares to cast,
But the fruitful ears to store
In His garner evermore.

Then, thou Church triumphant, come,
Raise the song of Harvest-Home!
All are safely gather'd in,
Free from sorrow, free from sin;
There for ever purified,
In God's garner to abide:
Come, ten thousand Angels, come,
Raise the glorious Harvest-Home!

Henry Alford. 1845.

III.

THE OLD AND NEW YEAR.

CCLXXV.

Another year hath fled ; renew,
   Lord, with our days Thy love !
Our days are evil here and few ;
   We look to live above :
We will not grieve, though day by day
We pass from earthly joys away ;
   Our joy abides in Thee ;
   Our joy abides in Thee !

Yet, when our sins we call to mind,
   We cannot fail to grieve ;
But Thou art pitiful and kind,
   And wilt our prayer receive :
O Jesu, evermore the same,
Our hope we rest upon Thy Name ;
   Our hope abides in Thee ;
   Our hope abides in Thee !

For all the future, Lord, prepare
   Our souls with strength Divine ;
Help us to cast on Thee our care,
   And on Thy servants shine :
Life without Thee is dark and drear ;
Death is not death if Thou art near ;
   Our life abides in Thee ;
   Our life abides in Thee !

Arthur Tozer Russell. 1851.

CCLXXVI.

Harp, awake! tell out the story
   Of our love and joy and praise;
Lute, awake! awake our glory!
   Join a thankful song to raise!
Join we, brethren faithful-hearted,
   Lift the solemn voice again
O'er another year departed
   Of our threescore years and ten!

Lo! a theme for deepest sadness,
   In ourselves with sin defiled;
Lo! a theme for holiest gladness,
   In our Father reconciled!
In the dust we bend before Thee,
   Lord of sinless hosts above;
Yet in lowliest joy adore Thee,
   God of mercy, grace, and love!

Gracious Saviour! Thou hast lengthen'd
   And hast blest our mortal span,
And in our weak hearts hast strengthen'd
   What Thy grace alone began!
Still, when danger shall betide us,
   Be Thy warning whisper heard;
Keep us at Thy feet, and guide us
   By Thy Spirit and Thy Word!

Let Thy favour and Thy blessing
   Crown the year we now begin;
Let us all, Thy strength possessing,
   Grow in grace, and vanquish sin!

Storms are round us, hearts are quailing,
  Signs in heaven and earth and sea;
But, when heaven and earth are failing,
  Saviour! we will trust in Thee!
                    Henry Downton. [1851.]

CCLXXVII.

Awake, ye saints, and raise your eyes,
  And raise your voices high;
Awake, and praise that sovereign love
  That shows Salvation nigh.

On all the wings of time it flies,
  Each moment brings it near;
Then welcome each declining day,
  Welcome each closing year!

Not many years their round shall run,
  Nor many mornings rise,
Ere all its glories stand reveal'd
  To our admiring eyes!

Ye wheels of nature, speed your course!
  Ye mortal powers, decay!
Fast as ye bring the night of death,
  Ye bring eternal day!
                    Philip Doddridge. 1755.

CCLXXVIII.

While with ceaseless course the sun
  Hasted through the former year,
Many souls their race have run,
  Never more to meet us here:
Fix'd in an eternal state,
  They have done with all below;
We a little longer wait,
  But how little, none can know.

As the wingèd arrow flies
  Speedily the mark to find;
As the lightning from the skies
  Darts, and leaves no trace behind;
Swiftly thus our fleeting days
  Bear us down life's rapid stream:
Upward, Lord! our spirits raise!
  All below is but a dream.

Thanks for mercies past receive;
  Pardon of our sins renew;
Teach us, henceforth, how to live
  With eternity in view:
Bless Thy word to young and old;
  Fill us with a Saviour's love;
And, when life's short tale is told,
  May we dwell with Thee above!
John Newton. 1779.

CCLXXIX.

For Thy mercy and Thy grace,
Faithful through another year,
Hear our song of thankfulness,
Father, and Redeemer, hear!

In our weakness and distress,
Rock of strength! be Thou our stay!
In the pathless wilderness
Be our true and living way!

Who of us death's awful road
In the coming year shall tread?
With Thy rod and staff, O God,
Comfort Thou his dying head!

Keep us faithful, keep us pure,
Keep us evermore Thine own !
Help, O help us to endure !
Fit us for the promised crown !

So within Thy palace gate
We shall praise, on golden strings,
Thee, the only Potentate,
Lord of lords, and King of kings !
Henry Downton. [1851.]

CCLXXX.

To-morrow, Lord, is Thine,
　Lodged in Thy sovereign hand,
And, if its sun arise and shine,
　It shines by Thy command.

The present moment flies,
　And bears our life away :
O make Thy servants truly wise,
　That they may live to-day !

Since on this wingèd hour
　Eternity is hung,
Waken by Thy Almighty power
　The aged and the young !

One thing demands our care :
　O ! be it still pursued !
Lest, slighted once, the season fair
　Should never be renew'd !

To Jesus may we fly
　Swift as the morning light ;
Lest life's young golden beams should die
　In sudden endless night !
Philip Doddridge. 1755.

IV.

BAPTISM AND CHILDHOOD.

CCLXXXI.

God of that glorious gift of grace
By which Thy people seek Thy face,
When in Thy presence we appear,
Vouchsafe us faith to venture near!

Confiding in Thy truth alone,
Here, on the steps of Jesus' throne,
We lay the treasure Thou hast given
To be received and rear'd for Heaven.

Lent to us for a season, we
Lend him for ever, Lord, to Thee!
Assured, that, if to Thee he live,
We gain in what we seem to give.

Large and abundant blessings shed,
Warm as these prayers, upon his head!
And on his soul the dews of grace,
Fresh as these drops upon his face!

Make him and keep him Thine own child,
Meek follower of the Undefil'd!
Possessor here of grace and love;
Inheritor of Heaven above!

John S. B. Monsell. 1837.

CCLXXXII.

Lord! may the inward grace abound
  Through Thine appointed outward sign;
A milder seal than Abraham found
  Of cov'nant blessings more Divine;

Which opens glory to our view
Beyond the brightest hope he knew!

Type of the Spirit's living flow,
   In faith we pour the hallow'd stream;
We sign the cross upon the brow,
   The solemn pledge of truth to Him,
Who shed for us His precious Blood
To seal the covenant of God.

Baptized into the Trinity,
   Adopted children of Thy grace,
O help us, Lord, to live to Thee
   A humble, pure, and faithful race!
Instruct us, sanctify, defend,
And crown with heavenly life our end!
                  Anon. [1855.]

CCLXXXIII.

In token that thou shalt not fear
   Christ Crucified to own,
We print the cross upon thee here,
   And stamp thee His alone.

In token that thou shalt not blush
   To glory in His Name,
We blazon here upon thy front
   His glory and His shame.

In token that thou shalt not flinch
   Christ's quarrel to maintain,
But 'neath His banner manfully
   Firm at thy post remain;

In token that thou too shalt tread
    The path He travell'd by,
Endure the cross, despise the shame,
    And sit thee down on high;

Thus, outwardly and visibly,
    We seal thee for His own:
And may the brow that wears His cross
    Hereafter share His crown!
                    Henry Alford. 1845.

CCLXXXIV.

Sweet baby, sleep! what ails my dear,
    What ails my darling thus to cry?
Be still, my child, and lend thine ear,
    To hear me sing thy lullaby.
My pretty lamb, forbear to weep;
Be still, my dear; sweet baby, sleep.

Thou blessèd soul, what canst thou fear?
    What thing to thee can mischief do?
Thy God is now thy Father dear,
    His holy Spouse, thy mother too.
Sweet baby, then forbear to weep;
Be still, my babe; sweet baby, sleep.

Though thy conception was in sin,
    A sacred bathing thou hast had;
And though thy birth unclean hath been,
    A blameless babe thou now art made.
Sweet baby, then forbear to weep;
Be still, my dear, sweet baby, sleep.

While thus thy lullaby I sing,
   For thee great blessings ripening be;
Thine eldest brother is a king,
   And hath a kingdom bought for thee.
Sweet baby, then forbear to weep;
Be still, my babe; sweet baby, sleep.

Sweet baby, sleep, and nothing fear;
   For whosoever thee offends
By thy protector threaten'd are,
   And God and angels are thy friends.
Sweet baby, then forbear to weep;
Be still, my babe; sweet baby, sleep.

When God with us was dwelling here,
   In little babes He took delight;
Such innocents as thou, my dear,
   Are ever precious in His sight.
Sweet baby, then forbear to weep;
Be still, my babe; sweet baby, sleep.

A little infant once was He;
   And strength in weakness then was laid
Upon His virgin mother's knee,
   That power to thee might be convey'd.
Sweet baby, then forbear to weep;
Be still, my babe; sweet baby, sleep.

In this thy frailty and thy need
   He friends and helpers doth prepare,
Which thee shall cherish, clothe, and feed,
   For of thy weal they tender are.
Sweet baby, then forbear to weep;
Be still, my babe; sweet baby, sleep.

The King of kings, when He was born,
   Had not so much for outward ease;
By Him such dressings were not worn,
   Nor such-like swaddling-clothes as these.
Sweet baby, then forbear to weep;
Be still, my babe; sweet baby, sleep.

Within a manger lodged thy Lord,
   Where oxen lay, and asses fed:
Warm rooms we do to thee afford,
   An easy cradle or a bed.
Sweet baby, then forbear to weep;
Be still, my babe; sweet baby, sleep.

The wants that He did then sustain
   Have purchased wealth, my babe, for thee;
And by His torments and His pain
   Thy rest and ease securèd be.
My baby, then forbear to weep;
Be still, my babe; sweet baby, sleep.

Thou hast, yet more, to perfect this,
   A promise and an earnest got
Of gaining everlasting bliss,
   Though thou, my babe, perceiv'st it not;
Sweet baby, then forbear to weep;
Be still, my babe; sweet baby, sleep.
            George Wither. 1641.

CCLXXXV.

Sleep well, my dear; sleep safe and free;
The holy Angels are with thee,
Who always see thy Father's face,
And never slumber, nights nor days.

Thou liest in down, soft every way;
Thy Saviour lay in straw and hay;
Thy cradle is far better drest
Than the hard crib where He did rest.

None dare disturb thy present ease;
He had a thousand enemies;
Thou liv'st in great security;
But He was punish'd, and for thee!

God make thy mother's health increase,
To see thee grow in strength and grace,
In wisdom and humility,
As infant Jesus did for thee!

God fill thee with His heavenly light
To steer thy Christian course aright;
Make thee a tree, of blessèd root,
That ever bends with godly fruit!

Sleep now, my dear, and take thy rest;
And if with riper years thou'rt blest,
Increase in wisdom, day and night,
Till thou attain'st th' eternal Light!

John Christian Jacobi. 1722.
From Martin Luther.

CCLXXXVI.

O Holy Lord, content to live
   In a poor home, a lowly child,
And in subjection meek to give
   Obedience to Thy mother mild;

Lead every child that bears Thy Name
   To walk in Thy pure upright way,
To dread the touch of sin and shame,
   And humbly, like Thyself, obey!

O let not this world's scorching glow
    Thy Spirit's quickening dew efface,
Nor blast of sin too rudely blow,
    And quench the trembling flame of grace.

Gather Thy lambs within Thine arm,
    And gently in Thy bosom bear;
Keep them, O Lord, from hurt and harm,
    And bid them rest for ever there!

So shall they, waiting here below,
    Like Thee, their Lord, a little span,
In wisdom and in stature grow,
    And favour both with God and man.
William Walsham How. [1860.]

CCLXXXVII.

Saviour, who Thy flock art feeding
    With the Shepherd's kindest care,
All the feeble gently leading,
    While the lambs Thy bosom share;

Now, these little ones receiving,
    Fold them in Thy gracious arm;
There, we know, Thy word believing,
    Only there, secure from harm!

Never, from Thy pasture roving,
    Let them be the lion's prey;
Let Thy tenderness so loving
    Keep them all life's dangerous way:

Then, within Thy fold eternal,
    Let them find a resting-place,
Feed in pastures ever vernal,
    Drink the rivers of Thy grace!
Anon. [1832.]

CCLXXXVIII.

Lamb of God, I look to Thee;
Thou shalt my example be;
Thou art gentle, meek, and mild;
Thou wast once a little child.

Fain I would be as Thou art;
Give me Thy obedient heart!
Thou art pitiful and kind;
Let me have Thy loving mind!

Meek and lowly may I be;
Thou art all humility!
Let me to my betters bow;
Subject to Thy parents Thou.

Let me above all fulfil
God my heavenly Father's will;
Never His good Spirit grieve;
Only to His glory live!

Thou didst live to God alone;
Thou didst never seek Thine own;
Thou Thyself didst never please;
God was all Thy happiness.

Loving Jesu, gentle Lamb,
In Thy gracious hands I am;
Make me, Saviour, what Thou art!
Live Thyself within my heart!

I shall then shew forth Thy praise;
Serve Thee all my happy days;
Then the world shall always see
Christ, the Holy Child, in me.

Charles Wesley. 1740.

CCLXXXIX.

When Jesus left His Father's throne,
   He chose an humble birth;
Like us, unhonour'd and unknown,
   He came to dwell on earth.

Like Him, may we be found below
   In wisdom's paths of peace;
Like Him, in grace and knowledge grow,
   As years and strength increase.

Jesus pass'd by the rich and great
   For men of low degree;
He sanctified our parents' state,
   For poor like them was He.

Sweet were His words, and kind His look,
   When mothers round Him press'd;
Their infants in His arms He took,
   And on His bosom bless'd.

Safe from the world's alluring harms,
   Beneath His watchful eye,
Thus in the circle of His arms
   May we for ever lie!

When Jesus into Salem rode,
   The children sang around;
For joy they pluck'd the palms, and strow'd
   Their garments on the ground.

Hosanna our glad voices raise,
   Hosanna to our King!
Should we forget our Saviour's praise,
   The stones themselves would sing!

        James Montgomery. 1825.

CCXC.

God of mercy, throned on high,
    Listen from Thy lofty seat;
Hear, O hear our feeble cry,
    Guide, O guide our wandering feet!

Young and erring travellers, we
    All our dangers do not know;
Scarcely fear the stormy sea,
    Hardly feel the tempest blow.

Jesus, lover of the young,
    Cleanse us with Thy Blood divine!
Ere the tide of sin grow strong,
    Save us, keep us, make us Thine!

When perplex'd in danger's snare,
    Thou alone our guide canst be;
When oppress'd with woe and care,
    Whom have we to trust but Thee?

Let us ever hear Thy voice,
    Ask Thy counsel every day;
Saints and angels will rejoice,
    If we walk in wisdom's way.

Saviour, give us faith, and pour
    Hope and love on every soul!
Hope, till time shall be no more!
    Love, while endless ages roll!

Anon. [1841.]

CCXCI.

Shepherd of Israel, from above
    Thy feeble flock behold;
And let us never lose Thy love,
    Nor wander from Thy fold.

Thou wilt not cast Thy lambs away;
    Thy hand is ever near,
To guide them lest they go astray,
    And keep them safe from fear.

Thy tender care supports the weak,
    And will not let them fall;
Then teach us, Lord, Thy praise to speak,
    And on Thy Name to call!

We want Thy help, for we are frail;
    Thy light, for we are blind;
Let grace o'er all our doubts prevail,
    To prove that Thou art kind.

Teach us the things we ought to know;
    And may we find them true;
And still, in stature as we grow,
    Increase in wisdom too.

Guide us through life; and when at last
    We enter into rest,
Thy tender arms around us cast,
    And fold us to Thy breast!
        William Hiley Bathurst. 1831.

V.

HOLY COMMUNION.

CCXCII.

With all the powers my poor soul hath
Of humble love, and loyal faith,
I come, dear Lord, to worship Thee,
Whom too much love bowed low for me.

Down, busy sense; discourses die;
And all adore faith's mystery!
Faith is my skill, faith can believe
As fast as love new laws shall give.

Faith is my eye, faith strength affords
To keep pace with those gracious words;
And words more sure, more sweet than they,
Love could not think, Truth could not say.

O dear memorial of that Death
Which still survives, and gives us breath!
Live ever, Bread of Life, and be
My food, my joy, my all to me!

Come, glorious Lord! my hopes increase,
And mix my portion with Thy peace!
Come, and for ever dwell in me
That I may only live to Thee!

Come, hidden life, and that long day
For which I languish, come away!
When this dry soul those eyes shall see,
And drink the unseal'd Source of Thee;

When Glory's Sun faith's shade shall chase,
And, for Thy vail, give me Thy face;
Then shall my praise eternal be
To the Eternal Trinity!
>   *Variation from Richard Crashaw.* 1646.
>   *By John Austin,* 1668,
>   *and Theophilus Dorrington.* 1686.

CCXCIII.

In memory of the Saviour's love,
   We keep the sacred feast,
Where every humble contrite heart
   Is made a welcome guest.

By faith we take the Bread of Life,
   With which our souls are fed;
And Cup, in token of His Blood
   That was for sinners shed.

Under His banner thus we sing
   The wonders of His love,
And thus anticipate by faith
   The heavenly feast above.
>   *Anon.* [1843.]

CCXCIV.

O God, unseen, yet ever near,
   Thy presence may we feel;
And thus, inspired with holy fear,
   Before Thine altar kneel.

Here may Thy faithful people know
   The blessings of Thy love;
The streams that through the desert flow;
   The manna from above.

We come, obedient to Thy word,
   To feast on heavenly food ;
Our meat, the Body of the Lord ;
   Our drink, His precious Blood.

Thus may we all Thy words obey ;
   For we, O God, are Thine ;
And go rejoicing on our way,
   Renewed with strength Divine !

Anon. [1836.]

CCXCV.

Lord, when before Thy throne we meet,
   Thy goodness to adore,
From Heaven, th' eternal mercy-seat,
   On us Thy blessing pour,
And make our inmost souls to be
An habitation meet for Thee !

The Body for our ransom given ;
   The Blood in mercy shed ;
With this immortal food from Heaven,
   Lord ! let our souls be fed !
And, as we round Thy table kneel,
Help us Thy quickening grace to feel !

Be Thou, O Holy Spirit, nigh !
   Accept the humble prayer,
The contrite soul's repentant sigh,
   The sinner's heartfelt tear !
And let our adoration rise,
As fragrant incense, to the skies !

Anon. [1853.]

CCXCVI.
Jesu, dulcedo cordium.

Jesus, thou Joy of loving hearts!
　Thou Fount of Life! Thou Light of men!
From the best bliss that earth imparts,
　We turn unfill'd to Thee again.

Thy truth unchanged hath ever stood;
　Thou savest those that on Thee call;
To them that seek Thee, Thou art good,
　To them that find Thee, All in All!

We taste Thee, O Thou Living Bread,
　And long to feast upon Thee still!
We drink of Thee, the Fountain Head,
　And thirst our souls from Thee to fill!

Our restless spirits yearn for Thee,
　Where'er our changeful lot is cast;
Glad, when Thy gracious smile we see,
　Blest, when our faith can hold Thee fast.

O Jesus, ever with us stay!
　Make all our moments calm and bright!
Chase the dark night of sin away,
　Shed o'er the world Thy holy light!
　　　　　　Anon. [1860.]
　　　　　　From St. Bernard.

CCXCVII.

They talk'd of Jesus, as they went;
　And Jesus, all unknown,
Did at their side Himself present
　With sweetness all His own.
Swift, as He op'd the sacred word,
　His glory they discern'd;
And swift, as His dear voice they heard,
　Their hearts within them burn'd.

He would have left them, but that they
    With prayers His love assail'd :
" Depart not yet ! a little stay !"
    They press'd Him, and prevail'd.
And Jesus was reveal'd, as there
    He bless'd and brake the bread :
But, while they mark'd His heavenly air,
    The matchless Guest had fled.

And thus at times, as Christians talk
    Of Jesus and His word,
He joins two friends amidst their walk,
    And makes, unseen, a third.
And oh ! how sweet their converse flows,
    Their holy theme how clear,
How warm with love each bosom glows,
    If Jesus be but near !

And they that woo His visits sweet,
    And will not let Him go,
Oft, while His broken bread they eat,
    His soul-felt presence know :
His gather'd friends He loves to meet
    And fill with joy their faith,
When they with melting hearts repeat
    The memory of His death.

But such sweet visits here are brief ;
    Dispens'd from stage to stage,
(A cheering and a prized relief,)
    Of faith's hard pilgrimage.
There is a scene where Jesus ne'er,
    Ne'er leaves His happy guests ;
He spreads a ceaseless banquet there,
    And love still fires their breasts.

Thomas Grinfield. 1836.

CCXCVIII.

Jesus, when near th' expected hour,
That Hell to grieve Him should have power,
As on His cross He kept His view,
Into an upper room withdrew,
With all His votaries there to meet
And celebrate the Paschal treat.

Then He Himself for death disposed;
Of dying well the art disclosed;
He wash'd with condescension sweet
And wiped His happy lovers' feet,
That from pollution cleansed they might
Approach the Eucharistic rite.

The Eucharist He then ordain'd;
With food immortal them sustain'd;
Then sang an hymn, the feast to close,
And sweeten His approaching woes,
Scattering truths heav'nly, high, and sweet,
As to the Mount He made retreat.

While death was lively in His thought,
He heavenly truths with vigour taught,
How to be loved of God, and love;
Promised sweet peace and joys above,
And the bless'd Spirit's constant aid;
And for them all with fervour pray'd.

He spent His preparation hours
To warn of dangers and hell-powers;
Their hearts to counsel, strengthen, cheer,
To arm against degenerate fear;
Pure love fraternal to instil,
And form them to His Father's will.

My soul ! O copy every line
Of this original divine !
On Jesus' votaries you must tend ;
To wash their feet must condescend ;
You pleasure for sweet Jesus' sake
In humble charities must take.

With zeal wash your own spirit clean
From all concupiscence terrene ;
When wash'd in penitential dew,
Then your baptismal vow renew ;
What Peter wish'd for, wash all o'er,
And take great care to sin no more.

Wash'd in heart-purifying tear
You must at Jesus' feast appear,
With food immortal to be fed,
That you nor Hell nor Death may dread ;
Then sing an hymn of the like strain
With that above of the Lamb Slain.

God's love to all with zeal suggest ;
And from the flame in your own breast
Fire other hearts, that they the Name
Of Jesus' friends may humbly claim ;
From God's love, love fraternal fire,
In which all Jesus' friends conspire.

Your foes both pray for, and forgive ;
And, when you ceasing are to live,
Strong cries to Love Paternal send ;
Into Love's hands your soul commend ;
In Love's soft hands to bliss you'll fly,
Taught by loved Jesus how to die.

Bishop Thomas Ken. [1721.]

VI.

HOLY MATRIMONY.

CCXCIX.

The voice that breathed o'er Eden,
    That earliest wedding day,
The primal marriage blessing,
    It hath not pass'd away.

Still in the pure espousal
    Of Christian man and maid,
The Holy Three are with us,
    The three-fold grace is said:

For dower of blessèd children,
    For love and faith's sweet sake,
For high mysterious union
    Which nought on earth may break!

Be present, awful Father,
    To give away this Bride,
As Eve thou gav'st to Adam
    Out of his own pierc'd side!

Be present, Son of Mary,
    To join their loving hands,
As Thou didst bind two natures
    In Thine eternal bands!

Be present, Holiest Spirit,
    To bless them as they kneel;
As Thou, for Christ the Bridegroom,
    The heavenly Spouse doth seal!

O spread Thy pure wing o'er them!
  Let no ill Power find place,
When onward to Thine altar
  The hallow'd path they trace,

To cast their crowns before Thee
  In perfect sacrifice,
Till to the home of gladness
  With Christ's own Bride they rise!

John Keble. 1857.

VII.

THE BURIAL OF THE DEAD.

CCC.

Thou God of Love! beneath thy sheltering wings
    We leave our holy dead,
To rest in hope! From this world's sufferings
    Their souls have fled!

Oh! when our souls are burden'd with the weight
    Of life, and all its woes,
Let us remember them, and calmly wait
    For our life's close!

Anon. [1861.]

CCCI.

Nunc suscipe, terra, fovendum.

Receive him, Earth, unto thine harbouring shrine;
    In thy soft tranquil bosom let him rest;
These limbs of man I to thy care consign,
    And trust the noble fragments to thy breast.

This house was once the mansion of a soul
  Brought into life by its Creator's breath ;
Wisdom did once this living mass control ;
  And Christ was there enshrined, who conquers death.

Cover this Body to thy care consign'd ;
  Its Maker shall not leave it in the grave ;
But His own lineaments shall bear in mind,
  And shall recall the image which He gave.

Isaac Williams. 1838.
(*From Prudentius.*)

CCCII.

There is a calm for those who weep ;
A rest for weary pilgrims found ;
And, while the mouldering ashes sleep,
    Low in the ground,

The Soul, of origin Divine,
God's glorious image, freed from clay,
In Heaven's eternal sphere shall shine,
    A Star of Day.

The sun is but a spark of fire,
A transient meteor in the sky ;
The Soul, immortal as its Sire,
    Shall never die !

James Montgomery. 1804.

CCCIII.

Must friends and kindred droop and die,
  And helpers be withdrawn,
While sorrow, with a weeping eye,
  Counts up our comforts gone ?

Be Thou our comfort, mighty God!
  Our Helper and our Friend!
Nor leave us, in this dangerous road,
  Till all our trials end!

O may our feet pursue the way
  Our pious fathers led;
With love and holy zeal obey
  The counsels of the dead!

Let us be wean'd from all below;
  Let hope our grief expel;
While death invites our souls to go
  Where our best kindred dwell.

Isaac Watts. 1709.

CCCIV.

Now let our mourning hearts revive,
  And all our tears be dry;
Why should those eyes be drown'd in grief,
  Which view a Saviour nigh?

What though the arm of conquering death
  Does God's own house invade?
What though the prophet and the priest
  Be number'd with the dead?

Though earthly shepherds dwell in dust,
  The aged and the young;
The watchful eye in darkness closed,
  And mute th' instructive tongue:

Th' Eternal Shepherd still survives,
  New comfort to impart;
His eye still guides us, and His voice
  Still animates our heart.

Lo, I am with you! saith the Lord;
  My Church shall safe abide;
For I will ne'er forsake My own,
  Whose souls in Me confide.

Through every scene, of life and death,
  This promise is our trust;
And this shall be our children's song
  When we are cold in dust.
Philip Doddridge. 1755.

CCCV.

Thou art gone to the grave: but we will not deplore thee,
  Though sorrows and darkness encompass the tomb:
The Saviour hath pass'd through its portal before thee,
  And the lamp of His love is thy guide through the gloom!

Thou art gone to the grave: we no longer behold thee,
  Nor tread the rough path of the world by thy side;
But the wide arms of Mercy are spread to enfold thee,
  And sinners may die, for the Sinless has died!

Thou art gone to the grave: and, its mansion forsaking,
  Perhaps thy weak spirit in fear linger'd long;
But the mild rays of Paradise beam'd on thy waking,
  And the sound which thou heard'st was the Seraphim's song!

Thou art gone to the grave: but we will not deplore
    thee;
  Whose God was thy ransom, thy Guardian, and
    Guide!
He gave thee, He took thee, and He will restore
    thee;
  And death has no sting, for the Saviour has died!
              Bishop Reginald Heber. 1827.

CCCVI.

Brother, thou art gone before us; and thy saintly
    soul is flown
Where tears are wiped from every eye, and sorrow
    is unknown;
From the burden of the flesh, and from care and
    fear releas'd,
Where the wicked cease from troubling, and the
    weary are at rest.

The toilsome way thou'st travelled o'er, and borne
    the heavy load;
But Christ hath taught thy languid feet to reach
    His blest abode:
Thou'rt sleeping now, like Lazarus upon his father's
    breast,
Where the wicked cease from troubling, and the
    weary are at rest.

Sin can never taint thee now, nor doubt thy faith
    assail,
Nor thy meek trust in Jesus Christ and the Holy
    Spirit fail:

And there thou'rt sure to meet the good, whom on
    earth thou lovedst best,
Where the wicked cease from troubling, and the
    weary are at rest.

Earth to earth, and dust to dust, the solemn priest
    hath said;
So we lay the turf above thee now, and we seal thy
    narrow bed;
But thy spirit, brother, soars away among the
    faithful blest,
Where the wicked cease from troubling, and the
    weary are at rest.

And when the Lord shall summon us, whom thou
    hast left behind,
May we, untainted by the world, as sure a welcome
    find!
May each, like thee, depart in peace, to be a
    glorious guest,
Where the wicked cease from troubling, and the
    weary are at rest!

Henry Hart Milman. 1822.

VIII.

CHURCH DEDICATION.

CCCVII.

Lord of hosts! to Thee we raise
Here a house of prayer and praise:
Thou Thy people's hearts prepare,
Here to meet for praise and prayer!

Let the living here be fed
With Thy Word, the heavenly bread;
Here, in hope of glory blest,
May the dead be laid to rest!

Here to Thee a temple stand
While the sea shall gird the land!
Here reveal Thy mercy sure,
While the sun and moon endure!

Hallelujah! earth and sky
To the joyful sound reply!
Hallelujah! hence ascend
Prayer and praise till time shall end!
James Montgomery. 1825.

CCCVIII.

Angulare Fundamentum.

Christ is our corner-stone,
On Him alone we build;
With His true saints alone
The courts of Heaven are fill'd:
  On His great love
    Our hopes we place
    Of present grace
  And joys above.

O then with hymns of praise
These hallow'd courts shall ring;
Our voices we will raise
The Three in One to sing;
  And thus proclaim
    In joyful song
    Both loud and long
  That glorious Name.

Here, gracious God, do Thou
For evermore draw nigh;
Accept each faithful vow,
And mark each suppliant sigh;
   In copious shower
    On all who pray
    Each holy day
   Thy blessings pour!

Here may we gain from Heaven
The grace which we implore;
And may that grace, once given,
Be with us evermore,
   Until that day
    When all the blest
    To endless rest
   Are call'd away!
          John Chandler. 1837.

CCCIX.

The lovely form of God's own Church,
  It riseth in all lands;
On mountain sides, in wooded vales,
  And by the desert sands.

There is it, with its solemn aisles,
  A heavenly, holy thing;
And round its walls lie Christian dead,
  Blessedly slumbering.

Though sects and factions rend the world,
  Peace is its heritage;
Unchanged, though empires by it pass,
  The same from age to age.

The hallow'd form our fathers built,
   That hallow'd form build we;
Let not one stone from its own place
   Removèd ever be!

Scoff as thou passest, if thou wilt,
   Thou man that hast no faith;
Thou, that no sorrows hast in life,
   Nor blessedness in death:

But we will build, for all thou scoff,
   And cry, "What waste is this!"
The Lord our God hath given us all,
   And all is therefore His.

Clear voices from above sound out
   Their blessing on the pile;
The dead beneath support our hands,
   And succour us the while.

Yea, when we climb the rising walls,
   Is peace and comfort given!
Because the work is not of earth,
   But hath its end in Heaven!
                    Henry Alford. 1845.

IX.

THE LORD'S DAY.

CCCX.

Welcome, sweet day, of days the best,
The time of holy mirth and rest,
   When to God's house the saints repair
To hear His word and see His face,
To learn His will and sing His grace,
   And vent their hearts in praise and prayer.

This is employment all Divine;
My soul, the blest assembly join,
  And from the world this day retire:
Go, bow before thy Maker's throne,
Thy risen Saviour's glories own,
  And feed thy love, and fan the fire.

Forget the trifles here below,
The shining heap, the gaudy show,
  All sensual mirth, and worldly cares;
On wings of strong devotion rise,
Pass every cloud, pass all the skies,
  And leave beneath Thy feet the stars.

To God direct thy steady flight,
Great Fund of bliss and Source of light;
  There fix, and there delight thine eyes:
View every shining wonder o'er,
And with transported heart adore,
  And feast on fruits of paradise.

This day was by our Lord ordain'd,
That thus His servants might be train'd
  For heavenly work, and heavenly joy:
My soul, be this thy day of rest,
And thus prepare thee to be blest,
  Thus all thy holy hours employ!
          Simon Browne. 1720.

CCCXI.

O day most calm, most bright!
The fruit of this, the next world's bud;
The indorsement of supreme delight,
Writ by a Friend, and with His blood;
The couch of time; care's balm and bay;
The week were dark, but for thy light;
  Thy torch doth show the way.

The other days and thou
Make up one man; whose face thou art,
Knocking at Heaven with thy brow:
The working days are the back part;
The burden of the week lies there,
Making the whole to stoop and bow,
   Till thy release appear.

Man had straight forward gone
To endless death; but thou dost pull
And turn us round to look on One,
Whom, if we were not very dull,
We could not choose but look on still,
Since there is no place so alone,
   The which He doth not fill!

Sundays the pillars are
On which Heav'n's palace archèd lies:
The other days fill up the spare
And hollow room with vanities:
They are the fruitful beds and borders
Of God's rich garden; that is bare,
   Which parts their ranks and orders.

The Sundays of man's life,
Threaded together on time's string,
Make bracelets to adorn the wife
Of the eternal glorious King:
On Sunday Heaven's gate stands ope;
Blessings are plentiful and rife,
   More plentiful than hope.

This day my Saviour rose,
And did enclose this light for His;
That, as each beast his manger knows,
Man might not of his fodder miss:

Christ hath took in this piece of ground,
And made a garden there, for those
  Who want herbs for their wound.

The rest of our Creation
Our great Redeemer did remove
With the same shake, which at His passion
Did th' earth, and all things with it, move:
As Samson bore the doors away,
Christ's hands, though nail'd, wrought our salvation,
  And did unhinge that day.

The brightness of that day
We sullied by our foul offence;
Wherefore that robe we cast away,
Having a new at His expense,
Whose drops of blood paid the full price
That was required to make us gay,
  And fit for Paradise.

George Herbert. 1632.

CCCXII.

My Lord, my love was crucified,
  He all the pains did bear;
But in the sweetness of His rest
  He makes His servants share.
How sweetly rest Thy saints above
  Which in Thy bosom lie!
The Church below doth rest in hope
  Of that felicity.

Thou, Lord, who daily feed'st Thy sheep,
  Mak'st them a weekly feast;
Thy flocks meet in their several folds
  Upon this day of rest:

Welcome and dear unto my soul
　　Are these sweet feasts of love;
But what a sabbath shall I keep
　　When I shall rest above!

I bless Thy wise and wondrous love,
　　Which binds us to be free ;
Which makes us leave our earthly snares,
　　That we may come to Thee!
I come, I wait, I hear, I pray !
　　Thy footsteps, Lord, I trace !
I sing to think this is the way
　　Unto my Saviour's face !
John Mason. 1683.

CCCXIII.

O time of tranquil joy and holy feeling !
When over earth God's Spirit from above
　　Spreads out His wings of love !
When sacred thoughts, like angels, come appealing
To our tent doors ; O eve, to earth and heaven
　　The sweetest of the seven !

How peaceful are thy skies ! thy air is clearer,
As on the advent of a gracious time :
　　The sweetness of its prime
Blesseth the world, and Eden's days seem nearer :
I hear, in each faint stirring of the breeze,
　　God's voice among the trees.

O while thy hallowed moments are distilling
Their fresher influence on my heart like dews,
　　The chamber where I muse
Turns to a temple ! He, whose converse thrilling
Honoured Emmaüs, that old eventide,
　　Comes sudden to my side.

'Tis light at evening time when Thou art present;
Thy coming to the eleven in that dim room
   Brightened, O Christ! its gloom:
So bless my lonely hour that memories pleasant
Around the time a heavenly gleam may cast,
   Which many days shall last!

Raise each low aim, refine each high emotion,
That with more ardent footstep I may press
   Toward Thy holiness;
And, braced for sacred duty by devotion,
Support my cross along that rugged road
   Which Thou hast sometime trod!

I long to see Thee, for my heart is weary:
O when, my Lord! in kindness wilt Thou come
   To call Thy banished home?
The scenes are cheerless, and the days are dreary;
From sorrow and from sin I would be free,
   And evermore with Thee!

Even now I see the golden city shining
Up the blue depths of that transparent air:
   How happy all is there!
There breaks a day which never knows declining;
A Sabbath, through whose circling hours the blest
   Beneath Thy shadow rest!

James D. Burns. 1855.

CCCXIV.
Psalm XCII.

Sweet is the work, my God, my King,
To praise Thy Name, give thanks and sing,
To show Thy love by morning light,
And talk of all Thy truth at night.

Sweet is the day of sacred rest;
No mortal cares shall seize my breast;
O may my heart in tune be found,
Like David's harp of solemn sound!

My heart shall triumph in my Lord,
And bless His works, and bless His word:
Thy works of grace, how bright they shine!
How deep Thy counsels, how divine!

Fools never raise their thoughts so high,
Like brutes they live, like brutes they die;
Like grass they flourish, till Thy breath
Blast them in everlasting death.

But I shall share a glorious part,
When grace hath well refined my heart,
And fresh supplies of joy are shed,
Like holy oil to cheer my head.

Sin, my worst enemy before,
Shall vex my eyes and ears no more;
My inward foes shall all be slain,
Nor Satan break my peace again.

Then shall I see and hear and know
All I desired or wish'd below,
And every power find sweet employ
In that eternal world of joy!
Isaac Watts. 1719.

CCCXV.

Psalm LXXXI.

Sing to the Lord, our might,
With holy fervour sing;
Let hearts and instruments unite
To praise our heavenly King.

This is His holy house,
  And this His festal day,
When He accepts the humblest vows
  That we sincerely pay.

The Sabbath to our sires
  In mercy first was given;
The Church her Sabbaths still requires
  To speed her on to Heaven.

We still, like them of old,
  Are in the wilderness;
And God is still as near His fold,
  To pity and to bless.

Then let us open wide
  Our hearts for Him to fill;
And He, that Israel then supplied,
  Will help His Israel still.
    Henry Francis Lyte. 1834—1841.

CCCXVI.

The day of rest once more comes round,
  A day to all believers dear;
The silver trumpets seem to sound,
  That call the tribes of Israel near;
    Ye people all,
    Obey the call,
  And in Jehovah's courts appear.

Obedient to Thy summons, Lord,
  We to Thy sanctuary come;
Thy gracious presence here afford,
  And send Thy people joyful home;

Of Thee our King
O may we sing,
And none with such a theme be dumb!

O hasten, Lord, the day when those,
   Who know Thee here, shall see Thy face;
When suffering shall for ever close,
   And they shall reach their destined place;
Then shall they rest
Supremely blest,
Eternal debtors to Thy grace!
Thomas Kelly. 1806.

CCCXVII.

Hail, thou bright and sacred morn,
   Risen with gladness in thy beams!
Light, which not of earth is born,
   From thy dawn in glory streams:
Airs of Heaven are breath'd around
And each place is holy ground.

Sad and weary were our way,
   Fainting oft beneath our load,
But for thee, thou blessed day,
   Resting-place on life's rough road!
Here flow forth the streams of grace,
Strengthen'd hence we run our race.

Great Creator! who this day
   From Thy perfect work didst rest;
By the souls that own Thy sway
   Hallow'd be its hours and blest;
Cares of earth aside be thrown,
This day giv'n to Heaven alone!

Saviour! who this day didst break
  The dark prison of the tomb;
Bid my slumbering soul awake,
  Shine through all its sin and gloom:
Let me, from my bonds set free,
Rise from sin, and live to Thee!

Blessed Spirit! Comforter!
  Sent this day from Christ on high;
Lord, on me Thy gifts confer,
  Cleanse, illumine, sanctify!
All Thine influence shed abroad,
Lead me to the truth of God!

Soon, too soon, the sweet repose
  Of this day of God will cease;
Soon this glimpse of Heaven will close,
  Vanish soon the hours of peace;
Soon return the toil, the strife,
All the weariness of life.

But the rest which yet remains
  For Thy people, Lord, above,
Knows nor change, nor fears, nor pains,
  Endless as their Saviour's love:
O may every Sabbath here
Bring us to that rest more near!
                Julia Anne Elliott. 1833.

CCCXVIII.

Lord of the Sabbath! hear our vows,
On this Thy day, in this Thy house;
And own as grateful sacrifice
The songs which from the desert rise.

Thine earthly Sabbaths, Lord, we love;
But there's a nobler rest above;
To that our labouring souls aspire
With ardent pangs of strong desire.

No more fatigue, no more distress;
Nor sin nor hell shall reach the place;
No groans to mingle with the songs
Which warble from immortal tongues.

No rude alarms of raging foes;
No cares to break the long repose;
No midnight shade, no clouded sun,
But sacred, high, eternal noon.

O long-expected day, begin!
Dawn on these realms of woe and sin!
Fain would we leave this weary road,
And sleep in death, to rest with God!
Philip Doddridge. 1755.

CCCXIX.

To Thy temple I repair;
Lord, I love to worship there;
When, within the veil I meet
Christ before the mercy-seat.

Thou, through Him, art reconciled;
I, through Him, became Thy child;
Abba, Father! give me grace
In Thy courts to seek Thy face!

While Thy glorious praise is sung,
Touch my lips, unloose my tongue,
That my joyful soul may bless
Thee, the Lord my Righteousness!

While the prayers of saints ascend,
God of love! to mine attend!
Hear me, for Thy Spirit pleads;
Hear, for Jesus intercedes!

While I hearken to Thy law,
Fill my soul with humble awe;
Till Thy Gospel bring to me
Life and immortality:

While Thy ministers proclaim
Peace and pardon in Thy Name,
Through their voice, by faith, may I
Hear Thee speaking from the sky!

From Thy house when I return,
May my heart within me burn;
And at evening let me say,
I have walk'd with God to-day!
James Montgomery. 1825.

CCCXX.

Ere another Sabbath's close,
Ere again we seek repose,
Lord! our song ascends to Thee;
At Thy feet we bow the knee.

For the mercies of the day,
For this rest upon our way,
Thanks to Thee alone be given,
Lord of earth, and King of Heaven!

Cold our services have been;
Mingled every prayer with sin;
But Thou canst and wilt forgive;
By Thy grace alone we live!

Whilst this thorny path we tread,
May Thy love our footsteps lead!
When our journey here is past,
May we rest with Thee at last!

Let these earthly Sabbaths prove
Foretastes of our joys above;
While their steps Thy pilgrims bend
To the rest which knows no end!

Anon. [1841.]

CCCXXI.

Of Thy love some gracious token
  Grant us, Lord, before we go;
Bless Thy word which has been spoken;
  Life and peace on all bestow!
When we join the world again,
Let our hearts with Thee remain:
    O direct us
    And protect us,
Till we gain the heavenly shore,
Where Thy people want no more!

Thomas Kelly. 1804.

END OF PART III.

PART IV.

SONGS OF THE HEART.

# The Book of Praise.

PART THE FOURTH.

SONGS OF THE HEART.

I.

THE CALL.

"*Rise; He calleth thee.*"—(MARK x. 49.)

CCCXXII.

Child of sin and sorrow,
 Fill'd with dismay,
Wait not for to-morrow,
 Yield thee to-day!
 Heaven bids thee come
 While yet there's room:
Child of sin and sorrow,
 Hear, and obey!

Child of sin and sorrow,
 Why wilt thou die?
Come, while thou canst borrow
 Help from on high!
 Grieve not that love
 Which from above,
Child of sin and sorrow,
 Would bring thee nigh!
  Thomas Hastings. [1842.]

CCCXXIII.

Poor child of sin and woe,
Now listen to thy Father's pleading voice;
   No longer need'st thou go
Without a friend to bid thy heart rejoice.

   I know thou canst not rest
Until thou art from guilt and sorrow free;
   Earth cannot make thee blest;
Come, bring thy suffering, bleeding heart to Me.

   How often, in the hour
Of weariness, would I have succoured thee!
   But thou didst spurn the power,
And scorn the heart that loved so tenderly.

   Oh, what on earth appears
To comfort thy distress and heal thy grief,
   To dry thy bitter tears,
And offer thy poor sinking soul relief?

   Thy life of sin has been
A toilsome path, without one cheering ray;
   Now on thy Father lean,
And He will guide thee in a better way.

   Come, leave the desert land,
And all the husks on which thy soul has fed;
   And trust the faithful Hand
That offers thee a feast of living Bread.

   O sinner! 'tis the voice
Of One, who long has loved and pitied thee!
   He would thy heart rejoice,
And set thee from all sin and suffering free.

Oh, canst thou turn away?
It is thy Father that invites thee near!
Nay, sinner! weep and pray!
And Heaven shall hail the penitential tear!
Eliza Fanny Morris. 1858.

CCCXXIV.

Return, O wanderer, to thy home;
  Thy Father calls for thee:
No longer now an exile roam,
  In guilt and misery:
    Return, return!

Return, O wanderer, to thy home;
  'Tis Jesus calls for thee:
The Spirit and the Bride say, Come:
  O now for refuge flee;
    Return, return!

Return, O wanderer, to thy home;
  'Tis madness to delay;
There are no pardons in the tomb,
  And brief is mercy's day:
    Return, return!
Thomas Hastings. [1842.]

CCCXXV.

Haste, traveller, haste! the night comes on,
And many a shining hour is gone;
The storm is gathering in the west,
And thou art far from home and rest;
    Haste, traveller, haste!

O far from home thy footsteps stray;
Christ is the Life, and Christ the Way;
And Christ the Light, thy setting Sun,
Sinks ere thy morning is begun;
   Haste, traveller, haste!

Awake, awake! pursue thy way
With steady course, while yet 'tis day;
While thou art sleeping on the ground,
Danger and darkness gather round;
   Haste, traveller, haste!

The rising tempest sweeps the sky;
The rains descend, the winds are high;
The waters swell, and death and fear
Beset thy path, nor refuge near;
   Haste, traveller, haste!

O yes! a shelter you may gain,
A covert from the wind and rain,
A hiding-place, a rest, a home,
A refuge from the wrath to come;
   Haste, traveller, haste!

Then linger not in all the plain,
Flee for thy life, the mountain gain;
Look not behind, make no delay,
O speed thee, speed thee on thy way;
   Haste, traveller, haste!

Poor, lost, benighted soul! art thou
Willing to find salvation now?
There yet is hope; hear mercy's call;
Truth! Life! Light! Way! in Christ is all!
   Haste to Him, haste!
    William Bengo Collyer. [1829.]

CCCXXVI.

Just as thou art, without one trace
Of love or joy or inward grace,
Or meetness for the heavenly place,
    O guilty sinner, come!

Burden'd with guilt, wouldst thou be blest?
Trust not the world, it gives no rest;
Christ brings relief to hearts opprest;
    O weary sinner, come!

Come, leave thy burden at the cross;
Count all thy gains but worthless dross;
His grace o'erpays all earthly loss;
    O needy sinner, come!

Come hither! bring thy boding fears,
Thy aching heart, thy bursting tears;
'Tis Mercy's voice salutes thine ears;
    O trembling sinner, come!
      Anon. [1862.]

CCCXXVII.
Rev. xxii. 17.

Sweet is the Spirit's strain;
Breath'd by soft pleadings inly heard,
By all the heart's deep fountains stirr'd,
By conscience, and the written Word;
 Come, wanderers, home again!

The Bride repeats the call ;
By high thanksgiving, lowly prayer,
By days of rest, and fostering care,
By holy rites, that all may share ;
   She whispers, Come ! to all.

Let him who hears say, Come !
If thou hast been sin's wretched slave ;
If thou art risen from that grave ;
Thy sleeping brethren seek to save,
   And call the wanderers home.

And let all come, who thirst !
Freely for every child of woe
The streams of living waters flow ;
And whosoever will, may go
   Where healing fountains burst.

There drink and be at rest ;
On Him who died for thee believe ;
The Spirit's quickening grace receive ;
No more the God who seeks thee grieve ;
   Be holy, and be blest !

Joseph Anstice. [1836.]

CCCXXVIII.

With tearful eyes I look around ;
   Life seems a dark and stormy sea ;
Yet midst the gloom I hear a sound,
   A heavenly whisper, Come to Me !

It tells me of a place of rest ;
   It tells me where my soul may flee :
Oh ! to the weary, faint, opprest,
   How sweet the bidding, Come to Me !

The Call.

When the poor heart with anguish learns
    That earthly props resign'd must be,
And from each broken cistern turns,
    It hears the accents, Come to Me!

When against sin I strive in vain,
    And cannot from its yoke get free,
Sinking beneath the heavy chain,
    The words arrest me, Come to Me!

When nature shudders, loth to part
    From all I love, enjoy, and see;
When a faint chill steals o'er my heart,
    A sweet voice utters, Come to Me!

Come, for all else must fail and die;
    Earth is no resting-place for thee;
Heavenward direct thy weeping eye;
    I am thy Portion; Come to Me!

O voice of mercy, voice of love!
    In conflict, grief, and agony,
Support me, cheer me from above,
    And gently whisper, Come to me!
                Hugh White. 1841.

CCCXXIX.

Come, take my yoke, the Saviour said;
To follow Me be not afraid;
For I in heart am lowly, meek,
And offer you the rest you seek.

The yoke of Pleasure may allure,
And promise bliss that will endure;
But, when it has thy youth despoil'd,
'Twill cast thee off as garment soil'd.

Take not on thee the yoke of Wealth;
'Twill eat thy soul, destroy thy health,
And make thee feel how cheap the cost,
If worlds could buy the peace it lost.

Ambition, too, its yoke displays,
And hangs out its perennial bays;
Be not, poor soul, by it misled;
I offer thee a crown instead.

Then take my yoke, 'tis soft and light,
'Twill ne'er disturb thy rest at night,
But guide thee to that world above
Where no restraint is known but love.
Robert Smith. 1862.

CCCXXX.

Behold! a Stranger's at the door!
He gently knocks, has knock'd before,
Has waited long, is waiting still;
You treat no other friend so ill.

But will He prove a Friend indeed?
He will! the very Friend you need!
The Man of Nazareth, 'tis He,
With garments dyed at Calvary.

Oh lovely attitude! He stands
With melting heart, and laden hands!
Oh matchless kindness! and He shows
This matchless kindness to His foes.

Rise, touch'd with gratitude Divine;
Turn out His enemy and thine,
That hateful, hell-born monster, Sin;
And let the Heavenly Stranger in.

The Call.

If thou art poor, (and poor thou art,)
Lo! He has riches to impart;
Not wealth, in which mean av'rice rolls;
O better far! the wealth of souls!

Thou'rt blind; He'll take the scales away,
And let in everlasting day:
Naked thou art; but He shall dress
Thy blushing soul in Righteousness.

Art thou a weeper? Grief shall fly;
For who can weep with Jesus by?
No terror shall thy hopes annoy;
No tear, except the tear of joy.

Admit Him, for the human breast
Ne'er entertain'd so kind a Guest:
Admit Him, for you can't expel;
Where'er He comes, He comes to dwell.

Admit Him, ere His anger burn;
His feet, departed, ne'er return!
Admit Him; or the hour's at hand,
When at His door denied you'll stand.

Yet know, (nor of the terms complain,)
If Jesus comes, He comes to reign;
To reign, and with no partial sway;
Thoughts must be slain, that disobey!

Sovereign of souls! Thou Prince of Peace!
O may Thy gentle reign increase!
Throw wide the door, each willing mind!
And be His empire all mankind!

Joseph Grigg. 1765.

CCCXXXI.

The winds were howling o'er the deep,
    Each wave a watery hill;
The Saviour waken'd from His sleep;
    He spake, and all was still.

The madman in a tomb had made
    His mansion of despair:
Woe to the traveller who stray'd
    With heedless footstep there!

The chains hung broken from his arm,
    Such strength can hell supply;
And fiendish hate, and fierce alarm,
    Flash'd from his hollow eye.

He met that glance, so thrilling sweet;
    He heard those accents mild;
And, melting at Messiah's feet,
    Wept like a weanèd child.

Oh! madder than the raving man!
    Oh! deafer than the sea!
How long the time since Christ began
    To call in vain on me!

He call'd me when my thoughtless prime
    Was early ripe to ill;
I pass'd from folly on to crime;
    And yet He call'd me still.

He call'd me in the time of dread,
    When death was full in view;
I trembled on my feverish bed,
    And rose to sin anew.

Yet, could I hear Him once again,
  As I have heard of old,
Methinks He should not call in vain
  His wanderer to the fold.

Oh Thou! that every thought canst know,
  And answer every prayer,
Oh! give me sickness, want, or woe;
  But snatch me from despair!

My struggling will by grace control!
  Renew my broken vow!
What blessed light breaks on my soul?
  My God! I hear Thee now!
        Bishop Reginald Heber. 1827.

CCCXXXII.

"Was du vor tausend Jahren."

A thousand years have fleeted;
  And, Saviour! still we see
Thy deed of love repeated
  On all who come to Thee.
As he who sat benighted,
  Afflicted, poor, and blind;
So now, (Thy word is plighted,)
  Joy, light, and peace I find.

Dark gloom my spirit filling,
  Beside the way I sat;
Desire my heart was thrilling;
  But anguish more than that.

To me no ray was granted,
  Although I heard the psalms
The faithful sweetly chanted,
  And felt the waving palms.

With grief my heart was aching;
  O'erwhelming were my woes,
Till, heaven-born courage taking,
  To Thee my cry arose:
" O David's Son, relieve me,
  " My bitter anguish quell;
" Thy promised succour give me,
  "And this dark night dispel!"

With tears that fast were flowing,
  I sought Thee through the crowd,
My heart more tender growing,
  Until I wept aloud:
Oh! then my grief diminish'd;
  For then they cried to me,
" Blind man, thy woe is finish'd;
  " Arise, He calleth thee!"

I came with steps that falter'd;
  Thy course I felt Thee check;
Then straight my mind was alter'd,
  And bow'd my stubborn neck:
Thou saidst, " What art thou seeking?"
  " O Lord! that I might see!"
Oh! then I heard Thee speaking;
  " Believe, and it shall be."

Our hope, Lord, faileth never,
  When Thou Thy word dost plight:
My fears then ceased for ever,
  And all my soul was light.

Thou gavest me Thy blessing;
From former guilt set free,
Now heavenly joy possessing,
O Lord! I follow Thee!
Frances Elizabeth Cox. 1841.
From Frederic de la Motte Fouqué.

CCCXXXIII.

I heard the voice of Jesus say,
"Come unto Me and rest;
"Lay down, thou weary one, lay down
"Thy head upon My breast!"
I came to Jesus as I was,
Weary, and worn, and sad;
I found in Him a resting-place,
And He has made me glad.

I heard the voice of Jesus say,
"Behold! I freely give
"The living water; thirsty one,
"Stoop down, and drink, and live!"
I came to Jesus, and I drank
Of that life-giving stream;
My thirst was quench'd, my soul revived,
And now I live in Him.

I heard the voice of Jesus say,
"I am this dark world's light;
"Look unto Me, thy morn shall rise,
"And all thy day be bright."
I look'd to Jesus, and I found
In Him my Star, my Sun;
And in that light of life I'll walk
Till travelling days are done.
Horatius Bonar. 1856.

CCCXXXIV.

In evil long I took delight,
  Unawed by shame or fear,
Till a new object struck my sight,
  And stopp'd my wild career:
I saw One hanging on a Tree,
  In agonies and blood,
Who fix'd His languid eyes on me,
  As near His Cross I stood.

Sure never till my latest breath
  Can I forget that look:
It seem'd to charge me with His death,
  Though not a word He spoke:
My conscience felt and own'd the guilt,
  And plunged me in despair;
I saw my sins His Blood had spilt,
  And help'd to nail Him there.

Alas! I knew not what I did!
  But now my tears are vain:
Where shall my trembling soul be hid?
  For I the Lord have slain!
A second look He gave, which said,
  " I freely all forgive;
" This Blood is for thy ransom paid;
  " I die, that thou may'st live."

Thus, while His death my sin displays
  In all its blackest hue,
Such is the mystery of grace,
  It seals my pardon too.
With pleasing grief, and mournful joy,
  My spirit now is fill'd,
That I should such a life destroy,
  Yet live by Him I kill'd.

John Newton. 1779.

II.

THE ANSWER.

"I will arise, and go to my Father."—(LUKE xv. 18.)

CCCXXXV.

And have I measured half my days,
    And half my journey run,
Nor tasted the Redeemer's grace,
    Nor yet my work begun?

The morning of my life is past,
    The noon is almost o'er;
The night of death approaches fast,
    When I can work no more.

Darkness He makes His secret place,
    Thick clouds surround His Throne;
Nor can I yet behold His face,
    Or find the God Unknown.

A God that hides Himself He is,
    Far off from mortal sight;
An inaccessible Abyss
    Of uncreated Light.

Far off He is, yet always near;
    He fills both earth and Heaven,
But doth not to my soul appear,
    My soul from Eden driven.

O'er earth a banish'd man I rove,
    But cannot feel Him nigh:
Where is the pardoning God of Love,
    Who stoop'd for me to die?

I sought Him in the secret cell
  With unavailing care:
Long did I in the desert dwell,
  Nor could I find Him there.

Still every means in vain I try;
  I seek Him far and near;
Where'er I come, constrain'd to cry,
  "My Saviour is not here."

God is in this, in every place:
  Yet oh! how dark and void
To me! 'tis one great wilderness,
  This earth without my God!

Empty of Him, who all things fills,
  Till He His Light impart,
Till He His glorious Self reveals,
  The veil is on my heart.

O Thou, who seest and know'st my grief,
  Thyself Unseen, Unknown!
Pity my helpless unbelief,
  And take away the stone!

Regard me with a gracious eye;
  The long-sought blessing give;
And bid me, at the point to die,
  Behold Thy face, and live!

A darker soul did never yet
  Thy promised help implore:
O! that I now my Lord might meet,
  And never lose Him more!

Charles Wesley. 1749.

CCCXXXVI.

O Thou, whose tender mercy hears
   Contrition's humble sigh,
Whose hand indulgent wipes the tears
   From sorrow's weeping eye;

See, low before Thy throne of grace,
   A wretched wanderer mourn;
Hast Thou not bid me seek Thy face?
   Hast Thou not said, Return?

And shall my guilty fears prevail
   To drive me from Thy feet?
Oh! let not this dear refuge fail,
   This only safe retreat!

Absent from Thee, my Guide, my Light,
   Without one cheering ray,
Through dangers, fears, and gloomy night,
   How desolate my way!

O shine on this benighted heart,
   With beams of mercy shine!
And let Thy healing voice impart
   A taste of joys Divine!

Thy presence only can bestow
   Delights which never cloy:
Be this my solace here below,
   And my eternal joy!

               Anne Steele. 1760.

CCCXXXVII.

When shall Thy love constrain
   And force me to Thy breast?
When shall my soul return again
   To her eternal rest?

Ah! what avails my strife,
   My wandering to and fro?
Thou hast the words of endless life;
   Ah! whither should I go?

Thy condescending grace
   To me did freely move;
It calls me still to seek Thy face,
   And stoops to ask my love.

Lord! at Thy feet I fall;
   I groan to be set free;
I fain would now obey the call,
   And give up all for Thee.

Though late, I all forsake,
   My friends, my life resign:
Gracious Redeemer, take, O take,
   And seal me ever Thine!

Come, and possess me whole,
   Nor hence again remove:
Settle, and fix my wavering soul
   With all Thy weight of love!

My one desire be this,
   Thy only love to know,
To seek and taste no other bliss,
   No other good below.

My Life, my Portion Thou,
  Thou all-sufficient art;
My Hope, my heavenly Treasure, now
  Enter, and keep my heart!
>> *Charles Wesley.* 1740.

CCCXXXVIII.

My spirit longeth for Thee
  Within my troubled breast,
Although I be unworthy
  Of so Divine a Guest.

Of so Divine a Guest
  Unworthy though I be,
Yet has my heart no rest
  Unless it come from Thee.

Unless it come from Thee,
  In vain I look around;
In all that I can see
  No rest is to be found.

No rest is to be found
  But in Thy blessèd love:
O let my wish be crown'd,
  And send it from above!
>> *John Byrom.* 1773.

CCCXXXIX.

Weary of wandering from my God,
  And now made willing to return,
I hear, and bow me to the rod;
  For Him, not without hope, I mourn:
I have an Advocate above,
A friend before the Throne of Love.

O Jesu, full of pardoning grace,
  More full of grace than I of sin;
Yet once again I seek Thy face,
  Open Thine arms and take me in,
And freely my backslidings heal,
And love the faithless sinner still!

Thou know'st the way to bring me back,
  My fallen spirit to restore;
O, for Thy Truth and Mercy's sake,
  Forgive, and bid me sin no more!
The ruins of my soul repair,
And make my heart an house of prayer!

The stone to flesh again convert,
  The veil of sin once more remove;
Drop Thy warm Blood upon my heart,
  And melt it with Thy dying love:
This rebel heart by love subdue,
And make it soft, and make it new!

Give to mine eyes refreshing tears,
  And kindle my relentings now;
Fill all my soul with filial fears,
  To Thy sweet yoke my spirit bow;
Bend by Thy grace, O! bend, or break
The iron sinew in my neck!

Ah! give me, Lord, the tender heart,
  That trembles at th' approach of sin;
A godly fear of sin impart,
  Implant, and root it deep within;
That I may dread Thy gracious power,
And never dare offend Thee more!

Charles Wesley. 1749.

CCCXL.

Hear, gracious God! a sinner's cry,
For I have nowhere else to fly;
My hope, my only hope's in Thee;
O God, be merciful to me!

To Thee I come, a sinner poor,
And wait for mercy at Thy door;
Indeed, I've nowhere else to flee:
O God, be merciful to me!

To Thee I come, a sinner weak,
And scarce know how to pray or speak;
From fear and weakness set me free;
O God, be merciful to me!

To Thee I come, a sinner vile;
Upon me, Lord, vouchsafe to smile!
Mercy alone I make my plea;
O God, be merciful to me!

To Thee I come, a sinner great,
And well Thou knowest all my state;
Yet full forgiveness is with Thee;
O God, be merciful to me!

To Thee I come, a sinner lost,
Nor have I ought wherein to trust;
But where Thou art, Lord, I would be;
O God, be merciful to me!

To glory bring me, Lord, at last;
And there, when all my fears are past,
With all the saints I'll then agree,
God has been merciful to me!

Samuel Medley. 1789.

CCCXLI.

Hear, gracious God! my humble moan;
    To Thee I breathe my sighs:
When will the mournful night be gone,
    And when my joys arise?

My God! Oh! could I make the claim,
    My Father and my Friend!
And call Thee mine, by every name
    On which Thy saints depend;

By every name of power and love
    I would Thy grace entreat;
Nor should my humble hopes remove,
    Nor leave Thy sacred seat.

Yet, though my soul in darkness mourns,
    Thy word is all my stay;
Here I would rest till light returns,
    Thy Presence makes my day.

Speak, Lord, and bid celestial peace
    Relieve my aching heart!
O smile, and bid my sorrows cease,
    And all the gloom depart!

Then shall my drooping spirit rise,
    And bless Thy healing rays,
And change these deep complaining sighs
    For songs of sacred praise!

Anne Steele. 1760.

CCCXLII.

And shall I sit alone,
  Oppress'd with grief and fear,
To God my Father make my moan,
  And He refuse to hear?

If He my Father be,
  His pity He will show,
From cruel bondage set me free,
  And inward peace bestow.

If still He silence keep,
  'Tis but my faith to try;
He knows and feels, whene'er I weep,
  And softens every sigh.

Then will I humbly wait,
  Nor once indulge despair;
My sins are great, but not so great
  As His compassions are.
          Benjamin Beddome. [1818.]

CCCXLIII.

O that my load of sin were gone!
  O that I could at last submit
At Jesus' feet to lay it down,
  To lay my soul at Jesus' feet!

When shall mine eyes behold the Lamb,
  The God of my salvation see?
Weary, O Lord, Thou know'st I am;
  Yet still I cannot come to Thee.

Rest for my soul I long to find;
  Saviour! (if mine indeed Thou art,)
Give me Thy meek and lowly mind,
  And stamp Thy image on my heart!

Fain would I learn of Thee, my God,
    Thy light and easy burden prove,
The cross, all stain'd with hallow'd blood,
    The labour of Thy dying love.

This moment would I take it up,
    And after my dear Master bear;
With Thee ascend to Calvary's top,
    And bow my head and suffer there.

I would; but Thou must give the power,
    My heart from every sin release:
Bring near, bring near the joyful hour,
    And fill me with Thy perfect peace!

Come, Lord, the drooping sinner cheer,
    Nor let Thy chariot-wheels delay!
Appear, in my poor heart appear!
    My God, my Saviour, come away!
              Charles Wesley. 1742.

CCCXLIV.

Come, let us to the Lord our God
    With contrite hearts return;
Our God is gracious, nor will leave
    The desolate to mourn.

His voice commands the tempest forth,
    And stills the stormy wave;
And, though His arm be strong to smite,
    'Tis also strong to save.

Long hath the night of sorrow reign'd;
    The dawn shall bring us light;
God shall appear, and we shall rise
    With gladness in His sight.

Our hearts, if God we seek to know,
  Shall know Him, and rejoice;
His coming like the morn shall be,
  Like morning songs His voice.

As dew upon the tender herb,
  Diffusing fragrance round;
As showers that usher in the spring,
  And cheer the thirsty ground;

So shall His Presence bless our souls,
  And shed a joyful light;
That hallow'd morn shall chase away
  The sorrows of the night.

John Morrison. 1770.

III.

FAITH.

*"Looking unto Jesus, the Author and Finisher of
  our Faith."*—(HEB. xii. 2.)

CCCXLV.

Come, O thou Traveller unknown,
  Whom still I hold, but cannot see
My company before is gone,
  And I am left alone with Thee;
With Thee all night I mean to stay,
And wrestle till the break of day.

I need not tell Thee who I am,
  My misery or sin declare;
Thyself hast call'd me by my name;
  Look on Thy hands, and read it there!
But Who, I ask Thee, Who art Thou?
Tell me Thy Name, and tell me now.

In vain Thou strugglest to get free,
  I never will unloose my hold;
Art Thou the Man that died for me?
  The secret of Thy love unfold.
Wrestling, I will not let Thee go,
Till I Thy Name, Thy Nature know.

Wilt Thou not yet to me reveal
  Thy new, unutterable Name?
Tell me, I still beseech Thee, tell:
  To know it now, resolved I am:
Wrestling, I will not let Thee go,
Till I Thy Name, Thy Nature know.

'Tis all in vain to hold Thy tongue,
  Or touch the hollow of my thigh;
Though every sinew be unstrung,
  Out of my arms Thou shalt not fly:
Wrestling, I will not let Thee go,
Till I Thy Name, Thy Nature know.

What though my shrinking flesh complain,
  And murmur to contend so long?
I rise superior to my pain;
  When I am weak, then I am strong:
And when my all of strength shall fail,
I shall with the God-Man prevail.

My strength is gone; my nature dies;
  I sink beneath Thy weighty hand,
Faint to revive, and fall to rise;
  I fall, and yet by faith I stand:
I stand, and will not let Thee go,
Till I Thy Name, Thy Nature know.

Yield to me now, for I am weak,
  But confident in self-despair;
Speak to my heart, in blessings speak,
  Be conquer'd by my instant prayer!
Speak, or Thou never hence shalt move,
And tell me, if Thy Name is Love?

'Tis Love! 'tis Love! Thou diedst for me!
  I hear Thy whisper in my heart!
The morning breaks, the shadows flee;
  Pure universal Love Thou art!
To me, to all, Thy bowels move;
Thy Nature, and Thy Name, is Love!

My prayer hath power with God; the grace
  Unspeakable I now receive;
Through faith I see Thee face to face,
  I see Thee face to face, and live:
In vain I have not wept and strove;
Thy Nature, and Thy Name, is Love.

I know Thee, Saviour, Who Thou art;
  Jesus, the feeble sinner's Friend!
Nor wilt Thou with the night depart,
  But stay, and love me to the end!
Thy mercies never shall remove,
Thy Nature, and Thy Name, is Love!

The Sun of Righteousness on me
  Hath rose, with healing in His wings;
Wither'd my nature's strength, from Thee
  My soul its life and succour brings;
My help is all laid up above;
Thy Nature, and Thy Name, is Love.

Contented now upon my thigh
  I halt, till life's short journey end ;
All helplessness, all weakness, I
  On Thee alone for strength depend ;
Nor have I power from Thee to move ;
Thy Nature, and Thy Name, is Love.

Lame as I am, I take the prey,
  Hell, earth, and sin, with ease o'ercome ;
I leap for joy, pursue my way,
  And as a bounding hart fly home !
Through all eternity to prove,
Thy Nature and Thy Name is Love !
Charles Wesley. 1742.

CCCXLVI.

Hark, my soul ! it is the Lord,
'Tis thy Saviour, hear His word :
Jesus speaks, and speaks to thee ;
" Say, poor sinner, lov'st thou Me ?

" I delivered thee when bound,
" And, when bleeding, heal'd thy wound ;
" Sought thee wandering, set thee right,
" Turn'd thy darkness into light.

" Can a woman's tender care
" Cease towards the child she bare ?
" Yes, she may forgetful be ;
" Yet will I remember thee !

" Mine is an unchanging love,
" Higher than the heights above,
" Deeper than the depths beneath,
" Free and faithful, strong as death.

"Thou shalt see my glory soon,
"When the work of grace is done;
"Partner of my throne shalt be;
"Say, poor sinner, lov'st thou Me?"

Lord! it is my chief complaint,
That my love is weak and faint;
Yet I love Thee and adore!
Oh! for grace to love Thee more!
William Cowper. 1779.

CCCXLVII.

And can it be, that I should gain
   An interest in the Saviour's blood?
Died He for me, who caus'd His pain,
   For me, who Him to death pursued?
Amazing Love! how can it be,
That Thou, my God, shouldst die for me?

'Tis mystery all! Th' Immortal dies!
   Who can explore His strange design?
In vain the first-born seraph tries
   To sound the depths of Love Divine.
'Tis mercy all! Let earth adore!
Let angel minds enquire no more!

He left His Father's throne above,
   (So free, so infinite His grace;)
Emptied Himself of all but love,
   And bled for Adam's helpless race.
'Tis mercy all, immense and free!
For O, my God! it found out me!

Long my imprison'd spirit lay,
   Fast bound in sin and nature's night;
Thine eye diffus'd a quickening ray;
   I woke; the dungeon flam'd with light:
My chains fell off, my heart was free,
I rose, went forth, and follow'd Thee!

Still the small inward voice I hear,
   That whispers all my sins forgiven;
Still the atoning Blood is near,
   That quench'd the wrath of hostile Heaven;
I feel the life His wounds impart;
I feel my Saviour in my heart.

No condemnation now I dread;
   Jesus, and all in Him, is mine!
Alive in Him, my living Head,
   And cloth'd in righteousness Divine,
Bold I approach th' Eternal Throne,
And claim the crown, through Christ my own.
Charles Wesley. 1739.

CCCXLVIII.

Now I have found the ground wherein
   Sure my soul's anchor may remain;
The wounds of Jesus, for my sin
   Before the world's foundation slain;
Whose mercy shall unshaken stay
When heaven and earth are fled away.

Father, Thine everlasting grace
   Our scanty thought surpasses far;
Thy heart still melts with tenderness;
   Thine arms of love still open are,
Returning sinners to receive,
That mercy they may taste and live.

O Love! Thou bottomless abyss!
  My sins are swallow'd up in thee:
Cover'd is my unrighteousness,
  Nor spot of guilt remains on me:
While Jesus' Blood, through earth and skies,
Mercy, free boundless mercy, cries!

With faith I plunge me in this sea;
  Here is my hope, my joy, my rest;
Hither, when hell assails, I flee,
  I look into my Saviour's breast:
Away, sad doubt, and anxious fear!
Mercy is all that's written there!

Though waves and storms go o'er my head;
  Though strength, and health, and friends be gone;
Though joys be wither'd all and dead;
  Though every comfort be withdrawn;
On this my steadfast soul relies;
Father! Thy mercy never dies.

Fix'd on this ground will I remain,
  Though my heart fail and flesh decay;
This anchor shall my soul sustain,
  When earth's foundations melt away:
Mercy's full power I then shall prove,
Loved with an everlasting love.
               John Wesley. 1740.
               From J. A. Rothe.)

CCCXLIX.

O Thou, the contrite sinners' Friend,
Who loving, lov'st them to the end,
On this alone my hopes depend,
  That Thou wilt plead for me!

When, weary in the Christian race,
Far off appears my resting-place,
And fainting I mistrust Thy grace,
   Then, Saviour, plead for me!

When I have err'd and gone astray
Afar from Thine and Wisdom's way,
And see no glimmering guiding ray,
   Still, Saviour, plead for me!

When Satan, by my sins made bold,
Strives from Thy cross to loose my hold,
Then with Thy pitying arms enfold,
   And plead, O plead for me!

And when my dying hour draws near,
Darken'd with anguish, guilt, and fear,
Then to my fainting sight appear,
   Pleading in Heaven for me!

When the full light of heavenly day
Reveals my sins in dread array,
Say Thou hast wash'd them all away;
   O say, Thou plead'st for me!
Charlotte Elliott. [1837.]

CCCL.

O Holy Saviour, Friend unseen,
The faint, the weak, on Thee may lean:
Help me, throughout life's varying scene,
   By faith to cling to Thee!

Blest with communion so Divine,
Take what Thou wilt, shall I repine,
When, as the branches to the vine,
   My soul may cling to Thee?

Faith.

Far from her home, fatigued, opprest,
Here she has found a place of rest,
An exile still, yet not unblest
   While she can cling to Thee!

Without a murmur I dismiss
My former dreams of earthly bliss;
My joy, my recompense be this,
   Each hour to cling to Thee!

What though the world deceitful prove,
And earthly friends and joys remove?
With patient uncomplaining love
   Still would I cling to Thee!

Oft when I seem to tread alone
Some barren waste with thorns o'ergrown,
A voice of love, in gentlest tone,
   Whispers, "Still cling to Me!"

Though faith and hope awhile be tried,
I ask not, need not, aught beside:
How safe, how calm, how satisfied,
   The souls that cling to Thee!

They fear not life's rough storms to brave,
Since Thou art near, and strong to save:
Nor shudder e'en at death's dark wave;
   Because they cling to Thee!

Blest is my lot, whate'er befal:
What can disturb me, who appal,
While, as my strength, my rock, my all,
   Saviour! I cling to Thee?

                Charlotte Elliott. 1836.

CCCLI.

Jesu, my strength, my hope,
  On Thee I cast my care,
With humble confidence look up,
  And know, Thou hear'st my prayer.
Give me on Thee to wait
  Till I can all things do,
On Thee, Almighty to create!
  Almighty to renew!

I want a sober mind,
  A self-renouncing will,
That tramples down and casts behind
  The baits of pleasing ill:
A soul inured to pain,
  To hardship, grief, and loss;
Bold to take up, firm to sustain,
  The consecrated cross.

I want a godly fear,
  A quick-discerning eye,
That looks to Thee when sin is near,
  And sees the Tempter fly;
A spirit still prepared,
  And arm'd with jealous care,
For ever standing on its guard,
  And watching unto prayer.

I want a heart to pray,
  To pray and never cease,
Never to murmur at Thy stay,
  Or wish my sufferings less;
This blessing, above all,
  Always to pray, I want,
Out of the deep on Thee to call,
  And never, never faint.

I want a true regard,
   A single, steady aim,
Unmov'd by threat'ning or reward,
   To Thee and Thy great Name ;
   A jealous, just concern
   For Thine immortal praise ;
A pure desire that all may learn
   And glorify Thy grace.

I rest upon Thy word ;
   Thy promise is for me ;
My succour and salvation, Lord,
   Shall surely come from Thee.
   But let me still abide,
   Nor from my hope remove,
Till Thou my patient spirit guide
   Into Thy perfect love !
             Charles Wesley. 1742.

IV.

LOVE.

"*If ye love Me, keep My commandments.*"
(JOHN xiv. 15.)

CCCLII.

Jesus, my all, to Heaven is gone ;
He that I placed my hopes upon ;
His track I see ; and I'll pursue
The narrow way, till Him I view.

The way the holy Prophets went,
The way that leads from banishment,
The King's high-way of holiness,
I'll go ; for all the paths are peace.

No stranger may proceed therein,
No lover of the world and sin;
No lion, no devouring care,
No ravenous tiger shall be there.

No: nothing may go up thereon
But travelling souls; and I am one:
Wayfaring men, to Canaan bound,
Shall only in the way be found.

Nor fools, by carnal men esteem'd,
Shall err therein; but they, redeem'd
In Jesu's blood, shall show their right
To travel there, till Heav'n's in sight.

This is the way I long have sought,
And mourn'd, because I found it not;
My grief, my burden, long have been
Because I could not cease from sin.

The more I strove against its power,
I sinn'd and stumbled but the more;
Till late I heard my Saviour say,
"Come hither, soul! for I'm the Way!"

Lo! glad I come; and Thou, dear Lamb,
Shall take me to Thee, as I am:
Nothing but sin I Thee can give;
Yet help me, and Thy praise I'll live!

I'll tell to all poor sinners round
What a dear Saviour I have found;
I'll point to Thy Redeeming blood.
And say, "Behold the Way to God!"

John Cennick. 1743.

CCCLIII.

Go, worship at Immanuel's feet;
See, in His face what wonders meet;
Earth is too narrow to express
His worth, His glory, or His grace!

The whole creation can afford
But some faint shadows of my Lord;
Nature, to make His beauties known,
Must mingle colours not her own.

Is He compared to Wine or Bread?
Dear Lord, our souls would thus be fed:
That flesh, that dying Blood of Thine,
Is Bread of Life, is heavenly Wine.

Is He a Tree? The world receives
Salvation from His healing leaves:
That righteous Branch, that fruitful bough,
Is David's root and offspring too.

Is he a Rose? Not Sharon yields
Such fragrancy in all her fields;
Or if the Lily He assume,
The valleys bless the rich perfume.

Is He a Vine? His heavenly root
Supplies the boughs with life and fruit:
O let a lasting union join
My soul the branch to Christ the Vine!

Is He the Head? Each member lives,
And owns the vital power He gives;
The Saints below and Saints above
Joined by His Spirit and His love.

Is He a Fountain? There I bathe,
And heal the plague of sin and death;
These waters all my soul renew,
And cleanse my spotted garments too.

Is He a Fire? He'll purge my dross;
But the true gold sustains no loss:
Like a Refiner shall He sit,
And tread the refuse with His feet.

Is He a Rock? How firm He proves!
The Rock of Ages never moves:
Yet the sweet streams, that from Him flow,
Attend us all the desert through.

Is He a Way? He leads to God;
The path is drawn in lines of Blood;
There would I walk with hope and zeal,
Till I arrive at Sion's hill.

Is He a Door? I'll enter in;
Behold the pastures large and green!
A paradise divinely fair;
None but the sheep have freedom there.

Is He design'd a Corner-stone,
For men to build their Heaven upon?
I'll make Him my Foundation too;
Nor fear the plots of hell below.

Is He a Temple? I adore
The indwelling majesty and power;
And still to His Most Holy Place,
Whene'er I pray, I turn my face.

Is He a Star? He breaks the night,
Piercing the shades with dawning light;
I know His glories from afar,
I know the bright, the morning Star!

Is He a Sun? His beams are grace,
His course is joy and Righteousness:
Nations rejoice, when He appears
To chase their clouds and dry their tears.

Oh! let me climb those higher skies
Where storms and darkness never rise!
There He displays His powers abroad,
And shines and reigns, th' incarnate God.

Nor earth, nor seas, nor sun, nor stars,
Nor heaven His full resemblance bears:
His beauties we can never trace,
Till we behold Him face to face.
Isaac Watts. 1709.

CCCLIV.

Compared with Christ, in all beside
   No comeliness I see;
The one thing needful, dearest Lord,
   Is to be one with Thee.
The sense of Thy expiring Love
   Into my soul convey;
Thyself bestow: for Thee alone
   I absolutely pray.

Whatever else Thy will withholds,
   Here grant me to succeed!
O let Thyself my portion be,
   And I am blest indeed!

Less than Thyself will not suffice
  My comfort to restore;
More than Thyself I cannot have;
  And Thou canst give no more.

Loved of my God, for Him again
  With love intense I burn;
Chosen of Thee ere time began,
  I choose Thee in return!
Whate'er consists not with Thy love,
  O! teach me to resign!
I'm rich to all th' intents of bliss,
  If Thou, O God, art mine!
        Augustus Montague Toplady. 1772.

CCCLV.

Jesu! who for my transgression
  Didst the shameful cross endure,
And didst there the blest possession
  Of Thy joys to me insure;
May my praise be ever telling
Of Thy love, all love excelling!

Wondrous woes that brought salvation!
  Wondrous grace to sinners shown!
Heaven is wrapt in contemplation
  Of His love, whom men disown!
Oh my soul! wilt thou disown Him?
Wilt not thou, my heart, enthrone Him?

Who but He can bless thy weeping?
  Who but He can soothe thy grief?
Only safe beneath His keeping,
  Thou in Him hast sure relief:

To the cross He came to bless thee;
Let His love, my soul, possess thee!

Lord! each thought and inclination,
   All my heart and will inspire,
That my soul, Thy new creation,
   Thee may serve with pure desire;
Daily Thy great love reviewing,
Daily thus my sins subduing!
               Arthur Tozer Russell. 1851.

CCCLVI.

Eternal God, of beings First,
   Of all created good the Spring,
For Thee I long, for Thee I thirst,
   My Love, my Saviour, and my King!
Thine is a never-failing store;
If God be mine, I ask no more.

The fairest world of light on high
   Reflection makes but faint of Thine;
The glorious tenants of the sky
   In God's own beams transported shine:
But, shouldst Thou wrap Thy face in shade,
Soon all their life and lustre fade.

Thy Presence makes celestial day,
   And fills each raptur'd soul with bliss;
Night would prevail, were God away,
   And spirits pine in Paradise!
In vain would all the angels try
To fill Thy room, Thy lack supply.

And, sure, from Heav'n we turn our eyes
   In vain, to seek for bliss below;
The tree of Life can't root nor rise,
   Nor in this blasted region grow:
The wealth of this poor barren clod
Can ne'er make up the want of God.

But, Lord! in Thee the thirsty soul
   Will meet with full, with rich supplies!
Thy smiles will all her fears control,
   Thy beauties feast her ravish'd eyes:
To failing flesh and fainting hearts
Thy favour life and strength imparts!
                Simon Browne. 1720.

CCCLVII.

Christ, my hidden Life, appear,
   Soul of my inmost soul!
Light of life, the mourner cheer,
   And make the sinner whole!
Now in me Thyself display;
Surely Thou in all things art;
I from all things turn away
   To seek Thee in my heart!

Open, Lord, my inward ear,
   And bid my heart rejoice!
Bid my quiet spirit hear
   Thy comfortable voice;
Never in the whirlwind found,
Or where earthquakes rock the place;
Still and silent is the sound,
   The whisper of Thy grace!

From the world of sin, and noise,
    And hurry, I withdraw;
For the small and inward Voice
    I wait with humble awe:
Silent am I now and still;
Dare not in Thy presence move:
To my waiting soul reveal
    The secret of Thy love!

Thou hast undertook for me;
    For me to death wast sold;
Wisdom in a mystery
    Of bleeding love unfold!
Teach the lesson of Thy cross;
Let me die, with Thee to reign!
All things let me count but loss,
    So I may Thee regain!

Show me, as my soul can bear,
    The depth of inbred sin;
All the unbelief declare,
    The pride that lurks within:
Take me, whom Thyself hast bought!
Bring into captivity
Every high aspiring thought,
    That would not stoop to Thee!

Lord, my time is in Thy hand;
    My soul to Thee convert!
Thou canst make me understand,
    Though I am slow of heart.
Thine, in whom I live and move,
Thine the work, the power is Thine!
Thou art Wisdom, Power, and Love;
    And all thou art is mine!

Charles Wesley. 1742.

CCCLVIII.

Source of good, whose power controls
Every movement of our souls;
Wind that quickens where it blows;
Comforter of human woes;
Lamp of God, whose ray serene
In the darkest night is seen;
Come, inspire my feeble strain,
That I may not sing in vain!

God's own Finger, skill'd to teach
Tongues of every land and speech;
Balsam of the wounded soul,
Binding up, and making whole;
Flame of pure and holy love;
Strength of all that live and move;
Come! Thy gifts and fire impart;
Make me love Thee from the heart!

As the hart, with longing, looks
For refreshing water-brooks,
Heated in the burning chace;
So my soul desires Thy grace:
So my heavy-laden breast,
By the cares of life opprest,
Longs Thy cooling streams to taste
In this dry and barren waste.

Mighty Spirit! by whose aid
Man a living soul was made;
Everlasting God! whose fire
Kindles chaste and pure desire;
Grant, in every grief and loss,
I may calmly bear the cross,
And surrender all to Thee,
Comforting and strengthening me!

Let not hell, with frowns or smiles,
Open force or cunning wiles,
Snap the thread of my brief days;
But, when gently life decays,
Take to Heaven Thy servant dear,
Who hath loved and served Thee here;
There eternal hymns to raise,
Mighty Spirit! to Thy praise!
    Richard Massie. 1854.
    (*From John Frank.*)

CCCLIX.

O Lamp of Life! that on the bloody Cross
 Dost hang, the Beacon of our wandering race,
 To guide us homeward to our resting-place,
And save our best wealth from eternal loss!
So purge my inward sight from earthly dross,
 That, fix'd upon Thy Cross, or near or far,
In all the storms this weary bark that toss,
 (Whate'er be lost in that tempestuous war,)
 Thee I retain, my Compass and my Star!
That, when arrived upon the wish'd-for strand,
 I pass of death th' irrevocable bar,
And at the gate of Heaven trembling stand,
The everlasting doors may open wide,
And give Thee to my sight, God glorified!
    Charles Dyson. 1816.

CCCLX.

A poor wayfaring man of grief
 Hath often cross'd me on my way,
Who sued so humbly for relief,
 That I could never answer, Nay·

I had not power to ask his name,
Whither he went, or whence he came,
Yet there was something in his eye
That won my love, I knew not why.

Once, when my scanty meal was spread,
   He entered; not a word he spake;
Just perishing for want of bread;
   I gave him all; he bless'd it, brake,
And ate; but gave me part again:
Mine was an angel's portion then;
For, while I fed with eager haste,
That crust was manna to my taste.

I spied him, where a fountain burst
   Clear from the rock; his strength was gone;
The heedless water mock'd his thirst,
   He heard it, saw it hurrying on:
I ran to raise the sufferer up;
Thrice from the stream he drain'd my cup,
Dipt, and return'd it running o'er;
I drank, and never thirsted more.

'Twas night; the floods were out; it blew
   A winter hurricane aloof;
I heard his voice abroad, and flew
   To bid him welcome to my roof;
I warmed, I clothed, I cheered my guest,
Laid him on my own couch to rest;
Then made the hearth my bed, and seem'd
In Eden's garden while I dream'd.

Stript, wounded, beaten, nigh to death,
   I found him by the highway-side:
I roused his pulse, brought back his breath,
   Revived his spirit, and supplied

Wine, oil, refreshment ; he was healed :
I had myself a wound concealed ;
But from that hour forgot the smart,
And peace bound up my broken heart.

In prison I saw him next, condemned
  To meet a traitor's death at morn :
The tide of lying tongues I stemmed,
  And honoured him midst shame and scorn ;
My friendship's utmost zeal to try,
He ask'd, if I for him would die ?
The flesh was weak, my blood ran chill ;
But the free spirit cried, " I will."

Then in a moment to my view
  The Stranger darted from disguise ;
The tokens in His hands I knew,
  My Saviour stood before mine eyes !
He spake ; and my poor name He named ;
" Of me thou hast not been ashamed ;
These deeds shall thy memorial be ;
Fear not ; thou didst them unto Me."

James Montgomery. 1826.

V.

HOPE.

"Set your affections on things above; not on things on the earth."—(COL. iii. 2.)

CCCLXI.

I praised the earth, in beauty seen
With garlands gay of various green ;
I praised the sea, whose ample field
Shone glorious as a silver shield ;
And earth and ocean seem'd to say,
" Our beauties are but for a day."

I praised the sun, whose chariot roll'd
On wheels of amber and of gold;
I praised the moon, whose softer eye
Gleam'd sweetly through the summer sky;
And moon and sun in answer said,
"Our days of light are numberèd."

O God! O Good beyond compare!
If thus Thy meaner works are fair,
If thus Thy bounties gild the span
Of ruin'd earth and sinful man,
How glorious must the mansion be,
Where Thy redeem'd shall dwell with Thee!
Bishop Reginald Heber. 1827.

CCCLXII.

Our life is but an idle play,
    And various as the wind;
We laugh and sport our hours away,
    Nor think of woes behind.

See the fair cheek of beauty fade,
    Frail glory of an hour;
And blooming youth, with sickening head,
    Droops like the dying flower.

Our pleasures, like the morning sun,
    Diffuse a flattering light;
But gloomy clouds obscure their noon,
    And soon they sink in night.

Wealth, pomp, and honour, we behold
    With an admiring eye;
Like summer insects, drest in gold,
    That flutter, shine, and die.

One little moment can destroy
    Our vast laborious schemes;
And all our heaps of solid joy
    Are sweet deceitful dreams.

Then rise, my soul! and soar away
    Above the thoughtless crowd;
Above the pleasures of the gay,
    And splendours of the proud;

Up where eternal beauties bloom,
    And pleasures all divine;
Where wealth, that never can consume,
    And endless glories shine!
Henry Moore. [1806.]

CCCLXIII.

Though, by sorrows overtaken,
Lord, thy servants seem forsaken,
Thy Almighty hand, we know,
Blendeth love with human woe.

Over earth, and over ocean,
Claiming sinful man's devotion,
Round the living and the dead,
Lord, Thy boundless love is shed.

All to death in this world hasteth;
Riches vanish, beauty wasteth;
Yet within the mourner's breast
Love is an undying guest.

Love, unlike all worldly pleasures,
Wraps in grief its golden treasures,
And to meek and wounded hearts
Deep and holy joy imparts.

Love, that strength and pardon bringest
Through His cross, from Whom thou springest!
May in us Thy gracious force
Heavenward turn our spirits' course!

Come, and while Salvation's morning
On our darken'd soul is dawning,
Sin's deep midnight roll away!
Pour on us the light of day!

Algernon Herbert. [1839.]

CCCLXIV.

We've no abiding city here:
   This may distress the worldling's mind;
But should not cost the saint a tear
   Who hopes a better rest to find.

We've no abiding city here:
   Sad truth! were this to be our home!
But let this thought our spirits cheer;
   We seek a city yet to come.

We've no abiding city here:
   Then let us live as pilgrims do!
Let not the world our rest appear,
   But let us haste from all below.

We've no abiding city here:
   We seek a city out of sight;
Zion its name, the Lord is there,
   It shines with everlasting light!

Zion! Jehovah is her strength;
   Secure she smiles at all her foes;
And weary travellers at length
   Within her sacred walls repose.

O! sweet abode of peace and love,
  Where pilgrims freed from toil are blest!
Had I the pinions of the dove,
  I'd fly to thee, and be at rest!
          Thomas Kelly. 1812—1836.

CCCLXV.

PSALM CXXXVII.

Far from my heavenly home,
  Far from my Father's breast,
Fainting I cry, "Blest Spirit! come
  And speed me to my rest!"

Upon the willows long
  My harp has silent hung:
How should I sing a cheerful song
  Till Thou inspire my tongue?

My spirit homeward turns,
  And fain would thither flee;
My heart, O Zion, droops and yearns,
  When I remember thee.

To thee, to thee I press,
  A dark and toilsome road:
When shall I pass the wilderness
  And reach the saints' abode?

God of my life, be near!
  On Thee my hopes I cast:
O guide me through the desert here,
  And bring me home at last!
          Henry Francis Lyte. 1834.

CCCLXVI.

O happy soul, that lives on high,
    While men lie grovelling here!
His hopes are fix'd above the sky,
    And faith forbids his fear.

His conscience knows no secret stings;
    While peace and joy combine
To form a life, whose holy springs
    Are hidden and divine.

He waits in secret on his God,
    His God in secret sees;
Let earth be all in arms abroad,
    He dwells in heavenly peace.

His pleasures rise from things unseen,
    Beyond this world and time,
Where neither eyes nor ears have been,
    Nor thoughts of sinners climb.

He wants no pomp, nor royal throne,
    To raise his figure here;
Content and pleased to live unknown,
    Till Christ, his Life, appear.

He looks to Heaven's eternal hill,
    To meet that glorious day;
And patient waits his Saviour's will,
    To fetch his soul away.

Isaac Watts. 1709.

CCCLXVII.

Fain would my thoughts fly up to Thee,
   Thy peace, sweet Lord, to find;
But when I offer, still the world
   Lays clogs upon my mind.

Sometimes I climb a little way
   And thence look down below;
How nothing, there, do all things seem,
   That here make such a show!

Then round about I turn my eyes
   To feast my hungry sight;
I meet with Heaven in every thing,
   In every thing delight.

I see Thy wisdom ruling all,
   And it with joy admire;
I see myself among such hopes
   As set my heart on fire.

When I have thus triumph'd awhile,
   And think to build my nest,
Some cross conceits come fluttering by,
   And interrupt my rest.

Then to the earth again I fall,
   And from my low dust cry,
'Twas not in my wing, Lord, but Thine,
   That I got up so high.

And now, my God, whether I rise,
   Or still lie down in dust,
Both I submit to Thy blest will;
   In both, on Thee I trust.

Guide Thou my way, who art Thyself
  My everlasting End,
That every step, or swift, or slow,
  Still to Thyself may tend!

To Father, Son, and Holy Ghost,
  One consubstantial Three,
All highest praise, all humblest thanks,
  Now and for ever be! Amen.

John Austin. 1668.

CCCLXVIII.

There is a pure and peaceful wave,
That rolls around the throne of love,
Whose waters gladden as they lave
  The peaceful shores above.

While streams, which on that tide depend,
Steal from those heavenly shores away,
And on this desert world descend
  O'er weary lands to stray;

The pilgrim faint, and nigh to sink
Beneath his load of earthly woe,
Refresh'd beside their verdant brink,
  Rejoices in their flow.

There, O my soul, do thou repair,
And hover o'er the hallowed spring,
To drink the crystal wave, and there
  To lave thy wearied wing!

There drop that wing, when far it flies
From human care, and toil, and strife,
And feed by those still streams, that rise
  Beneath the Tree of Life!

It may be that the waft of love
Some leaves on that pure tide have driven,
Which, passing from the shores above,
   Have floated down from Heaven.

So shall thy wounds and woes be healed,
By the blest virtue that they bring;
So thy parch'd lips shall be unsealed
   Thy Saviour's praise to sing!
Anon. [1828.]

CCCLXIX.

Calm me, my God, and keep me calm,
   While these hot breezes blow;
Be like the night-dew's cooling balm
   Upon earth's fevered brow!

Calm me, my God, and keep me calm,
   Soft resting on Thy breast;
Soothe me with holy hymn and psalm,
   And bid my spirit rest.

Calm me, my God, and keep me calm,
   Let thine outstretchèd wing,
Be like the shade of Elim's palm
   Beside her desert-spring.

Yes; keep me calm, though loud and rude
   The sounds my ear that greet;
Calm in the closet's solitude,
   Calm in the bustling street;

Calm in the hour of buoyant health,
   Calm in my hour of pain;
Calm in my poverty or wealth,
   Calm in my loss or gain;

Calm in the sufferance of wrong,
  Like Him who bore my shame;
Calm 'mid the threatening, taunting throng,
  Who hate Thy holy Name;

Calm when the great world's news with power
  My listening spirit stir:
Let not the tidings of the hour
  E'er find too fond an ear:

Calm as the ray of sun or star
  Which storms assail in vain,
Moving unruffled through earth's war
  Th' eternal calm to gain!

Horatius Bonar. 1856.

CCCLXX.

O send me down a draught of love,
Or take me hence to drink above!
Here, Marah's water fills my cup;
But there, all griefs are swallow'd up.

Love here is scarce a faint desire;
But there, the spark's a flaming fire;
Joys here are drops, that passing flee;
But there, an overflowing sea.

My faith, that sees so darkly here,
Will there resign to vision clear;
My hope, that's here a weary groan,
Will to fruition yield the throne.

Here fetters hamper freedom's wing;
But there, the captive is a king;
And grace is like a buried seed
But sinners there are saints indeed.

My portion here's a crumb at best;
But there, the Lamb's eternal feast;
My praise is now a smother'd fire;
But then, I'll sing and never tire.

Now dusky shadows cloud my day;
But then, the shades will flee away;
My Lord will break the dimming glass,
And show His glory face to face.

My numerous foes now beat me down;
But then, I'll wear the victor's crown;
Yet all the revenues I'll bring
To Zion's everlasting King!
Ralph Erskine. 1734.

CCCLXXI.

Fierce passions discompose the mind,
  As tempests vex the sea;
But calm content and peace we find,
  When, Lord, we turn to Thee.

In vain by reason and by rule
  We try to bend the will;
For none but in the Saviour's school
  Can learn the heavenly skill.

Since at His feet my soul has sat
  His gracious words to hear,
Contented with my present state,
  I cast on Him my care.

"Art thou a sinner, Soul?" He said;
  "Then how canst thou complain?
"How light thy troubles here, if weigh'd
  "With everlasting pain!

"If thou of murmuring wouldst be cured,
  "Compare thy griefs with Mine;
"Think what My love for thee endured,
  "And thou wilt not repine.

"'Tis I appoint thy daily lot,
  "And I do all things well:
"Thou soon shalt leave this wretched spot,
  "And rise with Me to dwell.

"In life My grace shall strength supply,
  "Proportion'd to thy day;
"At death thou still shalt find Me nigh,
  "To wipe thy tears away."

Thus I, who once my wretched days
  In vain repinings spent,
Taught in my Saviour's school of grace,
  Have learnt to be content.
               William Cowper. 1779.

CCCLXXII.

Let me be with Thee where Thou art,
  My Saviour, my eternal Rest!
Then only will this longing heart
  Be fully and for ever blest!

Let me be with Thee where Thou art,
  Thy unveil'd glory to behold;
Then only will this wandering heart
  Cease to be treacherous, faithless, cold!

Let me be with Thee where Thou art,
  Where spotless saints Thy Name adore;
Then only will this sinful heart
  Be evil and defiled no more!

Let me be with Thee where Thou art,
   Where none can die, where none remove;
There neither death nor life will part
   Me from Thy Presence and Thy love!
            Charlotte Elliott. 1836.

CCCLXXIII.

O Lord, how little do we know,
   How little of Thy Presence feel,
While we continue here below,
   And in these earthly houses dwell!

When will these veils of flesh remove,
   And not eclipse our sight of God?
When wilt Thou take us up above,
   To see Thy face without a cloud?

Show Thy omnipotence to save!
   The characters of sin efface!
Thine image on our hearts engrave,
   And let us feel Thy sweet embrace!

Dart in our hearts a heavenly ray,
   A ray which still may shine more bright,
Increasing to the perfect day,
   Till we awake in endless light!

Then shall each Star become a Sun,
   Fill'd with a lustre all Divine;
Each shall possess a radiant crown,
   And to eternal ages shine.
           William Hammond. 1745.

CCCLXXIV.

Go up, go up, my heart,
   Dwell with thy God above;
For here thou canst not rest,
   Nor here give out thy love.

Go up, go up, my heart,
   Be not a trifler here;
Ascend above these clouds,
   Dwell in a higher sphere.

Let not thy love flow out
   To things so soiled and dim;
Go up to Heaven and God,
   Take up thy love to Him.

Waste not thy precious stores
   On creature-love below;
To God that wealth belongs,
   On Him that wealth bestow.

Go up, reluctant heart,
   Take up thy rest above;
Arise, earth-clinging thoughts;
   Ascend, my lingering love!
Horatius Bonar. 1856.

CCCLXXV.

My soul, amid this stormy world,
   Is like some flutter'd dove,
And fain would be as swift of wing
   To flee to Him I love.

Hope.

The cords that bound my heart to earth
    Are broken by His hand;
Before His cross I found myself
    A stranger in the land.

That visage marr'd, those sorrows deep,
    The vinegar and gall,
These were His golden chains of love
    His captive to enthral.

My heart is with Him on His throne,
    And ill can brook delay,
Each moment listening for the voice,
    "Rise up, and come away!"

With hope deferr'd oft sick and faint,
    "Why tarries He?" I cry;
Let not the Saviour chide my haste,
    For then would I reply:

"May not an exile, Lord, desire
    "His own sweet land to see?
"May not a captive seek release,
    "A prisoner, to be free?

"A child, when far away, may long
    "For home and kindred dear;
And she, that waits her absent lord,
    "May sigh till he appear.

"I would, my Lord and Saviour, know
    "That which no measure knows!
"Would search the mystery of Thy love,
    "The depths of all Thy woes!

"I fain would strike my harp divine,
　"Before the Father's throne,
"There cast my crown of Righteousness,
　"And sing what grace has done!

"Ah! leave me not in this base world,
　"A stranger still to roam;
"Come, Lord, and take me to Thyself;
　"Come, Jesus, quickly come!"
　　　　　　Robert C. Chapman. 1837—1852.

CCCLXXVI.

Jesus, I my cross have taken,
　All to leave, and follow Thee;
Destitute, despised, forsaken,
　Thou, from hence, my all shalt be:
Perish every fond ambition,
　All I've sought, or hoped, or known;
Yet how rich is my condition!
　God and Heaven are still my own!

Let the world despise and leave me,
　They have left my Saviour too;
Human hearts and looks deceive me;
　Thou art not, like them, untrue:
And, while Thou shalt smile upon me,
　God of wisdom, love, and might,
Foes may hate, and friends may shun me;
　Show Thy face, and all is bright!

Go, then, earthly fame and treasure!
　Come, disaster, scorn, and pain!
In Thy service, pain is pleasure,
　With Thy favour, loss is gain!

Hope.

I have call'd Thee, Abba, Father!
   I have stay'd my heart on Thee!
Storms may howl, and clouds may gather,
   All must work for good to me.

Man may trouble and distress me,
   'Twill but drive me to Thy breast;
Life with trials hard may press me,
   Heaven will bring me sweeter rest!
O! 'tis not in grief to harm me,
   While Thy love is left to me!
O! 'twere not in joy to charm me,
   Were that joy unmix'd with Thee!

Take, my soul, thy full salvation;
   Rise o'er sin, and fear, and care;
Joy to find, in every station,
   Something still to do or bear:
Think what Spirit dwells within thee!
   What a Father's smile is thine!
What a Saviour died to win thee!
   Child of Heaven, shouldst thou repine?

Haste then on from grace to glory,
   Arm'd by faith, and wing'd by prayer;
Heaven's eternal day's before thee,
   God's own hand shall guide thee there!
Soon shall close thy earthly mission,
   Swift shall pass thy pilgrim days;
Hope soon change to glad fruition,
   Faith to sight, and prayer to praise!

              Henry Francis Lyte. [1833.]

VI.

JOY.

"In whom, though now ye see Him not, yet believing, ye rejoice with joy unspeakable, and full of glory."
—(1 PET. i. 8.)

CCCLXXVII.

My God, the Spring of all my joys,
    The Life of my delights,
The Glory of my brightest days,
    And Comfort of my nights:

In darkest shades if He appear,
    My dawning is begun;
He is my soul's sweet Morning-star,
    And He my rising Sun.

The opening heavens around me shine
    With beams of sacred bliss,
While Jesus shows, His heart is mine,
    And whispers, I am His.

My soul would leave this heavy clay
    At that transporting word,
Run up with joy the shining way
    T' embrace my dearest Lord.

Fearless of hell and ghastly death,
    I'd break through every foe:
The wings of love and arms of faith
    Should bear me conqueror through.

Isaac Watts. 1709.

CCCLXXVIII.

Far from the world, O Lord, I flee,
   From strife and tumult far;
From scenes where Satan wages still
   His most successful war.

The calm retreat, the silent shade,
   With prayer and praise agree,
And seem by Thy sweet bounty made
   For those who follow Thee.

There, if Thy Spirit touch the soul,
   And grace her mean abode,
Oh with what peace, and joy, and love,
   She communes with her God!

There, like the nightingale, she pours
   Her solitary lays,
Nor asks a witness of her song,
   Nor thirsts for human praise.

Author and Guardian of my life;
   Sweet Source of light Divine;
And, all harmonious names in one,
   My Saviour! Thou art mine!

What thanks I owe Thee, and what love,
   A boundless, endless store,
Shall echo through the realms above
   When time shall be no more!
               William Cowper. 1779.

CCCLXXIX.

There's not a bird, with lonely nest
In pathless wood or mountain crest,
Nor meaner thing, which does not share,
O God! in Thy paternal care!

There's not a being now accurst,
Who did not taste Thy goodness first ;
And every joy the wicked see
Received its origin from Thee.

Each barren crag, each desert rude,
Holds Thee within its solitude ;
And Thou dost bless the wanderer there,
Who makes his solitary prayer.

In busy mart and crowded street,
No less than in the still retreat,
Thou, Lord, art near, our souls to bless
With all a parent's tenderness !

And every moment still doth bring
Thy blessings on its loaded wing ;
Widely they spread through earth and sky,
And last to all eternity !

Through all creation let Thy Name
Be echoed with a glad acclaim !
That let the grateful Churches sing ;
With that let heaven for ever ring !

And we, where'er our lot is cast,
While life and thought and feeling last,
Through all our years, in every place,
Will bless Thee for Thy boundless grace !
Baptist Wriothesley Noel. [1841.]

CCCLXXX.

The child leans on its parent's breast,
Leaves there its cares, and is at rest ;
The bird sits singing by his nest,

   And tells aloud
His trust in God, and so is blest
    'Neath every cloud.

He has no store, he sows no seed;
Yet sings aloud, and doth not heed;
By flowing stream or grassy mead
    He sings to shame
Men, who forget, in fear of need,
    A Father's Name.

The heart that trusts for ever sings,
And feels as light as it had wings;
A well of peace within it springs:
    Come good or ill,
Whate'er to-day, to-morrow brings,
    It is His will!
    Isaac Williams. [1842.]

CCCLXXXI.

Why comes this fragrance on the summer breeze,
 The blended tribute of ten thousand flowers,
To me, a frequent wanderer 'mid the trees
 That form these gay, though solitary bowers!
One answer is around, beneath, above;
The echo of the voice, that God is Love!

Why bursts such melody from tree and bush,
 The overflowing of each songster's heart,
So filling mine, that it can scarcely hush
 Awhile to listen, but would take its part?
'Tis but one song I hear where'er I rove,
Though countless be the notes, that God is Love!

Why leaps the streamlet down the mountain's side,
　　Hastening so swiftly to the vale beneath,
To cheer the shepherd's thirsty flock, or glide
　　Where the hot sun has left a faded wreath,
Or, rippling, aid the music of the grove?
Its own glad voice replies, that God is Love!

In starry heavens, at the midnight hour,
　　In ever-varying hues at morning's dawn,
In the fair bow athwart the falling shower,
　　In forest, river, lake, rock, hill, and lawn,
One truth is written: all conspire to prove,
What grace of old reveal'd, that God is Love!

Nor less this pulse of health, far glancing eye,
　　And heart so moved with beauty, perfume, song,
This spirit, soaring through a gorgeous sky,
　　Or diving ocean's coral caves among,
Fleeter than darting fish or startled dove;
All, all declare the same, that God is Love!

Is it a fallen world on which I gaze?
　　Am I as deeply fallen as the rest,
Yet joys partaking, past my utmost praise,
　　Instead of wandering forlorn, unblest?
It is as if an unseen spirit strove
To grave upon my heart, that God is Love!

Yet wouldst thou see, my soul, this truth display'd
　　In characters which wondering angels read,
And read, adoring; go, imploring aid
　　To gaze with faith, behold the Saviour bleed!
Thy God, in human form! O, what can prove,
If this suffice thee not, that God is Love?

Cling to His cross ; and let thy ceaseless prayer
  Be, that thy grasp may fail not! and, ere long,
Thou shalt ascend to that fair Temple, where
  In strains ecstatic an innumerous throng
Of saints and seraphs, round the Throne above,
Proclaim for evermore, that God is Love!
Thomas Davis. 1859.

CCCLXXXII.

Shall I fear, O Earth, thy bosom?
  Shrink and faint to lay me there,
Whence the fragrant lovely blossom
  Springs to gladden earth and air?

Whence the tree, the brook, the river,
  Soft clouds floating in the sky,
All fair things come, whispering ever
  Of the love Divine on high?

Yea, whence One arose Victorious
  O'er the darkness of the grave,
His strong arm revealing, glorious
  In its might Divine to save?

No, fair Earth! a tender mother
  Thou hast been, and yet canst be:
And through Him, my Lord and Brother,
  Sweet shall be my rest in thee!
Thomas Davis. 1860.

CCCLXXXIII.

How vast the treasure we possess,
How rich Thy bounty, King of grace!
This world is ours, and worlds to come;
Earth is our lodge, and Heaven our home.

All things are ours, the gifts of God,
The purchase of a Saviour's Blood;
While the good Spirit shews us how
To use and to improve them too.

If peace and plenty crown my days,
They help me, Lord, to speak Thy praise;
If bread of sorrows be my food,
Those sorrows work my lasting good.

I would not change my blest estate
For all the world calls good or great;
And, while my faith can keep her hold,
I envy not the sinner's gold.

Father; I wait Thy daily will;
Thou shalt divide my portion still;
Grant me on earth what seems Thee best,
Till death and Heaven reveal the rest.
Isaac Watts. 1709.

CCCLXXXIV.

By faith in Christ I walk with God,
  With Heaven, my journey's end, in view;
Supported by His staff and rod,
  My road is safe, and pleasant too.

I travel through a desert wide
  Where many round me blindly stray;
But He vouchsafes to be my Guide,
  And will not let me miss my way.

Though snares and dangers throng my path,
  And earth and hell my course withstand,
I triumph over all by faith,
  Guarded by His Almighty hand.

The wilderness affords no food;
  But God for my support prepares,
Provides me every needful good,
  And frees my soul from wants and cares.

With him sweet converse I maintain;
  Great as He is, I dare be free;
I tell Him all my grief and pain;
  And He reveals His love to me.

Some cordial from His Word He brings,
  Whene'er my feeble spirit faints;
At once my soul revives and sings,
  And yields no more to sad complaints.

I pity all that worldlings talk
  Of pleasures, that will quickly end;
Be this my choice, O Lord, to walk
  With Thee, my Guide, my Guard, my Friend!
                    John Newton. 1779.

CCCLXXXV.

Sometimes a light surprises
  The Christian while he sings;
It is the Lord, who rises
  With healing in His wings:
When comforts are declining,
  He grants the soul again
A season of clear shining
  To cheer it after rain.

In holy contemplation
  We sweetly then pursue
The theme of God's salvation,
  And find it ever new:

Set free from present sorrow,
  We cheerfully can say,
E'en let the unknown to-morrow
  Bring with it what it may.

It can bring with it nothing,
  But He will bear us through;
Who gives the lilies clothing
  Will clothe His people too;
Beneath the spreading heavens
  No creature but is fed;
And He, who feeds the ravens,
  Will give His children bread.

Though vine nor fig-tree neither
  Their wonted fruit shall bear;
Though all the field should wither,
  Nor flocks nor herds be there;
Yet, God the same abiding,
  His praise shall tune my voice;
For, while in Him confiding,
  I cannot but rejoice.
            William Cowper. 1779.

CCCLXXXVI.

Long did I toil, and knew no earthly rest;
  Far did I rove, and found no certain home;
At last I sought them in His sheltering breast,
  Who opes His arms, and bids the weary come:
With Him I found a home, a rest Divine;
And I since then am His, and He is mine.

Yes! He is mine! and nought of earthly things,
  Not all the charms of pleasure, wealth, or power,
The fame of heroes, or the pomp of kings,
  Could tempt me to forego His love an hour.

Go, worthless world, I cry, with all that's thine!
Go! I my Saviour's am, and He is mine.

The good I have is from His stores supplied;
   The ill is only what He deems the best;
He for my Friend, I'm rich with nought beside;
   And poor without Him, though of all possest:
Changes may come; I take, or I resign;
Content, while I am His, while He is mine.

Whate'er may change, in Him no change is seen;
   A glorious Sun, that wanes not nor declines;
Above the clouds and storms He walks serene,
   And sweetly on his people's darkness shines:
All may depart; I fret not, nor repine,
While I my Saviour's am, while He is mine.

He stays me falling, lifts me up when down,
   Reclaims me wandering, guards from every foe;
Plants on my worthless brow the victor's crown;
   Which, in return, before His feet I throw,
Grieved that I cannot better grace His shrine,
Who deigns to own me His, as He is mine.

While here, alas! I know but half His love,
   But half discern Him, and but half adore;
But when I meet Him in the realms above,
   I hope to love Him better, praise Him more,
And feel, and tell, amid the choir Divine,
How fully I am His, and He is mine.

Henry Francis Lyte. 1833.

VII.

DISCIPLINE.

'Whom the Lord loveth, He chasteneth.'—(HEB. xii. 6.)

CCCLXXXVII.

When Christ, with all His graces crown'd,
   Sheds His kind beams abroad,
'Tis a young Heaven on earthly ground,
   And glory in the bud.

A blooming paradise of joy
   In this wild desert springs,
And every sense I straight employ
   On sweet celestial things.

But ah! how soon my joys decay!
   How soon my sins arise
And snatch the heavenly scene away
   From these lamenting eyes!

When shall the time, dear Jesus, when
   The shining day appear,
That I shall leave those clouds of sin
   And guilt and darkness here?

Up to the fields above the skies
   My hasty feet would go;
There everlasting flowers arise,
   And joys unwithering grow!

          Isaac Watts. 1709.

CCCLXXXVIII.

O for a closer walk with God,
   A calm and heavenly frame !
A light to shine upon the road
   That leads me to the Lamb !

Where is the blessedness I knew
   When first I saw the Lord ?
Where is the soul-refreshing view
   Of Jesus and His word ?

What peaceful hours I once enjoyed !
   How sweet their memory still !
But they have left an aching void
   The world can never fill.

Return, O holy Dove ! return,
   Sweet messenger of rest !
I hate the sins that made Thee mourn,
   And drove Thee from my breast.

The dearest idol I have known,
   Whate'er that idol be,
Help me to tear it from Thy throne,
   And worship only Thee !

So shall my walk be close with God,
   Calm and serene my frame ;'
So purer light shall mark the road
   That leads me to the Lamb !
        William Cowper. 1779.

CCCLXXXIX.

   The spring-tide hour
   Brings leaf and flower
With songs of life and love ;

And many a lay
Wears out the day
In many a leafy grove.
  Bird, flower, and tree
  Seem to agree
Their choicest gifts to bring;
  But this poor heart
  Bears not its part,
In it there is no spring.

  Dews fall apace,
  The dews of grace,
Upon this soul of sin
  And love Divine
  Delights to shine
Upon the waste within:
  Yet, year by year,
  Fruits, flowers, appear,
And birds their praises sing;
  But this poor heart
  Bears not its part,
Its winter has no spring.

  Lord, let Thy love,
  Fresh from above,
Soft as the south wind blow;
  Call forth its bloom,
  Wake its perfume,
And bid its spices flow!
  And when Thy voice
  Makes earth rejoice,
And the hills laugh and sing,
  Lord! make this heart
  To bear its part,
And join the praise of spring!

John S. B. Monsell. 1850.

CCCXC.

Psalm LXIII.

Early, my God, without delay,
    I haste to seek Thy face;
My thirsty spirit faints away
    Without Thy cheering grace.

So pilgrims on the scorching sand
    Beneath a burning sky
Long for a cooling stream at hand,
    And they must drink, or die.

I've seen Thy glory and Thy power
    Through all Thy temple shine;
My God! repeat that heavenly hour,
    That vision so divine!

Not life itself, with all her joys,
    Can my best passions move,
Or raise so high my cheerful voice,
    As Thy forgiving love.

Thus till my last expiring day
    I'll bless my God and King;
Thus will I lift my hands to pray,
    And tune my lips to sing.
              Isaac Watts. 1719.

CCCXCI.

God moves in a mysterious way
    His wonders to perform;
He plants his footsteps in the sea,
    And rides upon the storm.

Deep in unfathomable mines
    Of never-failing skill,
He treasures up His bright designs,
    And works His sovereign will.

Ye fearful saints, fresh courage take;
    The clouds ye so much dread
Are big with mercy, and shall break
    In blessings on your head.

Judge not the Lord by feeble sense,
    But trust Him for His grace;
Behind a frowning Providence
    He hides a smiling face.

His purposes will ripen fast,
    Unfolding every hour;
The bud may have a bitter taste,
    But sweet will be the flower.

Blind unbelief is sure to err,
    And scan His work in vain;
God is His own interpreter,
    And He will make it plain.
William Cowper. 1779.

CCCXCII.

The world can neither give nor take,
    Nor can they comprehend
The peace of God, which Christ has bought,
    The peace which knows no end.

The burning bush was not consumed
    Whilst God remainèd there;
The Three, when Jesus made the Fourth,
    Found fire as soft as air.

God's furnace doth in Zion stand;
  But Zion's God sits by,
As the refiner views his gold
  With an observant eye.

His thoughts are high, His love is wise,
  His wounds a cure intend;
And, though He does not always smile,
  He loves unto the end.
Cento by Selina, Countess of Huntingdon. 1780.
                 From John Mason. 1683.

CCCXCIII.

Let Jacob to his Maker sing,
And praise his great Redeeming King:
Call'd by a new, a gracious Name,
Let Israel loud his God proclaim.

He knows our souls in all their fears,
And gently wipes our falling tears;
Forms trembling voices to a song,
And bids the feeble heart be strong.

Then let the rivers swell around,
And rising floods o'erflow the ground;
Rivers and floods and seas divide,
And homage pay to Israel's Guide.

Then let the fires their rage display,
And flaming terrors bar the way;
Unburnt, unsinged, He leads them through,
And makes the flames refreshing too.

The fires but on their bonds shall prey;
The floods but wash their stains away;
And Grace Divine new trophies raise
Amidst the deluge and the blaze.
                Philip Doddridge. 1755.

CCCXCIV.

To Thee, my God, whose Presence fills
  The earth, and seas, and skies,
To Thee, whose Name, whose heart is Love,
  With all my powers I rise.

Troubles in long succession roll;
  Wave rushes upon wave;
Pity, O pity my distress!
  Thy child, Thy suppliant, save!

O bid the roaring tempest cease;
  Or give me strength to bear
Whate'er Thy holy will appoints,
  And save me from despair!

To Thee, my God, alone I look,
  On Thee alone confide;
Thou never hast deceived the soul
  That on Thy grace relied.

Though oft Thy ways are wrapt in clouds
  Mysterious and unknown,
Truth, Righteousness, and Mercy stand
  The pillars of Thy throne.
                    Thomas Gibbons. 1784.

CCCXCV.

The billows swell, the winds are high,
Clouds overcast my wintry sky;
Out of the depths to Thee I call,
My fears are great, my strength is small.

O Lord, the pilot's part perform,
And guide and guard me through the storm;
Defend me from each threatening ill,
Control the waves, say, "Peace, be still!"

Amidst the roaring of the sea
My soul still hangs her hopes on Thee;
Thy constant love, Thy faithful care
Is all that saves me from despair.

Dangers of every shape and name
Attend the followers of the Lamb,
Who leave the world's deceitful shore,
And leave it to return no more.

Though tempest-toss'd; and half a wreck,
My Saviour through the floods I seek:
Let neither winds nor stormy main
Force back my shatter'd bark again!
William Cowper. 1779.

CCCXCVI.

Why should I, in vain repining,
    Mourn the clouds that cross my way;
Since my Saviour's Presence shining
    Turns my darkness into day?

Earthly honour, earthly treasure,
    All the warmest passions win,
And the silken wings of pleasure
    Only waft us on to sin.

But, within the vale of sorrow,
    All with tempests overblown,
Purer light and joy we borrow
    From the face of God alone.

Welcome, then, each darker token!
  Mercy sent it from above!
So the heart, subdued, not broken,
  Bends in fear, and melts with love.

James Edmeston. 1820.

CCCXCVII.

Why should I fear the darkest hour,
Or tremble at the Tempter's power?
Jesus vouchsafes to be my Tower.

Though hot the fight, why quit the field?
Why must I either fly or yield,
Since Jesus is my mighty Shield?

When creature-comforts fade and die,
Worldlings may weep, but why should I?
Jesus still lives, and still is nigh.

Though all the flocks and herds were dead,
My soul a famine need not dread,
For Jesus is my living Bread.

I know not what may soon betide,
Or how my wants shall be supplied;
But Jesus knows, and will provide.

Though Sin would fill me with distress,
The throne of Grace I dare address,
For Jesus is my Righteousness.

Though faint my prayers, and cold my love,
My stedfast hope shall not remove,
While Jesus intercedes above.

Against me earth and hell combine;
But on my side is Power divine;
Jesus is all, and He is mine!
                    John Newton. 1779.

CCCXCVIII.

When gathering clouds around I view,
And days are dark and friends are few,
On Him I lean, who not in vain
Experienced every human pain;
He sees my wants, allays my fears,
And counts and treasures up my tears.

If aught should tempt my soul to stray
From heavenly wisdom's narrow way;
To fly the good I would pursue,
Or do the sin I would not do;
Still He, who felt temptation's power,
Shall guard me in that dangerous hour.

If wounded love my bosom swell,
Deceived by those I prized too well;
He shall His pitying aid bestow,
Who felt on earth severer woe;
At once betrayed, denied, or fled,
By those who shared His daily bread.

If vexing thoughts within me rise,
And, sore dismayed, my spirit dies;
Still He, who once vouchsafed to bear
The sickening anguish of despair,
Shall sweetly soothe, shall gently dry,
The throbbing heart, the streaming eye.

When sorrowing o'er some stone I bend,
Which covers what was once a friend,
And from his voice, his hand, his smile,
Divides me for a little while;
Thou, Saviour, mark'st the tears I shed,
For Thou didst weep o'er Lazarus dead!

And O! when I have safely past
Through every conflict but the last;
Still, still unchanging, watch beside
My painful bed, for Thou hast died!
Then point to realms of cloudless day,
And wipe the latest tear away!
Sir Robert Grant. [1839.]

CCCXCIX.

Whate'er my God ordains is right;
  His will is ever just;
Howe'er He orders now my cause,
  I will be still and trust.
    He is my God;
    Though dark my road,
He holds me that I shall not fall;
Wherefore to Him I leave it all.

Whate'er my God ordains is right;
  He never will deceive;
He leads me by the proper path,
  And so to Him I cleave,
    And take content
    What He hath sent;
His hand can turn my griefs away,
And patiently I wait His day.

Whate'er my God ordains is right;
  He taketh thought for me;
The cup that my Physician gives
  No poisoned draught can be,
    But medicine due;
    For God is true;
And on that changeless truth I build,
And all my heart with hope is fill'd.

Whate'er my God ordains is right;
  Though I the cup must drink
That bitter seems to my faint heart,
  I will not fear nor shrink;
    Tears pass away
    With dawn of day;
Sweet comfort yet shall fill my heart,
And pain and sorrow all depart.

Whate'er my God ordains is right;
  My Light, my Life is He,
Who cannot will me aught but good;
  I trust Him utterly;
    For well I know,
    In joy or woe,
We soon shall see as sunlight clear,
How faithful was our Guardian here.

Whate'er my God ordains is right;
  Here will I take my stand,
Though sorrow, need, or death make earth
  For me a desert land.
    My Father's care
    Is round me there;
He holds me that I shall not fall,
And so to Him I leave it all.

              Catherine Winkworth. 1858.
              (*From S. Rodigast.*)

VIII.

PATIENCE.

"Be patient, therefore, brethren, unto the coming of the Lord."—(JAMES v. 7.)

CCCC.

When languor and disease invade
  This trembling house of clay,
'Tis sweet to look beyond the cage,
  And long to fly away.

Sweet to look inward, and attend
  The whispers of His love;
Sweet to look upward to the place
  Where Jesus pleads above.

Sweet to look back, and see my Name
  In Life's fair book set down;
Sweet to look forward, and behold
  Eternal joys my own.

Sweet to reflect, how Grace Divine
  My sins on Jesus laid;
Sweet to remember, that His Blood
  My debt of sufferings paid.

Sweet on His Righteousness to stand
  Which saves from second death;
Sweet to experience, day by day,
  His Spirit's quickening breath.

Sweet on His faithfulness to rest,
  Whose love can never end;
Sweet on His covenant of grace
  For all things to depend.

Sweet in the confidence of faith
   To trust His firm decrees;
Sweet to lie passive in His hand,
   And know no will but His.

Sweet to rejoice in lively hope,
   That, when my change shall come,
Angels will hover round my bed,
   And waft my spirit home.

There shall my disimprison'd soul
   Behold Him, and adore;
Be with His Likeness satisfied,
   And grieve and sin no more;

Shall see Him wear that very Flesh
   On which my guilt was lain;
His Love intense, His Merit fresh,
   As though but newly slain!

Soon, too, my slumbering dust shall hear
   The Trumpet's quickening sound;
And, by my Saviour's Power rebuilt,
   At His right hand be found.

These eyes shall see Him in that day,
   The God that died for me!
And all my rising bones shall say,
   Lord, who is like to Thee?

If such the views which grace unfolds,
   Weak as it is below,
What raptures must the Church above
   In Jesus' Presence know!

If such the sweetness of the stream,
   What must the Fountain be,
Where saints and angels draw their bliss
   Immediately from Thee!

O! may the unction of these truths
   For ever with me stay,
Till, from her sinful cage dismiss'd,
   My spirit flies away!
        Augustus Montague Toplady. 1777.

CCCCI.

We're bound for yonder land
   Where Jesus reigns supreme;
We leave the shore at His command,
   Forsaking all for Him.

The perils of the sea,
   The rocks, the waves, the wind,
Are small, whatever they may be,
   To those we leave behind.

Nor have we cause to fear;
   The God, who rules the sea,
In every danger will be near,
   And our protector be.

The Lord Himself will keep
   His people safe from harm,
Will hold the helm, and guide the ship,
   With His Almighty arm.

Then let the tempests roar,
   The billows heave and swell;
We trust to reach the peaceful shore
   Where all the ransom'd dwell:

  And, when we gain the land,
   How happy shall we be!
  How shall we bless the mighty Hand
   That led us through the sea!
      Thomas Kelly. 1809.

CCCCII.

Rejoice, though storms assail thee;
 Rejoice, when skies are bright;
Rejoice, though round thy pathway
 Is spread the gloom of night:
If the good hope be in thee
 That all at last is well,
Then let thy happy spirit
 With joyful feelings swell!

Look back on early childhood,
 And let thy soul rejoice!
Who then upheld thy goings,
 And tuned thy feeble voice?
Look back on youth's gay visions
 When life one glory seem'd:
Who pour'd those rays of gladness
 Which on thy prospect beam'd?

Recall the hours of anguish,
 And let thy soul rejoice,
Though wave on wave of sorrow
 Rush on with fearful noise:
Was not the Bow of Promise
 Still seen amidst the gloom,
Shedding its hallow'd lustre
 E'en round the silent tomb?

Rejoice, rejoice for ever,
  Though earthly friends be gone!
For silently and swiftly
  The wheels of time roll on;
And still they bear thee forward
  Nearer that happy shore,
While the triumphant song is,
  Rejoice for evermore!

Anon. [1853.

CCCCIII.

Nearer, my God, to Thee,
  Nearer to Thee!
E'en though it be a cross
  That raiseth me;
Still all my song shall be,
Nearer, my God, to Thee,
  Nearer to Thee!

Though like the wanderer,
  The sun gone down,
Darkness be over me,
  My rest a stone;
Yet in my dreams I'd be
Nearer, my God, to Thee,
  Nearer to Thee!

There let the way appear
  Steps unto Heaven;
All that Thou send'st to me
  In mercy given;
Angels to beckon me
Nearer, my God, to Thee,
  Nearer to Thee!

Then with my waking thoughts
  Bright with Thy praise,
Out of my stony griefs
  Bethel I'll raise ;
So by my woes to be
Nearer, my God, to Thee,
  Nearer to Thee !

Or if on joyful wing
  Cleaving the sky,
Sun, moon, and stars forgot,
  Upwards I fly,
Still all my song shall be,
Nearer, my God, to Thee,
  Nearer to Thee !
Sarah Flower Adams. 1848.

CCCCIV.

Lead, kindly Light, amid th' encircling gloom,
    Lead Thou me on ;
The night is dark, and I am far from home ;
    Lead Thou me on ;
Keep Thou my feet ; I do not ask to see
The distant scene ; one step enough for me.

I was not ever thus, nor pray'd, that Thou
    Shouldst lead me on ;
I loved to choose and see my path ; but now
    Lead Thou me on !
I loved the garish day, and, spite of fears,
Pride ruled my will : Remember not past years!

So long Thy Power has blest me, sure it still
  Will lead me on
O'er moor and fen, o'er crag and torrent, till
  The night is gone,
And with the morn those angel faces smile
Which I have loved long since, and lost awhile!
    John Henry Newman. 1833.

CCCCV.

Abide with me! fast falls the even-tide;
The darkness deepens; Lord, with me abide!
When other helpers fail, and comforts flee,
Help of the helpless, O abide with me!

Swift to its close ebbs out life's little day;
Earth's joys grow dim; its glories pass away;
Change and decay in all around I see;
O Thou, who changest not, abide with me!

Not a brief glance I beg, a passing word;
But, as Thou dwell'st with Thy disciples, Lord,
Familiar, condescending, patient, free,
Come, not to sojourn, but abide, with me!

Come not in terrors, as the King of kings;
But kind and good, with healing in Thy wings;
Tears for all woes, a heart for every plea;
Come, Friend of sinners, and thus 'bide with me!

Thou on my head in early youth didst smile;
And, though rebellious and perverse meanwhile,
Thou hast not left me, oft as I left Thee
On to the close, O Lord, abide with me!

I need Thy Presence every passing hour:
What but Thy grace can foil the Tempter's power?
Who like Thyself my guide and stay can be?
Through cloud and sunshine, O abide with me!

I fear no foe, with Thee at hand to bless:
Ills have no weight, and tears no bitterness:
Where is death's sting? where, Grave, thy victory?
I triumph still, if Thou abide with me!

Hold then Thy cross before my closing eyes!
Shine through the gloom, and point me to the skies!
Heaven's morning breaks, and earth's vain shadows flee;
In life and death, O Lord, abide with me!
Henry Francis Lyte. 1847.

CCCCVI.

Commit thou all thy griefs
  And ways into His hands,
To His sure Truth and tender care,
  Who earth and Heaven commands.

Who points the clouds their course,
  Whom winds and seas obey,
He shall direct thy wandering feet,
  He shall prepare thy way.

Thou on the Lord rely;
  So safe shalt thou go on;
Fix on His Work thy stedfast eye,
  So shall thy work be done.

No profit canst thou gain
 By self-consuming care ;
To Him commend thy cause ; His ear
 Attends the softest prayer.

Thy everlasting Truth,
 Father ! Thy ceaseless love,
Sees all Thy children's wants, and knows
 What best for each will prove.

And whatsoe'er Thou will'st
 Thou dost, O King of kings ;
What Thy unerring Wisdom chose,
 Thy Power to being brings.

Thou everywhere hast sway,
 And all things serve Thy might ;
Thy every act pure blessing is,
 Thy path unsullied light.

When Thou arisest, Lord,
 Who shall Thy work withstand ?
When all Thy children want Thou giv'st,
 Who, who shall stay Thy hand ?

Give to the winds thy fears ;
 Hope, and be undismay'd ;
God hears thy sighs, and counts thy tears,
 God shall lift up thy head.

Through waves and clouds and storms,
 He gently clears thy way ;
Wait thou His time ; so shall this night
 Soon end in joyous day.

Still heavy is thy heart?
Still sink thy spirits down?
Cast off the weight, let fear depart,
  And every care be gone.

What though thou rulest not?
Yet Heaven and earth and hell
Proclaim, God sitteth on the Throne,
  And ruleth all things well!

Leave to His sovereign sway
To choose and to command;
So shalt thou wondering own, His way
  How wise, how strong His hand!

Far, far above thy thought
His counsel shall appear,
When fully He the work hath wrought
  That caused thy needless fear.

Thou seest our weakness, Lord!
Our hearts are known to Thee:
Oh! lift Thou up the sinking hand,
  Confirm the feeble knee!

Let us, in life, in death,
Thy stedfast Truth declare,
And publish, with our latest breath,
  Thy love and guardian care!
John Wesley. 1739.
(From Paul Gerhardt.)

CCCCVII.

Your harps, ye trembling saints,
  Down from the willows take;
Loud to the praise of Love divine,
  Bid every string awake.

Though in a foreign land,
  We are not far from home;
And nearer to our house above,
  We every moment come.

His Grace will to the end
  Stronger and brighter shine;
Nor present things, nor things to come,
  Shall quench the spark divine.

Fasten'd within the vail,
  Hope be your anchor strong;
His loving Spirit the sweet gale
  That wafts you smooth along.

Or, should the surges rise,
  And peace delay to come,
Blest is the sorrow, kind the storm,
  That drives us nearer home.

The people of His choice
  He will not cast away;
Yet do not always here expect
  On Tabor's mount to stay.

When we in darkness walk,
  Nor feel the heavenly flame,
Then is the time to trust our God,
  And rest upon His Name.

Soon shall our doubts and fears
  Subside at His control;
His loving-kindness shall break through
  The midnight of the soul.

No wonder, when His Love
    Pervades your kindling breast,
You wish for ever to retain
    The heart-transporting Guest.

Yet learn, in every state,
    To make His will your own;
And, when the joys of sense depart,
    To walk by faith alone.

By anxious fear depress'd,
    When from the deep ye mourn,
" Lord, why so hasty to depart,
    " So tedious in return ?"

Still on His plighted Love
    At all events rely;
The very hidings of His face
    Shall train thee up to joy.

Wait, till the shadows flee;
    Wait thy appointed hour;
Wait, till the Bridegroom of thy soul
    Reveal His Love with power.

The time of Love will come,
    When thou shalt clearly see,
Not only that He shed His Blood,
    But that it flowed for thee!

Tarry His leisure, then,
    Although He seem to stay;
A moment's intercourse with Him
    Thy grief will overpay.

Blest is the man, O God,
    That stays himself on Thee!
Who wait for Thy salvation, Lord,
    Shall Thy salvation see!
Augustus Montague Toplady. 1772.

CCCCVIII.

Through the love of God our Saviour
    All will be well;
Free and changeless is His favour;
    All, all is well!
Precious is the Blood that heal'd us,
Perfect is the grace that seal'd us,
Strong the Hand stretch'd forth to shield us;
    All must be well!

Though we pass through tribulation,
    All will be well;
Ours is such a full salvation,
    All, all is well!
Happy, still to God confiding,
Fruitful, if in Christ abiding,
Holy, through the Spirit's guiding;
    All must be well!

We expect a bright to-morrow,
    All will be well;
Faith can sing through days of sorrow,
    All, all is well!
On our Father's love relying,
Jesus every need supplying,
Or in living, or in dying,
    All must be well!
Mary Bowly. 1847.

CCCCIX.

Rest weary soul !
The penalty is borne, the ransom paid,
For all thy sins full satisfaction made ;
Strive not to do thyself what Christ has done,
Claim the free gift, and make the joy thine own ;
No more by pangs of guilt and fear distrest,
    Rest, sweetly rest !

Rest, weary heart,
From all thy silent griefs, and secret pain,
Thy profitless regrets, and longings vain ;
Wisdom and love have ordered all the past,
All shall be blessedness and light at last ;
Cast off the cares that have so long opprest ;
    Rest, sweetly rest !

Rest, weary head !
Lie down to slumber in the peaceful tomb:
Light from above has broken through its gloom ;
Here, in the place where once thy Saviour lay,
Where He shall wake thee on a future day,
Like a tired child upon its mother's breast,
    Rest, sweetly rest !

Rest, spirit free !
In the green pastures of the heavenly shore,
Where sin and sorrow can approach no more,
With all the flock by the Good Shepherd fed,
Beside the streams of Life eternal led,
For ever with thy God and Saviour blest,
    Rest, sweetly rest !

Anon. "*H. L. L.*" 1859.

CCCCX.

For ever with the Lord!
  Amen! so let it be!
Life from the dead is in that word,
  And immortality!

Here in the body pent,
  Absent from Him I roam,
Yet nightly pitch my moving tent
  A day's march nearer home.

My Father's house on high,
  Home of my soul! how near,
At times, to faith's foreseeing eye,
  Thy golden gates appear!

Ah! then my spirit faints
  To reach the land I love,
The bright inheritance of saints,
  Jerusalem above!

Yet clouds will intervene,
  And all my prospect flies;
Like Noah's dove, I flit between
  Rough seas and stormy skies.

Anon the clouds depart,
  The winds and waters cease;
While sweetly o'er my gladden'd heart
  Expands the bow of peace!

Beneath its glowing arch,
  Along the hallow'd ground,
I see cherubic armies march,
  A camp of fire around.

I hear at morn and even,
  At noon and midnight hour,
The choral harmonies of Heaven
  Earth's Babel tongues o'erpower.

Then, then I feel, that He,
  Remember'd or forgot,
The Lord, is never far from me,
  Though I perceive Him not.
                    James Montgomery. 1853.

CCCCXI.

The God of Abraham praise,
  Who reigns enthroned above,
Ancient of everlasting days,
    And God of Love!
  Jehovah! Great I Am!
  By earth and Heaven confest;
I bow and bless the sacred Name,
    For ever blest!

The God of Abraham praise!
  At whose supreme command
From earth I rise, and seek the joys
    At His right hand:
  I all on earth forsake,
    Its wisdom, fame, and power,
And Him my only portion make,
    My Shield and Tower.

The God of Abraham praise!
  Whose all-sufficient grace
Shall guide me all my happy days
    In all my ways:

He calls a worm His friend!
He calls Himself my God!
And He shall save me to the end
    Through Jesus' Blood.

He by Himself hath sworn,
    I on His oath depend;
I shall, on eagle's wings upborne,
    To Heaven ascend;
    I shall behold His face,
    I shall His power adore,
And sing the wonders of His grace
    For evermore!

Though nature's strength decay,
    And earth and hell withstand,
To Canaan's bounds I urge my way
    At His command:
    The watery deep I pass
    With Jesus in my view,
And through the howling wilderness
    My way pursue.

The goodly land I see,
    With peace and plenty blest,
A land of sacred liberty,
    And endless rest:
    There milk and honey flow,
    And oil and wine abound,
And trees of life for ever grow,
    With Mercy crown'd.

There dwells the Lord our King,
    The Lord our Righteousness,
Triumphant o'er the world and sin,
    The Prince of Peace!

On Sion's sacred height
　His kingdom still maintains,
And, glorious with His saints in light,
　　For ever reigns!

He keeps His own secure;
　He guards them by His side;
Arrays in garments white and pure
　　His spotless Bride;
　With streams of sacred bliss,
　With groves of living joys,
With all the fruits of Paradise,
　　He still supplies.

Before the great Three-One
　They all exulting stand,
And tell the wonders He hath done
　　Through all their land;
　The listening spheres attend
　And swell the growing fame,
And sing, in songs which never end,
　　The wondrous Name!

The God, who reigns on high,
　The great Archangels sing,
And, "Holy, holy, holy," cry,
　　"Almighty King!
"Who Was, and Is, the same,
"And evermore shall be!
"Jehovah! Father! Great I Am!
　　"We worship Thee!"

Before the Saviour's face
　The ransom'd nations bow,
O'erwhelm'd at His Almighty grace,
　　For ever new:

　　　　He shows His prints of love;
　　　　They kindle to a flame,
　　And sound, through all the worlds above,
　　　　The slaughter'd Lamb!

　　　　The whole triumphant host
　　　　Give thanks to God on high;
　　"Hail! Father, Son, and Holy Ghost!"
　　　　They ever cry:
　　　　Hail! Abraham's God, and mine!
　　　　I join the heavenly lays;
　　All might and majesty are Thine,
　　　　And endless praise!
　　　　　　　　　　Thomas Olivers. 1772.

　　　　　　　　CCCCXII.

　　　　　　Rev. vii. 9—17.

　　I saw, and lo! a countless throng,
Th' elect of every nation, name, and tongue,
Assembled round the everlasting Throne;
　　　　With robes of white endued,
　　　　The Righteousness of God;
　　　　And each a palm sustain'd
　　　　In his victorious hand;
When thus the bright melodious choir begun:
　　　　"Salvation to Thy Name,
"Eternal God, and co-eternal Lamb!
"In power, in glory, and in Essence, One!"

　　　So sung the Saints. Th' Angelic train
Second the anthem with a loud Amen:
　　(These in the outer circle stood,
　　　　The Saints were nearest God;)

And prostrate fall, with glory overpower'd,
   And hide their faces with their wings,
  And thus address the King of kings:
" All hail! by Thy triumphant Church adored!
   " Blessing and thanks and honour too
" Are Thy supreme, Thy everlasting due,
" Our Triune Sovereign, our propitious Lord!"

   While I beheld th' amazing sight,
A Seraph pointed to the Saints in white,
And told me who they were, and whence they came:
   " These are they, whose lot below
   " Was persecution, pain, and woe;
  " These are the chosen purchased Flock,
    " Who ne'er their Lord forsook;
" Through His imputed Merit free from blame;
   " Redeem'd from every sin;
"And, as thou seest, whose garments were made
    clean,
" Wash'd in the Blood of yon Exalted Lamb.

   " Saved by His Righteousness alone,
   " Spotless they stand before the Throne,
" And in th' ethereal Temple chant His praise:
   " Himself among them deigns to dwell,
   " And face to face His Light reveal:
   " Hunger and thirst, as heretofore,
   " And pain, and heat, they know no more,
" Nor need, as once, the sun's prolific rays:
   " Immanuel here His people feeds,
   " To streams of joy perennial leads,
"And wipes, for ever wipes, the tears from every face."

   Happy the souls released from fear,
    And safely landed there!

Some of the shining number once I knew,
    And travell'd with them here :
      Nay some, my elder brethren now,
Set later out for Heaven, my junior saints below :
    Long after me, they heard the call of Grace
      Which waked them unto Righteousness :
        How have they got beyond !
    Converted last, yet first with glory crown'd !
      Little, once, I thought that these
        Would first the Summit gain,
And leave me far behind, slow journeying through the Plain.

    Loved while on earth ! nor less belov'd, tho' gone !
      Think not I envy you your crown :
    No ! if I could, I would not call you down !
        Though slower is my pace,
        To you I'll follow on,
      Leaning on Jesus all the way ;
      Who, now and then, lets fall a ray
        Of comfort from His Throne :
        The shinings of His grace
Soften my passage through the wilderness ;
And vines, nectareous, spring where briers grew :
      The sweet unveilings of His Face
Make me, at times, near half as blest as you !
O ! might His Beauty feast my ravish'd eyes,
    His gladdening Presence ever stay,
      And cheer me all my journey through !
But soon the clouds return ; my triumph dies ;
    Damp vapours from the valley rise,
And hide the hill of Sion from my view.

    Spirit of Light ! thrice holy Dove !
Brighten my sense of interest in that Love

Patience.

Which knew no birth, and never shall expire!
   Electing Goodness, firm and free,
   My whole salvation hangs on thee,
Eldest and fairest daughter of Eternity!
   Redemption, grace, and glory too,
   Our bliss above, and hopes below,
   From her, their parent-fountain, flow.
Ah! tell me, Lord, that Thou hast chosen me!
Thou, who hast kindled my intense desire,
Fulfil the wish Thy influence did inspire,
   And let me my election know!
Then, when Thy summons bids me come up higher,
   Well pleased I shall from life retire,
And join the burning hosts, beheld at distance now.
   Augustus Montague Toplady. 1759—1774.

NOTES.

HYMN

II.—Part of Hymn No. 100 in Mant's *Ancient Hymns*, &c. Three stanzas out of eight are omitted.

IV.—The text of this hymn, as now corrected (see *Errata*), is from *The Devout Chorister* (Masters; Third Edition, 1854); in which book it was first published; and the author's name is given, by his kind permission.

V.—From the *General Psalmody*, compiled by the late Rev. William Carus Wilson. Author and original text unknown.

VII.—From *Hymns for the Church of England* (Longman, 1857). Author and original text unknown.

VIII.—From John and Charles Wesley's *Collection of Psalms and Hymns* (the first edition published in 1741). The Psalm, as rendered by Watts, is in six stanzas, of which the Wesleys omitted the first and fourth, and varied the second by substituting the well-known lines,
"Before Jehovah's awful throne,
Ye nations, bow with sacred joy;"
for Watts' original,
"Nations, attend before his throne
With solemn fear, with sacred joy."
The only other change is the word "shall" instead of "must,' in the third line of the last stanza.

XII.—Three stanzas out of six. The first, second, and fifth of Watts' are omitted.

XV.—Nine stanzas out of twelve (the first, third, and eleventh of Watts' being omitted). The word "God" is brought down into the first line, from the first (omitted) stanza, instead of "Him."

XVI.—The four first stanzas of Hymn No. 11, Book II. in Gibbons' *Hymns adapted to Divine Worship* (London, 1784); sometimes wrongly ascribed to Berridge. Gibbons has seven stanzas.

XXIII.—Four out of five stanzas, Lyte's fourth being omitted.

XXVIII.—The first thirteen out of forty-two stanzas. The poem is the last of several in Skelton's *Appeal to Common Sense on the Subject of Christianity*. (Dublin, 1784.)

XXXII.—Stanzas 1, 6, 9, and 10, of a poem in ten stanzas (No. 68 of T. Grinfield's *Century of Sacred Songs*). I have adhered to the selection made by the late Rev. John Hampden Gurney in the Marylebone Hymn-Book of 1851.

XXXIII.—My only authority for ascribing this to Tate is the late Rev. Edward Bickersteth; but the authorship seems probable, as this is one of the hymns included in the "Supplement to the New Version," for the use of which Brady and Tate obtained from Queen Anne an Order in Council, dated the 30th July, 1703.

HYMN
XXXIV.—The text is that of the fourth edition (1743) of *Hymns and Sacred Poems*, by John and Charles Wesley; differing in one word only ("Heavenly," instead of "Inner," in the second line of the last stanza) from the first edition, published in 1739. The common variation, beginning, "Hark, the herald angels sing," is probably by Martin Madan (1760), who, besides altering several lines, has left out part (but not the whole) of the two last stanzas, which are usually omitted at the end of modern editions of the New Version of the Psalms. The word "welkin," in the first line, is open to criticism, but in other respects I prefer Wesley's original to Madan's variation.

XXXVIII.—From *Christian Lyrics* (Norwich: J. Fletcher; 1860). Mr. Sears is an American writer, and I have not been able to obtain access to his original text.

XL.—This text is genuine; but I have not been able to discover the author of the volume, published in 1829, under the title *Spirit of the Psalms*, which is not to be confounded with the work of the Rev. H. F. Lyte, afterwards published under the same title, in 1834.

XLI.—This hymn is from *Hymns Ancient and Modern, for Use in the Services of the Church* (London: Novello; 1861). I am indebted to the Rev. Sir Henry Baker, Bart. (one of the editors of that collection), for the permission, which he has kindly obtained for me from the author, to publish his name, as well as for the authentication of the text. I am also indebted to him and his co-editors for their consent to the use which I have made of this hymn, and of three others, contributed by Sir Henry Baker himself to the same collection, to which he has allowed me to affix his name.

XLII.—Five out of seven stanzas. Those omitted are Doddridge's second and sixth.

XLVI.—Five stanzas out of a hymn which, as first published in 1740 (then beginning "Glory to God, and praise, and love"), consisted of eighteen stanzas; and which, in the seventeenth edition of *Hymns and Spiritual Songs* (Pine, Bristol; 1773), was reduced to eleven stanzas; then beginning as in the present text. In the *Hymn-Book for Methodists*, it consists of ten stanzas; one of which is taken from the earlier edition, and is not in that of 1773.

XLVIII.—Four out of five stanzas. That omitted is the fourth of Watts.

LII.—Five out of eight stanzas. Those omitted are the fourth, fifth, and seventh of Watts.

LV.—Six out of seven stanzas. That omitted is the third of Newton.

LVII.—This hymn, as here given, was introduced into the Marylebone Collection (1851) from a poem of some length, published in 1831, in *The Iris*, a volume edited by the Rev. Thomas Dale. The text (which will be found at page 139 of that volume) is unaltered, except that the first word "Saviour," has been brought down from a preceding line, in substitution for the words "And then," so as to give to these stanzas an independent beginning.

HYMN
LVIII.—Nine out of eleven stanzas. Those omitted are the fifth and seventh of Mrs. Barbauld.

LX.—I have not succeeded in tracing the author, or the original text of this hymn. The earliest edition of the *New Version of the Psalms*, to which Mr. Sedgwick has been able to find it appended, was published in 1796. The three first stanzas were printed, with music, in the *Christian's Magazine*, vol. 3, 1762. The "Gloria," which constitutes the fourth stanza, goes with the hymn in some modern books, and suits it so well, that I have ventured to retain it. This "Gloria" is certainly by Charles Wesley; it will be found at page 242 of the fourth edition (1743) of the *Hymns and Sacred Poems*, by the two brothers.

LXI.—This hymn (No. 2, in the Rev. John Chandler's *Hymns of the Primitive Church*) is, as stated by himself in his Preface to that work, a variation from a translation from the same Latin original, by the Rev. Isaac Williams; which had previously appeared in the *British Magazine*, and which is No. 2 in Mr. Williams' *Hymns Translated from the Parisian Breviary* (Rivingtons; 1839).

LXII.—From the Marylebone Collection of 1851, edited by the late Rev. J. H. Gurney, the present Bishop of Durham, and the present Dean of Lincoln. It is there attributed to "A. Gray." I have not been able to learn anything about the author, nor to discover the original text, if previously published.

LXIV.—Mr. Neale's hymn is divided into thirteen unequal parts, the first seven of which constitute the present text.

LXV.—From the *Hymns for Public Worship*, of the Society for Promoting Christian Knowledge. I have not been able to trace the author, nor the original text, if previously published.

LXVI.—I have taken this hymn from Mr. Martineau's *Hymns for the Christian Church and Home* (Longman; twelfth edition; 1856), in which it is No. 234. I have not met with it elsewhere; but, from the internal evidence, I presume the text to be genuine.

LXIX.—Four out of nine stanzas, of unequal length, from Bishop Mant's *Holydays of the Church: or, Scriptural Narratives and Biographical Notices*, vol. ii. p. 536 (Oxford: Parker; 1831).

LXX.—The *Offices* of John Austin, containing hymns of striking excellence, were adapted to the use of members of the Church of England, first by Theophilus Dorrington, and afterwards by the Nonjuring Bishop Hickes. Dorrington, in some cases, altered Austin's hymns; Hickes almost always reprinted them without alteration. This hymn is No. 31 in Austin's *Offices*, where it consists of seven stanzas; the first of which was omitted, and some of the others slightly altered, by Charles Wesley. The present text is taken from the first edition (1739) of the Wesleys' *Hymns and Sacred Poems*, page 130, where it is entitled *Hymn to Christ; altered from Dr. Hickes' "Reformed Devotions."*

LXXI.—The text of this hymn is given from Toplady's Collection, published in 1776, the original having been given to Toplady by the author, Mr. Bakewell, himself. It had been previously published, in a shorter and altered form, by Martin Madan, in 1760.

LXXIII.—Twenty-three out of twenty-eight stanzas, communicated by Mr. Turner, one of the authors, to Dr. Rippon in 1791 (See Rippon's *Baptist Annual Register*, vol. iii. p. 471). The first four stanzas of the text are by Fanch, who also wrote the three which follow them in the original, but which are here omitted, because they are repeated in substance towards the end of the part contributed by Turner. The stanzas, from "Blest angels," to the end, are by Turner, and were published by him separately, with variations (not improvements), in a little volume, printed in 1794. Abridgments of this hymn, more or less varied (usually beginning "Beyond the glittering starry skies"), occur in several modern hymn-books; one of the first of them appeared in Dr. Rippon's own Collection.

LXXIV.—The three last out of five stanzas (Hymn LVIII. in Book I. of Watts' *Hymns and Spiritual Songs*, beginning "Let mortal tongues attempt to sing").

XXIX.—From the Rev. William Carus Wilson's *General Psalmody*. I have not been able to discover the author, or the original text.

LXXX.—Seven stanzas out of eight. That omitted is Montgomery's third.

LXXXI.—This is one of a small number of compositions by Michael Bruce (a Scottish schoolmaster, who died very young), which have been the subject of much controversy in Scotland, and, indeed, of a kind of literary romance. They appear to have been intrusted in manuscript by Michael Bruce, or by his father, to John Logan, who, some time after Bruce's death, published them with variations, in his own name. The eighteenth "Paraphrase" is a variation of this hymn; no doubt contributed by Logan. The present is Bruce's original text, as given in Mr. Mackelvie's collection of his poems (Edinburgh: Paterson; 1837).

LXXXII.—Six out of eight stanzas. The second and third of Watts' are omitted.

LXXXIII.—Four out of six stanzas. The second and third of Watts', are omitted.

LXXXVI.—The text of this hymn, and of No. CIII. as now corrected (see *Errata*), is from the first edition of *Psalms and Hymns* (Ipswich, 1813), by the author, the Rev. William Hurn, formerly Vicar of Debenham.

XC.—This popular hymn is a cento, composed by Martin Madan, with some variations, out of two hymns by Charles Wesley (Nos. 38 and 39 of *Hymns of Intercession for all Mankind*), and one by John Cennick (No. 965 in the *Collection of Hymns for the Use of the Protestant Church of the United Brethren, revised and enlarged:* Bath; 1801). The choice and arrangement of the stanzas, as made by Madan, is here preserved, as are his variations of the third and fourth stanzas (Cennick's), of which the last lines do not rhyme in the original. The two first stanzas and the last are from Wesley's No. 39, a hymn of four stanzas. Madan made some alterations in the first and the last, which (with the exception of "O come quickly," instead of Wesley's "Jah, Jehovah!") I have not retained.

Notes. 453

HYMN

The second, and the fifth (which is the concluding stanza of Wesley's No. 38), he did not alter.

XCI.—The preceding hymn is generally, by a popular error, attributed to Olivers, the only foundation for that error being, that he adopted its first line as the beginning of one of his stanzas, which (though the first of those selected here) is not the first in either edition of his Judgment Hymn. His hymn was greatly altered and enlarged in its second edition, from which the present text is taken; being a selection of eleven out of thirty-six stanzas.

XCIV.—This translation of *Veni Creator* (by an unknown hand) was first introduced into the Office for the Ordination of Priests upon the revision of the Liturgy of the Church of England, in 1662.

XCVIII.—Seven out of nine stanzas. Hart's seventh and eighth are omitted.

C.—Jacobi's translation will be found at page 43 of Haberkorn's *Psalmodia Germanica* (London, 1765). It consists of ten stanzas, of which Toplady adopted and altered six. Toplady's third stanza is here omitted.

CI.—Five out of six stanzas; from Mant's *Holydays of the Church* (vol. ii. page 317). The Bishop's first stanza is omitted.

CIV.—The seven last out of eleven stanzas (No. 24 of John Mason's *Songs of Praise*).

CVI.—Four out of eight stanzas: (the fourth, fifth, sixth, and seventh of Watts' are omitted).

CVIII.—Fourteen out of twenty-six stanzas. This is the most ancient of all the compositions included in this volume, and it is the true English source of all the "New Jerusalem Hymns" of the seventeenth and eighteenth centuries. It is printed at length in Dr. Bonar's interesting Preface to his edition, published in 1852 (Edinburgh: Johnstone and Hunter), of David Dickson's *New Jerusalem*, which is itself a mere variation of this hymn, with thirty-six more stanzas added to it. The original hymn is contained in a MS. quarto volume, numbered 15,225, in the British Museum, the date of which seems (from the internal evidence, as stated by Dr. Bonar), to be about 1616. The hymn itself (which is entitled, *A Song by F. B. P. to the tune of Diana*) is, probably, of Queen Elizabeth's time.

CX.—I have been unable to trace this hymn higher than to the Collection of Dr. Williams and Mr. Boden, first published in 1801, in which it is stated to be from "*Eckinton Collection;*" and I have not discovered the author, or the original text. In the collections which give it most fully, there are seven stanzas; of which one, the third (a stanza of inferior merit, and borrowed directly from an older hymn), is here omitted.

CXIII.—Five out of six stanzas; from Hymn CXLIII. of Berridge's *Sion's Songs*. The stanza omitted is Berridge's fourth. The last couplet of the second stanza is taken by Berridge, with very little alteration, from Ralph Erskine's *Gospel Sonnets* (Part V. section 6); and the whole hymn follows so closely in Erskine's

HYMN

track, that it might properly be described as a variation from him.

CXIV.—The text is that of the 66th Scotch Paraphrase, in which Cameron, taking the general plan, and much of the detail and expression of Watts' hymn (No. 41 of Watts' Book I.), has recast the whole composition, with excellent effect.

CXVI.—Four out of five stanzas. That omitted is Newton's fourth.

CXXII.—The first ten lines of this hymn were left a fragment by Kirke White, written on the back of one of his mathematical papers. They came after his death into the hands of Dr. Collyer, who published them, with six (not very successful) lines of his own added, in his Hymn-Book of 1812, where the hymn is numbered 867. The task of finishing it was more happily accomplished by Miss Maitland, in the form in which it is here given, and which first appeared in a volume published by Hatchard in 1827, under the title of *Hymns for Private Devotion, selected and original.*

CXXIII.—Five out of ten stanzas.

CXXV.—Six out of seven stanzas. That omitted is Newton's third.

CXXVI.—Eight out of twelve stanzas. Those omitted are the third, ninth, tenth, and eleventh of Cennick.

CXXVII.—Hammond's hymn (which will be found at page 85 of his *Psalms, Hymns, and Spiritual Songs;* London, 1745) is in fourteen stanzas. Of these, the first, second, and thirteenth, are the same, except some very slight verbal changes, with the three first stanzas of Madan's variation. The two last stanzas of the variation are an expansion by Madan of Hammond's concluding stanza.

CXXVIII.—Chandler concludes this hymn with a "Gloria," which is omitted here.

CXXXIII.—Three out of seven stanzas.

CXLII.—Six out of eight stanzas.

CXLVIII.—This and No. CLXIII. are taken, by permission of the authoress, from *The Legend of the Golden Prayers, and other Poems* (London: Bell and Daldy; 1859; pages 139—142). Both hymns had been previously published at or before the dates marked in the text.

CLV.—This is a variation from the four first and the two last stanzas of James Montgomery's *Verses to the Memory of the late Joseph Browne, of Lethersdale,* a poem in fourteen stanzas (of four lines each), which was written about 1803, and published in *The Wanderer of Switzerland, and other Poems,* in 1806. The hymn, in its present form, seems to have first appeared in Dr. Collyer's Collection, published in 1812; but I have not been able to ascertain whether the variation is due to Dr. Collyer, or (as, from the internal evidence, I should have thought very probable) to Montgomery himself. It is not, however, included in Montgomery's Collection of his own hymns, published in 1853, nor is it in his *Christian Psalmist,* published in 1825.

CLVIII.—The last four out of five stanzas. (The hymn is No. 86, Book II. of Watts.)

CLX.—Eight out of eleven stanzas. (*Theodosia's Poems,* vol. i. page

159; Bristol edition of 1780.) The stanzas omitted are the fourth, fifth, and sixth of the authoress.

CLXVIII.—Seven out of nine stanzas. The fourth and eighth of Watts are omitted.

CLXXI.—Four out of six stanzas. The fourth and fifth of Watts' are omitted.

CLXXVI.—From *Hymns for the Church of God* (Leicester, 1852). The author and the original text (if previously published) unknown.

CLXXVIII.—The first five out of six stanzas.

CLXXX.—The text of this hymn is from Dr. Raffles' Collection, whom I understand (on Mr. Sedgwick's authority) to have had it from the author.

CLXXXII.—Mr. Ray Palmer is an American writer, and I have not had access to any original publication containing this hymn, the text of which I have taken from the late Dr. Andrew Reed's Collection.

CLXXXVI.—Eight out of eleven four-line stanzas, which constitute the latter part of *The Covenant and Confidence of Faith*, in Baxter's Poems (Pickering's edition, 1821; page 71). The stanzas omitted are the first, third, and fifth, at the page referred to.

CLXXXIX.—Four stanzas out of eight. The hymn is No. 32 in John Austin's *Offices*. The stanzas omitted are the three first, and the "Gloria" at the end.

CXC.—Five stanzas out of six. The stanza omitted is Cowper's fifth.

CXCI.—Five stanzas out of eight. Those omitted are Wesley's fifth, sixth, and seventh. The hymn is at page 30 of the *Hymns and Sacred Poems* (Second Edition; Bristol, 1743).

CXCIII.—The last stanza is wanting in Miss Elliott's *Hours of Sorrow cheered and comforted* (Fourth Edition, 1849; page 136). But I have ventured to retain it, because it is found in the Collection published by the brother of the authoress (the Rev. H. V. Elliott, of Brighton), with her initials attached.

CXCIV.—From a memoir of the Life of Oberlin, published anonymously in 1830 (London, Ball). The translator is Mrs. Daniel Wilson, of Islington; who, since this edition was prepared for the press, has kindly permitted me to give her name.

CXCV.—Five out of ten stanzas (*Theodosia's Poems*; vol. i. p. 134, of the edition of 1780). The stanzas omitted are the third to the seventh inclusive.

CCII.—From *The Rivulet* (Longman and Co.; Second Edition, 1856).

CCIII.—Five out of ten stanzas, from Mant's *Holydays of the Church* (vol. ii. page 563). The Bishop's fifth, sixth, seventh, ninth, and tenth stanzas are omitted.

CCVI.—A curious example of a successful cento. Each stanza is taken from a different hymn by Mason; the four hymns which have each contributed one stanza, being Nos. 6, 7, 9,

HYMN

and 8, of Mason's *Songs of Praise*. Mr. Gurney (who had been to some extent anticipated in this operation, by former Collections *e.g.* Montgomery, in the *Christian Psalmist*, gives a composite hymn of greater length, from the same sources) has introduced some slight verbal alterations, which are here retained.

CCIX.—Five out of eight stanzas (*Conder's Hymns*; London, Snow, p. 140). The stanzas omitted are Conder's second, third, and fourth.

CCXIII.—The text is that of the second Scotch Paraphrase. It is slightly different from that printed in Logan's works, where some of the pieces, now ascertained to be by Michael Bruce, are still ascribed to Logan, who originally published them as his own. The true original (which begins, "O God of Jacob," &c.) is No. 4 of Doddridge's hymns; it has been re-written and certainly improved, by Logan.

CCXIX.—The first five out of six stanzas.

CCXX.—The five first out of six stanzas (from Watts' *Divine Songs for Children*; Song 9).

CCXXIII.—Six stanzas out of eight (from Lyte's *Poems, chiefly Religious*; London, Nisbet; p. 158). The stanzas omitted are the fourth and eighth of Lyte.

CCXXIV.—The text of this hymn is from Le Bas' *Life of Bishop Middleton* (Rivingtons, 1831).

CCXXVI.—John Mardley's original is the *Humble Lamentation of a Sinner*; usually appended to the "Old Version" of the Psalms. In Bishop Heber's book, it is erroneously ascribed to Sternhold; and no notice is there taken of the Bishop's extensive variations.

CCXXVIII.—Three out of four stanzas. The stanza omitted is Mr. Russell's third.

CCXXIX.—This and No. CCLII. were communicated to me in manuscript by the kindness of my friend, Mr. Palgrave.

CCXXXI.—Three out of four stanzas; the fourth is that omitted.

CCXLIII.—From the Marylebone Hymn-Book of 1851. The two first and the fourth lines are by Waring, the rest by a different hand, but whose, I have not been able to ascertain.

CCXLVI.—The text of this, and of Nos. CCLVII. and CCLXV. is from an edition published soon after Bishop Ken's death, by Charles Brome, the proprietor of the copyright; containing (as I believe) the author's latest corrections. The text of the editions of 1700 and 1705, published in the Bishop's lifetime, is materially different, both from that here given, and from all the modern variations. It will be found in Mr. Anderdon's *Life of Ken*.

CCXLVIII.—The twelve last of sixteen stanzas, from the first poem in the *Christian Year*.

CCLIII.—I am indebted for the communication of this hymn and No. CCLXVI. to the kindness of the author, the Rev. James Ford, Prebendary of Exeter.

CCLVI.—A variation from Watts' "Dread Sovereign, let my evening song" (No. VII. of Watts' Hymns, Book II.). Browne has altered the metre, and has re-written and improved the whole composition.

HYMN
CCLI.—The twelve last of fourteen stanzas, from the second poem in the *Christian Year*.

CCLX.—From *The New Congregational Hymn Book* (Jackson, Walford, and Co.) This is not in the only volume of Park's Hymns, which I have seen; I have, therefore, been unable to verify the text.

CCLXIV.—One couplet only is omitted; viz. that which, in Doddridge's text, follows the sixteenth line. The hymn, as originally, and generally, printed, is divided into three unequal parts; the first consisting of eighteen lines, the second of twenty-eight, and the third of twenty-four. I have ventured to adopt a division into stanzas, as being more suitable for music.

CCLXVII.—Five out of seven stanzas. The omitted stanzas are Doddridge's second and fifth.

CCLXIX.—This, and No. CCXCIX. were first published in Lord Nelson's *Salisbury Hymnal*; from whence they are taken, and the author's name now for the first time added, by Mr. Keble's and Lord Nelson's kind permission.

CCLXX.—The repeated couplet is taken from Milton's translation of the 136th Psalm; with the change of Milton's word "aye," into "still."

CCLXXVI. CCLXXIX.—Both these are taken (with four of his own hymns), by the permission of the Rev. Arthur Tozer Russell, from his Hymn Book (*Psalms and Hymns*, &c.; Cambridge; Deighton, 1851), in which they were first published. The author is the Rev. Henry Downton, formerly of Chatham, and now of Geneva.

CCLXXXI.—This, and No. CCCLXXXIX. are from *Parish Musings*, by the Rev. Dr. J. S. B. Monsell, Vicar of Egham (Rivingtons; Fifth Edition; 1860), and are inserted by his kind permission.

CCLXXXII.—From the Islington collection; *Psalms and Hymns for Public Worship* (Ewins, 1855). The author and the original text unknown.

CCLXXXV.—Six out of twelve stanzas. Those omitted are the sixth to the eleventh, inclusive, of Jacobi. The hymn is at page 189 of Haberkorn's *Psalmodia Germanica* (London, 1765).

CCLXXXVII.—From the Hymn Book of the Society for Promoting Christian Knowledge. I have not ascertained the Author, or verified the text: but I believe the Hymn first appeared in the *Protestant Episcopal Collection of Hymns* (1832), appended to the version of the Psalms at the end of the American Prayer-Book.

CCLXXXVIII.—The seven last out of fourteen stanzas. (*Hymns and Sacred Poems by J. & C. Wesley*; second edition: 1843: page 192).

CCLXXXIX.—Seven out of eight stanzas. Montgomery's last stanza is omitted.

CCXC.—From the late Rev. Edward Bickersteth's *Christian Psalmody*. The author, and the original text, unknown.

CCXCII.—Crashaw's hymn is a translation from the *Adoro te devote* of Thomas Aquinas. It consists of fifty-six lines; from which most of the lines of the present hymn are adopted, with more or less variation. The first abridgment (less varied than the present, and containing only six stanzas), was Hymn 18 in Austin's *Offices*; and was repeated, with the change of one or two words, by Hickes (*Devotions*; 1706; page 210). The

HYMN present text is that of Dorrington's variation from Austin: in whose *Reformed Devotions* it is Hymn 23.

CCXCIII.—From the collection of the Rev. R. Whittingham (Simpkin and Marshall: fourth edition, 1843). I have not been able to trace the author, or the original text.

CCXCIV.—From Hall's collection: *Psalms and Hymns adapted to the Services of the Church of England* (London: Wix, 1838). I have not been able to trace the author, or the original text.

CCXCV.—From the Hymn-Book of the Society for Promoting Christian Knowledge. The author, and the original text, unknown.

CCXCVI.—From the Rev. R. H. Baynes' *Lyra Anglicana* (Houlston & Wright, 1862, page 67). Mr. Baynes took it from an American collection, in which this and some other translations from the Latin are said to be by *Palmer*. In all probability the translator is Mr. Ray Palmer, the author of the hymn No. CLXXXII. of this Collection. But I have not been able to verify the name or the text.

CCXCVIII.—Ten out of twenty-eight stanzas; from a poem entitled *Jesus teaches to die;* at page 80 of the fourth volume of Bishop Ken's works (London; 1721). The stanzas omitted, are the first four; the tenth to the eighteenth inclusive; the twenty-second to the twenty-fifth inclusive; and the twenty-eighth.

CCC.—This was given to me by a friend in manuscript; but had, I believe, been previously in print. I have not been able to discover the author, nor the original text.

CCCI.—Three out of forty-three stanzas. The poem (a translation from the Hymn of Prudentius, *Circa exequias defuncti*) is in Williams' *Thoughts in Past Years* (Rivingtons; third edition, 1843; page 290). The stanzas selected are at pages 304-5.

CCCII.—The three last stanzas of James Montgomery's *The Grave* (Montgomery's *Poetical Works complete in one volume;* Longman: page 261). They now constitute, I believe, part of the epitaph on the poet's tomb.

CCCVIII.—Four out of five stanzas. The omitted stanza, a "Gloria," is Chandler's last.

CCCX.—Five out of six stanzas. The omitted stanza is Browne's last. (Browne's *Hymns and Spiritual Songs*, No. 203.)

CCCXI.—Eight out of nine stanzas. The omitted stanza is Herbert's last.

CCCXII.—In Mason's *Songs of Praise* (No. 19), this hymn ends (as many of Mason's hymns do) with a half-stanza; the general scheme of division being into stanzas of eight lines. The concluding half-stanza is omitted here.

CCCXVII.—This hymn was first privately printed in 1833. It was afterwards subdivided into three distinct hymns, in the collection of the Rev. H. V. Elliott (the husband of the authoress); by whose kindness I have been enabled to reunite, in this place, the parts so separated.

CCCXX.—From the late Rev. Edward Bickersteth's *Christian Psalmody*. I have not been able to discover the author, or the original text. It is sometimes erroneously attributed to the Hon. & Rev. B. W. Noel.

CCCXXII. CCCXXIV.—The text of both these is from the late Dr.

Andrew Reed's collection. Mr. Hastings is an American author; and, on comparing them with his original text, since the first edition of the present volume was published, they appear to be correctly given; except that the refrain, "Return, return," in No. cccxxiv. is not in Mr. Hastings' book: (*Hymns and Poems*, New York, 1850.)

CCCXXIII.—I am indebted to Mr. Morris, of Worcester, for the communication of Mrs. Morris' volume, entitled, "The Voice and the Reply" (Worcester; Grainger), from which this hymn is taken.

CCCXXV.—From the twenty-ninth edition (published about 1826) of Dr. Rippon's Hymn-Book; where it is attributed to Dr. Collyer. It is not in Dr. Collyer's own collection, of 1812; and I have not succeeded in tracing it beyond Dr. Rippon's book.

CCCXXVI.—By an American author, whose name I have not been able to ascertain. It was communicated by him to Miss Elliott, the authoress of the hymn by which it was suggested, "Just as I am," &c. (No. CXLVII. of this volume), and the text (which I have not had the means of verifying), is from a small printed tract, without date, placed in my hands by a friend.

CCCXXIX.—This was kindly communicated to me in manuscript, by the author, Robert Smith, Esq. of Holloway.

CCCXXXV.—Thirteen out of sixteen stanzas, from *Hymns and Sacred Poems*, by Charles Wesley; vol. i. p. 40 (Farley, Bristol; second edition, 1755).

CCCXXXVII.—The hymn from which these eight stanzas are taken, was first published in twenty-two stanzas in *Spiritual Songs* by J. and C. *Wesley* (vol. i. p. 224, fourth edition, 1743). Afterwards in the seventeenth edition (Pine, Bristol, 1773; p. 80) it was reduced to sixteen stanzas. In both it begins, "And wilt Thou yet be found."

CCCXLIX.—Miss Elliott's name is now (through the kindness of her brother, the Rev. H. V. Elliott, in obtaining for me her permission) first made public, as the authoress of this hymn. Through some accidental error it is ascribed in the Rev. H. V. Elliott's Collection to Wesley; and the same mistake has been transferred to Ryle's *Spiritual Songs*, Bourchier's *Solace in Sickness and Sorrow*, and probably other books.

CCCLI.—Six out of seven stanzas (*Hymns and Sacred Poems*, vol. ii. p. 146; second edition, 1743). Wesley's last stanza is omitted; and a change of arrangement, which the Wesleys themselves sanctioned in the *Hymn Book for Methodists*, is adopted, by placing as last of the six the stanza which is second in the original text.

CCCLVI.—Five out of six stanzas. Browne's last is omitted.

CCCLVIII.—Five out of eight stanzas. Those omitted are Mr. Massie's third, fourth, and seventh. (From *Martin Luther's Spiritual Songs; translated by R. Massie, Esq. of Eccleston*: Hatchard, 1854.)

CCCLXIII.—From the original, as printed, with music, by the late Baron Bunsen, and communicated to me by a friend.

CCCLXIV.—In most of the editions of Kelly's hymns (including that

HYMN

of 1836), this is a hymn of ten stanzas; of which the fifth, sixth, seventh, and tenth, are here omitted. In the edition of 1812, it was reduced by the author himself to six stanzas; being (except the last), the same with the present text. The last stanza of that edition was unequal to the rest; and was omitted by the author in all the later editions.

CCCLXVIII.—From *Sacred Poetry* (Oliphant, Edinburgh; seventh edition; 1828). I have not been able to trace the author, or the original text.

CCCLXX.—The seven last of twenty stanzas; from Erskine's *Gospel Sonnets* (twentieth edition; Berwick: Phorson; 1788: page 272).

CCCLXXVI.—(From Lyte's *Poems, chiefly Religious;* page 41). This hymn had been in circulation several years before the publication of that volume, and will be found in the *Christian Psalmist* (1825), and in *Hymns for Private Devotion, Selected and Original* (Hatchard, 1827). It has sometimes been erroneously attributed to Miss Grenfell.

CCCLXXXI. CCCLXXXII.—I am indebted for the communication of the volumes from which these two pieces are taken (*Songs for the Suffering;* and *The Family Hymnal;* London: Hamilton, Adams, & Co.), to the kindness of the author, the Rev. Thomas Davis, Incumbent of Roundhay, Yorkshire.

CCCLXXXVII.—Five out of nine stanzas (from Watts' Hymn 59, of Book 2). The stanzas omitted are the first, second, fifth, and sixth.

CCCXC.—Five out of six stanzas. The omitted stanza is the fourth of Watts.

CCCXCII.—This has been made up by putting together two stanzas taken from No. 23 (with some slight variation), and two others taken (without variation) from No. 28 of Mason's *Songs of Praise.* Lady Huntingdon added two stanzas more from the latter hymn, which are here omitted.

CCCCI.—Six out of eight stanzas. The stanzas omitted are Kelly's second and third.

CCCCII.—From the Rev. R. Burgess' Collection (*Psalms and Hymns for Public Worship:* Seeleys; second edition; 1853): where it bears the name of "Newton." Besides John Newton (who is certainly not the author), there were two others of that name, mentioned in Mr. Sedgwick's catalogue of hymnwriters; viz. Henry Newton (among whose works I do not find this), and James Newton, whose works I have not seen, but whose date (1800) is earlier than that, to which, from internal evidence, I should be disposed to refer the present composition. I have, therefore, marked it as the work of an unknown author, to whose original text I have not had access.

CCCCIII.—From *Hymns and Anthems* (Fox, Paternoster Row); a volume edited by the late Mr. William Johnson Fox; to whom this hymn was given for publication by the authoress, who afterwards left England for America.

CCCCIX.—From *Thoughts for Thoughtful Hours* (Nelson, Edinburgh 1859). "H. L. L." is the signature of the translators of *Hymns from the Land of Luther.*

LIST OF AUTHORS.

ADAMS, Sarah Flower (1840) CCCCIII
ADDISON, Joseph (1728) XIII, CLXXIII, CCXVI
ALEXANDER, Cecil Frances (1853—1858) CXLVIII, CLXIII
ALFORD, Henry (1845) XCII, CXXX, CCLXXIV, CCLXXXIII, CCCIX
ANSTICE, Joseph [1841] CCLXXIII, CCCXXVII
AUSTIN, John (1668) XXVI, LXX, CLXXXIX, CCXCII, CCCLXVII

BAKER, Sir Henry (1857—1961) CLXII, CXCII, CCLXX
BAKEWELL, John (1760) LXXI
BARBAULD, Anna Lætitia [1825] LVIII, CXXXVIII, CCLXXI
BATHURST, William Hiley (1831) LVI, CII, CLXXV, CLXXXIV, CCXCI
BAXTER, Richard (1681) CLXXXVI
BEDDOME, Benjamin [1818] CCCXLII
BERRIDGE, John (1785) CXIII, CC
BICKERSTETH, Edward Henry (1858) CCXXII
BONAR, Horatius (1856) CXCVII, CCCXXXIII, CCCLXIX, CCCLXXIV
BOWDLER, John (1814) XXII, CCXXXIV
BOWLY, Mary (1847) CCCCVIII
BROWNE, Simon (1720) XCVI, CCLVI, CCCX, CCCLVI
BROWNE, T. B. (1844) XXV
BRUCE, Michael (1768) LXXXI
BURNS, James D. (1856) CCCXIII
BYROM, John (1773) CCCXXXVIII

CAMERON, William (1770) CXIV
CENNICK, John (1742) XC, CXXVI, CCCLII
CHANDLER, John (1837) LXI, CXXVIII, CXXXIX, CCLI, CCCVIII
CHAPMAN, Robert C. (1837) CCCLXXV
CONDER, Josiah (1856) LXXVI, LXXXVIII, CCIX
COLLYER, William Bengo [1829] CCCXXV
COWPER, William (1779) CV, CXXXVI, CXLIII, CXC, CCCXLVI, CCCLXXI, CCCLXXVIII, CCCLXXXV, CCCLXXXVIII, CCCXCI, CCCXCV
CRASHAW, Richard (1646) CCXCII
CROSSMAN, Samuel (1664) CIX, CLIII
Cox, Frances Elizabeth (1841) CCCXXXII

DAVIS, Thomas (1859, 1860) CCCLXXXI, CCCLXXXII
DIX, William Chatterton (1861) XLI
DODDRIDGE, Philip (1755) XLII, CXVIII, CXXIX, CXXXI, CLIX, CCVII, CCXII, CCXIII, CCLXIV, CCLXVII, CCLXXVII, CCLXXX, CCCIV, CCCXVIII, CCCXCIII
DORRINGTON, Theophilus (1686) CCXCII
DOWNTON, Henry (1851) CCLXXVI, CCLXXIX
DRENNAN, William (1815) CXXXVII
DYSON, Charles (1816) CCCLIX

EDMESTON, James (1820) CCXXVII, CCCXCVI
ELLIOTT, Charlotte (1836) CXLVII, CXCIII, CCCXLIX, CCCL, CCCLXXII
ELLIOTT, Julia Anne (1833) CCCXVII
ERSKINE, Ralph (1734) CCCLXX

FANCH, James (1791) LXXIII
FLOWERDEW, Anne (1811) CCLXVIII
FORD, James (1856) CCLIII, CCLXVI

GIBBONS, Thomas (1784) XVI, CCCXCIV
GISBORNE, Thomas (1803) CXIX
GRANT, Sir Robert (1839) XXI, LXVIII, CVII, CCCXCVIII
GRAY, A. (1851) LXII
GRIGG, Joseph (1765) CCCXXX
GRINFIELD, Thomas (1836) XXXII, CCVIII, CCXCVII
GURNEY, John Hampden (1851) XVIII, CXLIX, CCVI, CCLXXII

HAMMOND, William (1745) XCV, CXXVII, CCCLXXIII
HART, Joseph (1759) XCVIII
HASTINGS, Thomas [1842] CCCXXII, CCCXXIV
HAWEIS, Thomas (1792) CCXXXIX
HEBER, Bishop Reginald (1827) I, LXXXIV, LXXXVII, CXVII, CXLI, CLXXVII, CCXIV, CCXXV, CCXXVI, CCXLII, CCLXI, CCCV, CCCXXXI, CCCLXI
HERBERT, Algernon [1839] CCCLXIII
HERBERT, George (1632) XX, CCCXI
HILL, Rowland (1783—1796) CXII, CLII
HOW, William Walsham (1860) L, CCLXXXVI
HUNT, John (1853) X
HUNTINGDON, Selina, Countess of (1780) CCCXCII
HURN, William (1813) LXXXVI, CIII

IRONS, William Joseph (1853) CXCVI

JACOBI, John Christian (1722) C, CCLXXXV

KEBLE, John (1827—1857) XIV, XXXI, XCIII, CCXLVIII, CCLIX, CCLXIX, CCXCIX
KELLY, Thomas (1804—1836) XXXV, XLIII, XLV, XLIX, LXXVIII, LXXXV, CXX, CXXI, CXXIV, CLXXIX, CCXV, CCLXII, CCCXVI, CCCXXI, CCCLXIV, CCCCI
KEN, Bishop Thomas (1700—1721), CCXLVI, CCLVII, CCLXV, CCXCVIII
KIRKE-WHITE, Henry (1803—1806) CXXII, CCLVIII

LOGAN, John (1770) CCXIII
LYNCH, Thomas Toke (1855) CCII
LYTE, Henry Francis (1833—1847) XI, XXIII, XXIV, LIII, CXXXII, CLXXXIII, CLXXXVIII, CCXXIII, CCXXXV, CCXXXVI, CCXXXVII, CCCXV, CCCLXV, CCCLXXVI, CCCLXXXVI, CCCCV

MADAN, Martin (1760) XC, CXXVII
MAITLAND, Fanny Fuller (1827) CXXII
MANT, Bishop Richard (1831—1837) II, LXIX, CI, CCIII
MARDLEY, John (1562), CCXXVI
MARRIOTT, John (1816) CLXXX
MASON, John (1683) CIV, CCVI, CCCXII, CCCXCII

MASSIE, Richard (1854) CCCLVIII
MEDLEY, Samuel (1789—1800) CLI, CCCXL
MIDDLETON, Bishop Thomas Fanshaw [1831] CCXXIV
MILES, Sibella Elizabeth [1840] LXVI
MILLARD, James Elwin (1848) IV
MILMAN, Henry Hart (1822—1827) CCXXXVIII, CCCVI
MONSELL, John S. B. (1837—1850) CCLXXXI, CCCLXXXIX
MONTGOMERY, James (1803—1853) III, XXXVI, LXXX, XCIX, CXI
    CXV, CLV, CLXIV, CLXIX, CLXX, CLXXVIII, CCXXI, CCLXXXIX
    CCCII, CCCVII, CCCXIX, CCCLX, CCCCX
MOORE, Henry [1806] CCCLXII
MORRIS, Eliza Fanny [1858] CCCXXIII
MORRISON, John (1770) XXXIX, CCCXLIV

NEALE, John Mason (1851—1854) XXIX, LXIV, CCLIV
NEWMAN, John Henry (1833) CCCCIV
NEWTON, John (1779) XLVII, LV, LXXVII, CXVI, CXXV,
    CLXVI, CLXXXI, CXCIX, CCXIX, CCXLI, CCLXXVIII, CCCXXXIV,
    CCCLXXXIV, CCCXCVII
NOEL, Baptist Wriothesley (1841) CCCLXXIX

OLIVERS, Thomas (1757—1772) XCI, CCCCXI

PALGRAVE, Francis Turner (1862) CCXXIX, CCLII
PALMER, Ray [1840] CLXXXII
PARK, Thomas (1797) CCLX

REED, Andrew (1842) CLXVII
RICKARDS, Samuel (1825) XXXVII
RUSSELL, Arthur Tozer (1851) LXVII, CCXXVIII, CCLXXV, CCCLV
RYLAND, John (1777) CCX, CCXI

SEAGRAVE, Robert (1748) CLXV
SEARS, Edmund H. [1860] XXXVIII
SCOTT, Robert Allan (1839) CLXXII
SKELTON, Philip (1784) XXVIII
SMITH, Robert (1862) CCCXXIX
STEELE, Anne (1760) CLX, CXCV, CCCXXXVI, CCCXLI
SWAIN, Joseph (1792) CXXXIV

TATE, Nahum (1703) XXXIII
TAYLOR, Bishop Jeremy (1653) CLXXIV
TOPLADY, Augustus Montague (1759—1777) C, CXLV, CLVI, CCI,
    CCCLIV, CCCC, CCCCVII, CCCCXII
TURNER, Daniel (1791) LXXIII

WARING, Anna Lætitia (1850—1860) CXCVIII
WARING, Samuel Miller (1827) CCXLIII
WATTS, Isaac (1709—1720) VI, VIII, IX, XII, XV, XVII, XLIV, XLVIII,
    LII, LXIII, LXXII, LXXIV, LXXXII, LXXXIII, XCVII, CVI, CXIV,
    CXXIII, CXXXIII, CXLII, CLIV, CLVIII, CLXI, CLXVIII, CLXXI,
    CCIV, CCXVII, CCXVIII, CCXX, CCXXXIII, CCXLV, CCXLVII, CCLVI,
    CCCIII, CCCXIV, CCCLIII, CCCLXVI, CCCLXXVII, CCCLXXXIII,
    CCCLXXXVII, CCCXC
WESLEY, Charles (1739—1762) VIII, XXXIV, XLVI, LIV, LIX, LXXV,
    LXXXIX, XC, CXL, CXLIV, CXLVI, CLVII, CLXXXV, CLXXXVII,
    CXCI, CCXL, CCL, CCLXIII, CCLXXXVIII, CCCXXXV, CCCXXXVII,
    CCCXXXIX, CCCXLIII, CCCXLV, CCCXLVII, CCCLI, CCCLVII

List of Authors.

WESLEY, John (1739—1743) LXX, CXXXV, CCXXX, CCCXLVIII, CCCCVI
WHITE, Henry Kirke (see Kirke White)
WHITE, Hugh (1841) CCCXXVIII
WILLIAMS, Isaac (1838—1842) XIX, XXX, CCCI, CCCLXX
WILLIAMS, William (1759—1774) LI, CCXXXI, CCXXXII
WILSON, Mrs. Daniel (1830) CXCIV
WINKWORTH, Catherine (1858) CCCXCIX
WITHER, George (1641) XXVII, CCXLIX, CCLV, CCLXXXIV

ANONYMOUS, from miscellaneous Collections, V, VII, LX, LXV, LXXIX, CX, CL, CLXXVI, CCV, CCXLIV, CCLXXXII, CCLXXXVII, CCXC, CCXCIII, CCXCIV, CCXCV, CCC, CCCXX, CCCXXVI, CCCLXVIII, CCCCII
DITTO, "F. B. P." [1616] CVIII
DITTO, "H. L. L." [1859] CCCCIX
DITTO, "M. G. T." (1831) LVII
DITTO, translated from St. Bernard [1860] CCXCVI
DITTO, from Ordination Service [1662] XCIV
DITTO, from "Spirit of the Psalms" (1829) XL

INDEX OF FIRST LINES.

	PAGE
Abide with me! fast falls the even-tide	432
Accept, my God, my evening song	270
Again the Lord of Life and Light	61
All praise to Him who dwells in bliss	278
All praise to Thee, my God, this night.	271
Almighty God, Thy piercing eye	235
And can it be, that I should gain	369
And have I measured half my days	355
And shall I sit alone	363
Another year has fled; renew	294
A poor wayfaring man of grief	385
Approach, my soul, the mercy-seat	234
As o'er the past my memory strays	238
A soldier's course, from battles won	134
As with gladness men of old	46
A thousand years have fleeted	361
Awake, and sing the song	142
Awake, my soul, and with the sun	257
Awake, my soul, awake to prayer	283
Awake, ye saints, and raise your eyes	296
Away with sorrow's sigh	32
Before Jehovah's awful throne	7
Behold! a Stranger's at the door	348
Behold, the morning sun	118
Behold! the Mountain of the Lord	91
Behold the sun, that seem'd but now	269
Beneath Thy cross I lay me down	55
Beyond the glittering starry globe	79
Blest are the humble souls that see	220
Blest be Thy love, dear Lord	205
Blow ye the trumpet, blow	57
Bright was the guiding star that led	46
Brother, thou art gone before us; and thy saintly soul is flown	322
By faith in Christ I walk with God	410
Calm me, my God, and keep me calm	395
Child of sin and sorrow	341
Children of the Heavenly King	141
Christ is our corner-stone	324
Christ, my hidden Life, appear	382
Christ the Lord is risen to-day	62

Index of First Lines.

	PAGE
Christ, whose glory fills the skies	263
Come, Holy Ghost, our souls inspire	106
Come, Holy Spirit, come	110
Come, Holy Spirit, heavenly Dove	108
Come, Holy Spirit, heavenly Dove	109
Come, let us join our friends above	153
Come, let us to the Lord our God	364
Come, my soul, Thy suit prepare	198
Come, O come! in pious lays	27
Come, O thou Traveller unknown	365
Come, take my yoke, the Saviour said	347
Come, we that love the Lord	138
Come, ye thankful people, come	292
Commit thou all thy griefs	433
Compared with Christ, in all beside	379
Day of anger, that dread Day	102
Dearest of names, our Lord, our King	163
Deathless principle, arise	169
Early, my God, without delay	417
Earth to earth, and dust to dust	162
Ere another Sabbath's close	337
Eternal God, of beings First	381
Eternal source of every joy	286
Exalted high at God's right hand	127
Fain would my thoughts fly up to Thee	393
Far from my heavenly home	391
Far from these narrow scenes of night	173
Far from the world, O Lord, I flee	405
Father, I know that all my life	213
Father of Love, our Guide and Friend	211
Fierce passions discompose the mind	397
For ever with the Lord	440
Forth from the dark and stormy sky	238
Forth in Thy Name, O Lord, I go	201
For Thy mercy and Thy grace	297
Fountain of mercy! God of love	286
Friend after friend departs	177
From all that dwell below the skies	254
From Egypt lately come	139
From Greenland's icy mountains	93
Full of weakness and of sin	114
Glorious things of thee are spoken	131
God eternal, Lord of all	3
God is our Refuge, tried and proved	247
God moves in a mysterious way	417
God of mercy, throned on high	308
God of my salvation, hear	159
God of that glorious gift of grace	299
God of the morning, at whose voice!	259
God, that madest earth and heaven	277
Go up, go up, my heart	400

Index of First Lines.

	PAGE
Go, worship at Immanuel's feet	377
Gracious Spirit, dwell with me	218
Great God, Whose universal sway	93
Guide me, O Thou great Jehovah	243
Hail, thou bright and sacred morn	334
Hail, Thou once despised Jesus	76
Hail to the Lord's Anointed	89
Happy soul! thy days are ended	171
Happy the man, whose hopes rely	11
Hark! how all the welkin rings	38
Hark, my soul, how every thing	25
Hark, my soul! it is the Lord	368
Hark, the glad sound! the Saviour comes	47
Hark, 'tis a martial sound!	135
Harp, awake! tell out the story	295
Haste, traveller, haste! the night comes on	343
He, Who on earth as man was known	86
Hear, gracious God! a sinner's cry	361
Hear, gracious God! my humble moan	362
Hear my prayer, O heavenly Father	276
Heavenly Father, to Whose eye	224
Holy Ghost, dispel our sadness	112
Holy, holy, holy, Lord	2
Holy, holy, holy, Lord God Almighty	1
Holy Spirit, gently come	107
Holy Spirit, in my breast	113
Hosanna! raise the pealing hymn	88
Hosanna to the Living Lord!	154
How blest the sacred tie that binds	151
How bright these glorious spirits shine	129
How gentle God's commands	228
How rich thy favours, God of grace	145
How sweet the Name of Jesus sounds	51
How vast the treasure we possess	409
I give immortal praise	5
I heard the voice of Jesus say	353
I praised the earth, in beauty seen	387
I saw, and lo! a countless throng	444
I sing th' almighty power of God	16
In evil long I took delight	354
In memory of the Saviour's love	311
Interval of grateful shade	278
In token that thou shalt not fear	300
It came upon the midnight clear	43
Jerusalem, my happy home	120
Jerusalem, my happy home	125
Jesu! behold, the Wise from far	74
Jesu! guide our way	241
Jesu, lover of my soul	251
Jesu, my strength, my hope	374
Jesu, Thou art my Righteousness	157
Jesu! who for my transgression	380
Jesus, cast a look on me	215
Jesus Christ is risen to-day	64

Index of First Lines.

	PAGE
Jesus, I my cross have taken	402
Jesus! lead us with Thy power	244
Jesus, my all, to Heaven is gone	375
Jesus shall reign where'er the sun	92
Jesus, the Shepherd of the sheep	230
Jesus, thou Joy of loving hearts	313
Jesus, Thy Church with longing eyes	191
Jesus, when near th' expected hour	315
Jesus, where'er Thy people meet	150
Join all the glorious names	77
Joy to the world, the Lord is come	49
Just as I am, without one plea	160
Just as thou art, without one trace	345
Lamb of God, I look to Thee	306
Lead, kindly Light, amid th' encircling gloom	431
Lead us, heavenly Father, lead us	240
Let all the world in every corner sing	19
Let all the world rejoice	9
Let Jacob to his Maker sing	419
Let me be with Thee where Thou art	398
Light of the lonely pilgrim's heart	192
Lo! God is here! Let us adore	149
Lo! He comes! let all adore Him	48
Lo! He comes, with clouds descending	99
Lo! He comes with clouds descending	100
Long did I toil, and knew no earthly rest	412
Lord! come away	191
Lord God of morning and of night	266
Lord God the Holy Ghost	111
Lord, I feel a carnal mind	216
Lord, in the day Thou art about	222
Lord, in Thy Name Thy servants plead	237
Lord Jesu, when we stand afar	54
Lord! may the inward grace abound	299
Lord of hosts! to Thee we raise	323
Lord of my life, whose tender care	222
Lord of the harvest! once again	292
Lord of the harvest! Thee we hail	291
Lord of the Sabbath! hear our vows	335
Lord of the worlds above	147
Lord, Thou hast form'd mine every part	188
Lord, when before Thy throne we meet	312
Lord, when I lift my voice to Thee	201
Mercy alone can meet my case	235
Much in sorrow, oft in woe	137
Must friends and kindred droop and die	319
My faith looks up to Thee	199
My God and Father, while I stray	208
My God, my King, Thy various praise	187
My God, now I from sleep awake	281
My God, the Spring of all my joys	404
My life's a shade, my days	166
My Lord, my love was crucified	329
My Shepherd will supply my need	232
My soul, amid this stormy world	400

Index of First Lines.

	PAGE
My soul, repeat His praise	155
My spirit longeth for Thee	359
My spirit on Thy care	204
My trust is in the Lord	246
Nearer, my God, to Thee	430
Not unto us, Almighty Lord	10
Now I have found the ground wherein	370
Now is the hour of darkness past	83
Now it belongs not to my care	202
Now let our mourning hearts revive	320
Now let us join with hearts and tongues	58
Now may He, who from the dead	252
Now morning lifts her dewy veil	64
Now to Him, who loved us, gave us	253
O day most calm, most bright	327
O for a closer walk with God	415
O for an heart to praise my God	206
O for a thousand tongues to sing	51
O God of Bethel, by whose hand	228
O God, Thou art my God alone	186
O God, Thy grace and blessing give	163
O God, unseen, yet ever near	311
O happy saints, who dwell in light	128
O happy soul, that lives on high	392
O Holy Saviour, Friend unseen	372
O Holy Lord, content to live	304
O house of Jacob, come	95
O how kindly hast Thou led me	224
O Israel, to thy tents repair	164
O Jesu, Lord of heavenly grace	263
O Jesus, Saviour of the lost	236
O King of earth, and air, and sea	229
O King of kings, before whose throne	6
O Lamp of Life! that on the bloody Cross	385
O Lord, another day is flown	273
O Lord, how good, how great art Thou	56
O Lord, how joyful 'tis to see	152
O Lord, how little do we know	399
O Lord, I would delight in Thee	227
O Lord, my best desire fulfil	205
O Lord, Thy heavenly grace impart	209
O Lord, turn not Thy face away	239
O most merciful	253
O Saviour! is Thy promise fled	193
O Saviour, may we never rest	59
O send me down a draught of love	396
O Spirit of the living God	194
O that my load of sin were gone	363
O Thou, from whom all goodness flows	250
O Thou, the contrite sinners' Friend	371
O Thou, to whose all-searching sight	242
O Thou, who camest from above	203
O Thou, whose tender mercy hears	357
O time of tranquil joy and holy feeling	330
O timely happy, timely wise	260

Index of First Lines.

	PAGE
O worship the King	20
Of Thy love some gracious token	338
Oh help us, Lord! each hour of need	249
Oh what, if we are Christ's	207
On God the race of man depends	14
On the mountain's top appearing	94
Our God, our help in ages past	181
Our life is but an idle play	388
Our praise Thou need'st not; but Thy love	19
Palms of glory, raiment bright	130
Pleasant are Thy courts above	146
Plunged in a gulf of dark despair	56
Poor child of sin and woe	342
Praise, my soul, the King of heaven	23
Praise, O praise our God and King	288
Praise the Lord, His glories show	24
Praise the Lord of Heaven, praise Him in the height	25
Praise to God, immortal praise	289
Praise to the radiant Source of bliss	143
Prayer is the soul's sincere desire	185
Quiet, Lord, my froward heart	214
Receive him, Earth, unto thine harbouring shrine	318
Redeem'd from guilt, redeem'd from fears	200
Rejoice, the Lord is King	83
Rejoice, though storms assail thee	420
Rest, weary soul	439
Return, O wanderer, to thy home	343
Rise, my soul, and stretch thy wings	173
Rock of Ages, cleft for me	153
Round the Lord in glory seated	2
Salvation! oh! the joyful sound	67
Saviour, I lift my trembling eyes	60
Saviour, when in dust to Thee	71
Saviour, who, exalted high	73
Saviour, who Thy flock art feeding	305
See, the ransomed millions stand	97
Shall I fear, O Earth, thy bosom	400
Shepherd of Israel, from above	309
Shine on our souls, eternal God	223
Since Thou hast added now, O God	262
Sing to the Lord, our might	332
Sing to the Lord with cheerful voice	22
Sleep well, my dear; sleep safe and free	303
Sometimes a light surprises	411
Source of good, whose power controls	384
Sovereign Ruler of the skies	225
Speed Thy servants, Saviour, speed them	195
Spirit! leave thine house of clay	168
Star of morn and even	241
Sun of my soul, Thou Saviour dear	274
Sweet baby, sleep! what ails my dear	301
Sweet is the Spirit's strain	345
Sweet is the work, my God, my King	331
Sweet place, sweet place alone	122

Index of First Lines.

First Line	Page
The child leans on its parent's breast	406
The billows swell, the winds are high	420
The day, O Lord, is spent	269
The day of rest once more comes round	333
The foe behind, the deep before	67
The God of Abraham praise	441
The Head that once was crown'd with thorns	87
The heaven of heavens cannot contain	151
The Lord is King! lift up your voice	85
The Lord Jehovah reigns	8
The Lord my pasture shall prepare	231
The Lord my Shepherd is	233
The Lord of Might from Sinai's brow	96
The lovely form of God's own Church	325
The race that long in darkness pined	45
The roseate hues of early dawn	177
The scene around me disappears	41
The Son of God goes forth to war	132
The Son of God! the Lord of Life	66
The spacious firmament on high	12
The spring-tide hour	415
The starry firmament on high	118
The strain upraise of joy and praise	30
The voice that breathed o'er Eden	317
The waves of trouble, how they rise	172
The winds were howling o'er the deep	350
The world can neither give nor take	418
Thee we adore, eternal Lord	4
There is a blessed Home	176
There is a book, who runs may read	13
There is a calm for those who weep	319
There is a dwelling-place above	219
There is a fountain fill'd with blood	156
There is a land of pure delight	175
There is a pure and peaceful wave	394
There is a River, deep and broad	115
There is a safe and secret place	248
There is a Stream, which issues forth	116
There is an hour, when I must part	180
There's not a bird, with lonely nest	405
They talk'd of Jesus, as they went	313
Thou art gone to the grave: but we will not deplore thee	321
Thou art gone up on high	69
Thou God of Love! beneath thy sheltering wings	318
Thou, great Creator, art possest	143
Thou Judge of quick and dead	97
Thou, who didst stoop below	70
Thou, Whose Almighty word	197
Though, by sorrows overtaken	389
Though rude winds usher thee, sweet day	42
Through the day Thy love hath spared us	277
Through the love of God our Saviour	438
Thus saith God of His Anointed	50
Thy goodness, Lord, our souls confess	16
Thy way, not mine, O Lord	212
'Tis come, the time so oft foretold	36
'Tis Heaven begun below	148

	PAGE
To God, ye choir above, begin	28
To Heaven I lift mine eye	246
To Him, who for our sins was slain	71
To-morrow, Lord, is Thine	298
To Thee, my God, whose Presence fills	420
To Thy temple I repair	336
Up to the hills I lift mine eyes	245
We seek a rest beyond the skies	180
We sing His love, Who once was slain	165
We sing the praise of Him Who died	63
Weary of wandering from my God	359
Welcome, sweet day, of days the best	326
We'll sing, in spite of scorn	40
We're bound for yonder land	428
We've no abiding city here	390
What are these in bright array	126
What sudden blaze of song	34
Whate'er my God ordains is right	424
When all Thy mercies, O my God	189
When at mid-day my task I ply	266
When at Thy footstool, Lord, I bend	237
When Christ the Lord would come on earth	144
When Christ, with all His graces crown'd	414
When gathering clouds around I view	423
When God of old came down from Heaven	104
When languor and disease invade	426
When I survey life's varied scene	210
When I survey the wondrous cross	53
When Israel, by Divine command	140
When Jesus left His Father's throne	307
When shall Thy love constrain	358
When wounded sore the stricken heart	161
While shepherds watched their flocks by night	37
While with ceaseless course the sun	296
Why comes this fragrance on the summer breeze	407
Why do we mourn departing friends	167
Why should I fear the darkest hour	422
Why should I, in vain repining	421
With all the powers my poor soul hath	310
With tearful eyes I look around	346
Worship, honour, glory, blessing	253
Ye golden lamps of heaven, farewell	172
Ye servants of the Lord	133
Ye sons of earth, prepare the plough	117
Yes, God is good; in earth and sky	18
Your harps, ye trembling saints	435

www.ingramcontent.com/pod-product-compliance
Lightning Source LLC
Chambersburg PA
CBHW021425300426
44114CB00010B/654